HISTORICAL ATLAS OF KANSAS

UNIVERSITY OF OKLAHOMA PRESS : NORMAN AND LONDON

HISTORICAL ATLAS OF KANSAS

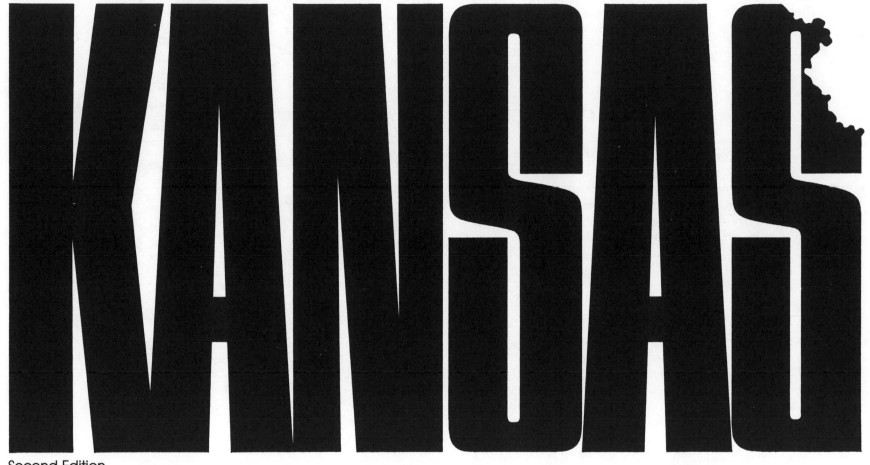

Second Edition

BY HOMER E. SOCOLOFSKY AND HUBER SELF

BOOKS BY HOMER E. SOCOLOFSKY

(ed. and comp.) *Kansas in Graduate Study* (Manhattan, 1959: To-
   peka, 1970)
Arthur Capper, Publisher, Politician, Philanthropist (Lawrence,
   1962)
The Cimarron Valley (New York, 1969)
(with Huber Self) *Historical Atlas of Kansas* (Norman, 1972, 1988)
Landlord William Scully (Lawrence, 1979)
(ed. with C. Clyde Jones) *Science and Technology in Agriculture*
   (Washington, D.C., 1985)
*From the Beginning: A History of the First United Methodist
   Church, Manhattan, Kansas, 1855–1985* (Manhattan, 1985)
(with Allen Spetter) *The Presidency of Benjamin Harrison* (Lawrence, 1987)

BOOKS BY HUBER SELF

Geography of Kansas (Norman, 1959)
Atlas of Kansas (Norman, 1961)
Introductory Physical Geography (Manhattan, 1962)
World Regional Geography (Manhattan, 1963)
Geography of Kansas Syllabus and Atlas (Dubuque, 1967)
(with Homer Socolofsky) *Historical Atlas of Kansas* (Norman, 1972,
   1988)
Environment and Man in Kansas: A Geographical Analysis (Law-
   rence, 1978)

Library of Congress Cataloging-in-Publication Data

Socolofsky, Homer Edward, 1922–
   Historical atlas of Kansas.

   Bibliography: p. ix.
   Includes index.
   1. Kansas—Historical geography—Maps.   I. Self,
Huber.   II. Title.
G1456.S1S6   1988   911′.781   88–40209
ISBN 0–8061–2157–2

PREFACE

KANSAS HAS HAD A LONG and eventful history. The Great Seal of the state of Kansas, adopted soon after statehood was approved on January 29, 1861, shows the feelings and conditions of that day. The sun was rising, Indians on horseback were pursuing buffalo, smoke was ascending from a log cabin chimney and from the stack of a river boat, two ox-drawn wagons were heading west, and in the foreground a farmer was plowing. This seal depicts the heritage of early Kansas in a prairie landscape. Visible were its background and its beginnings in commerce, settlement, and agriculture. The Latin motto, "*Ad Astra Per Aspera*," translated as "To the stars through difficulties," refers to the troublous territorial days. Had Kansas adopted the seal a hundred years later, no doubt there would have been included railroads, factories, cities, highways with automobiles, and even aircraft. Still, the components of a historical atlas of Kansas are evident in this Great Seal, used to emboss the official documents of the state.

Geography and history support each other. A proper knowledge of the history of Kansas requires an understanding of the state's geography. The lay of the land, the routes available for easy travel, the location of population concentrations, and the unfolding of economic and political development are all shown on the following maps. Because the state's boundaries are artificial and man-made, except for the northeast corner where the Missouri River provides a natural border, this atlas shows some of the geographical and historical development of neighboring areas which have a bearing on Kansas geography and history. All present-day population centers are included in this atlas. Lack of space has made it necessary to leave out most of the lost towns and ghost communities that are a feature of Kansas history.

Each map is accompanied by a page of text providing a brief narration which describes the map. Spellings and names have changed through the years. An effort has been made on each map to use the spelling and the proper names in use at that time. Topics and maps are numbered consecutively; there are no page numbers in that part of the atlas.

Among the numerous persons contributing to the preparation of this historical atlas are the staff of the Kansas State Historical Society, particularly Mrs. Lela Barnes, Nyle H. Miller, Ed Langsdorf, and Robert Richmond; the staff of many Kansas state offices; the librarians of the Farrell Library at Kansas State University; and the faculty of the Departments of Geography and of History at Kansas State University.

The long, exciting history of Kansas is of great interest to the authors and they sincerely hope that this atlas will aid all those seeking wider acquaintance of Kansas geography and history. We have prepared this atlas for the professional scholar, as well as the amateur historian and the elementary, secondary, or college student. At each level of understanding there are materials of use for a better conception of the relationship between geography and history in the development of the state of Kansas.

We thank all of you who have commented on the first edition of *The Historical Atlas of Kansas*. Especially, we thank Don McCoy, University of Kansas, and Stephen White, Kansas State University, for suggestions for additional maps.

Homer E. Socolofsky
Huber Self

CONTENTS

HISTORICAL ATLAS OF KANSAS

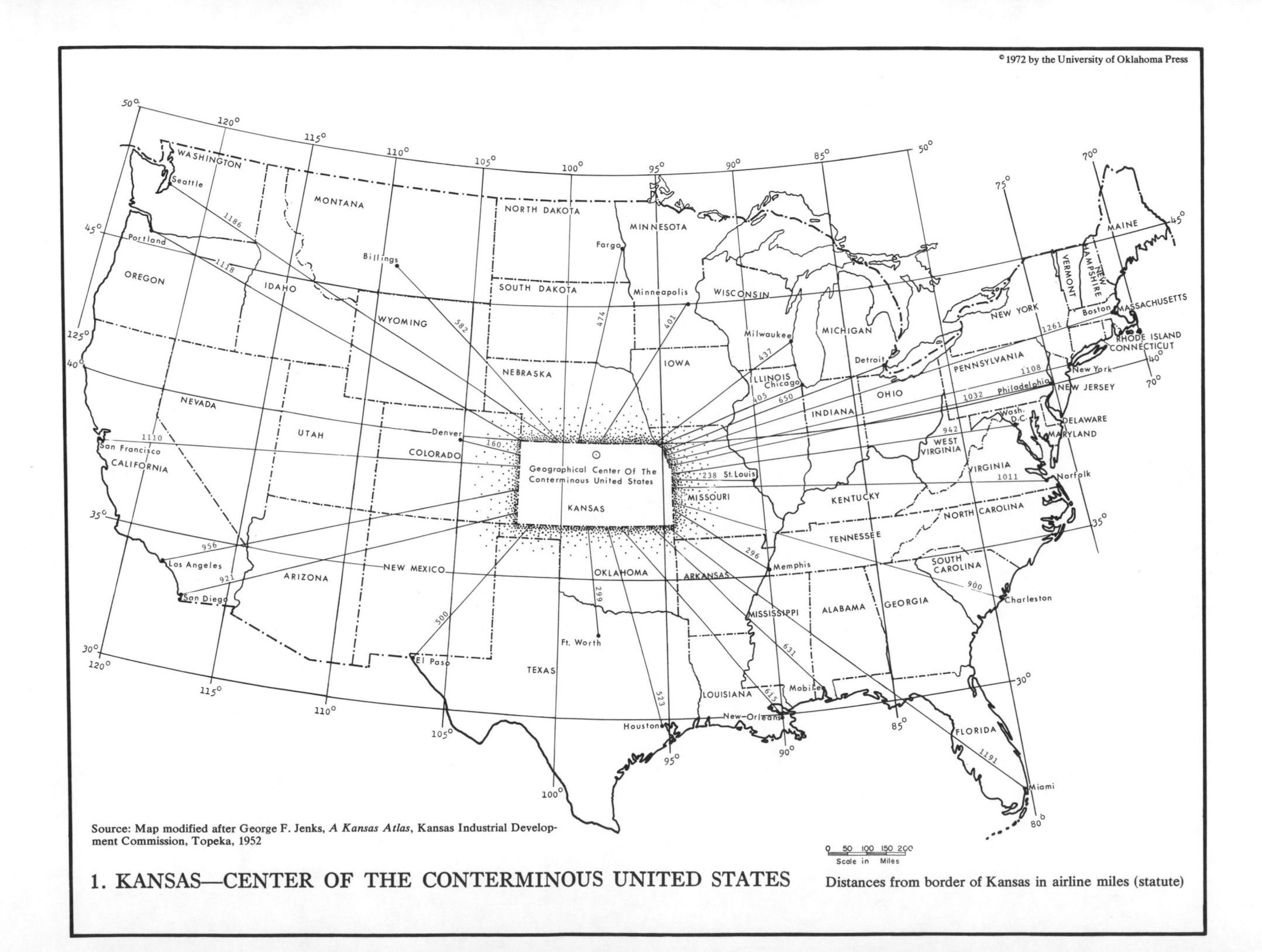

Geographical Center Of The
Conterminous United States

Source: Map modified after George F. Jenks, *A Kansas Atlas*, Kansas Industrial Development Commission, Topeka, 1952

0 50 100 150 200
Scale in Miles

1. KANSAS—CENTER OF THE CONTERMINOUS UNITED STATES

Distances from border of Kansas in airline miles (statute)

1. KANSAS—CENTER OF THE CONTERMINOUS UNITED STATES

KANSAS IS LOCATED in the center of the conterminous United States, that part of the country which has a common external border. The area is bounded on the east by the state of Missouri at 94°37′03.4″ West Longitude and the mid-channel of the Missouri River; on the north by the state of Nebraska at 40° North Latitude; on the west by the state of Colorado at 102°3′02.3″ West Longitude; and on the south by the state of Oklahoma at 37° North Latitude.

Except for the northeast boundary, established by the meandering Missouri, the area of Kansas is basically a rectangle stretching slightly more than 400 miles east–west and slightly more than 200 miles north–south. The fourteenth largest state in the country, Kansas has an area of 82,264 square miles. National capitals in the same latitude as the state of Kansas include Seoul, South Korea; Beijing, China; Ankara, Turkey; Lisbon, Portugal; and Washington, D.C.

As the home of two and a half million people of diverse origins but of considerable homogeneity, Kansas has the potential for a wide range of cultural developments. The size of the state and distance from the equator have profound influence on the variety of conditions existing within its borders.

The geographical center of the conterminous United States is also known as the geographical center of the historic United States. It is located near Lebanon, in Smith County in north central Kansas. Of more scientific interest is the North American geodetic datum, established on Meade's Ranch (later known as Robinson's Farm), Osborne County, some forty miles south and east of the historic geographical center. This geodetic datum of North America is the controlling point for all land surveys in the United States, Canada, and Mexico. The geodetic center remains as the initial point for North American surveys, whereas the geographical center of the nation was shifted to the state of South Dakota with the admission of the new states of Alaska and Hawaii.

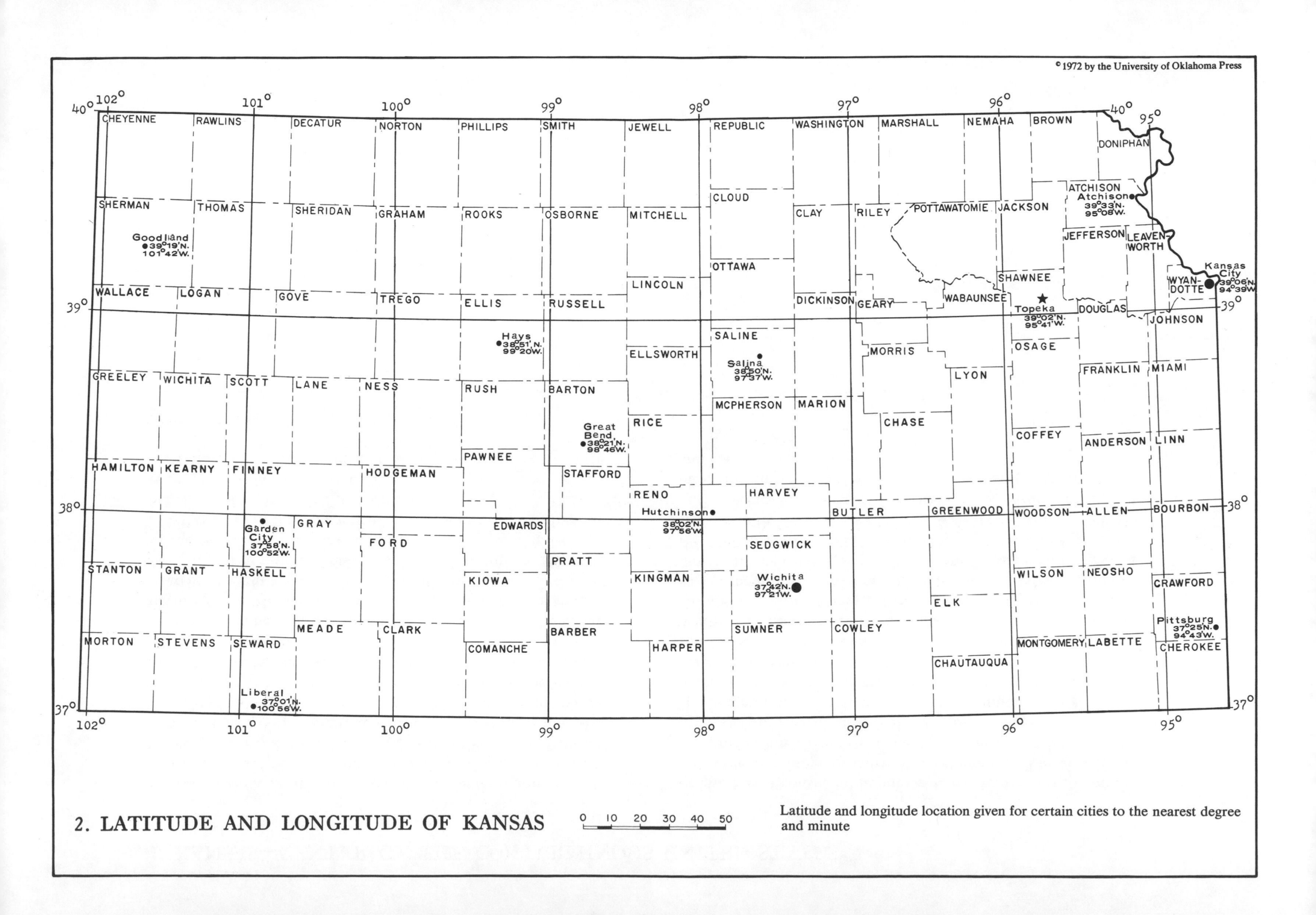

2. LATITUDE AND LONGITUDE OF KANSAS

0 10 20 30 40 50

Latitude and longitude location given for certain cities to the nearest degree and minute

2. LATITUDE AND LONGITUDE OF KANSAS

KANSAS RANGES three degrees north–south, from 37° to 40° North Latitude, and almost seven and a half degrees east–west, 94°37′03.4″ to 102°3′02.3″ West Longitude. The southern border is 411.18 miles, a reduction from the territorial southern boundary by slightly more than 51 miles. The western boundary, at 25° west of Washington, is 207.33 miles, and the northern border has a length of 356.66 miles. The Missouri River boundary, from the mouth of the Kansas River to the fortieth parallel is 101 miles, and from that point to the thirty-seventh parallel is 142.84 miles. The total length of the boundary is 1,219.01 miles. The center of the state is about 15 miles northeast of Great Bend in Barton County. The maximum distance, from the southeast corner to the northwest corner, is about 435 miles.

The great east–west distance of Kansas, approximately seven and one-half degrees, means that the sun rises and sets on the eastern border approximately thirty minutes earlier than on the western border. Prior to the establishment of time zones most towns used local solar time. Development of railroads, the telegraph, and eventually the telephone, prompted use of standardized time zones for scientific purposes. The railroads led in 1883, with railroad division points at Phillipsburg, Plainville, Ellis, Hoisington, and Dodge City serving as boundaries between "Railroad Standard Central Time" and "Railroad Standard Mountain Time." Elkhart, in southwest Kansas, was part of the central time zone in this arrangement. Subsequent changes in standard time zones moved the boundary in northwest Kansas farther west, and by 1950 only six counties—Cheyenne, Sherman, Wallace, Greeley, Kearny, and Hamilton—remained in the mountain time zone. Communities in the western part of Kansas frequently decided by consensus to use mountain time, since the western boundary of the central time zone, strictly on a longitudinal basis, would have run through Halstead, located only half a minute in solar time west of the sixth principal meridian. The state legislature, responding to the federal Uniform Time Act of 1966, petitioned Congress to make the western border of Kansas the boundary between Central Standard and Mountain Standard Time.

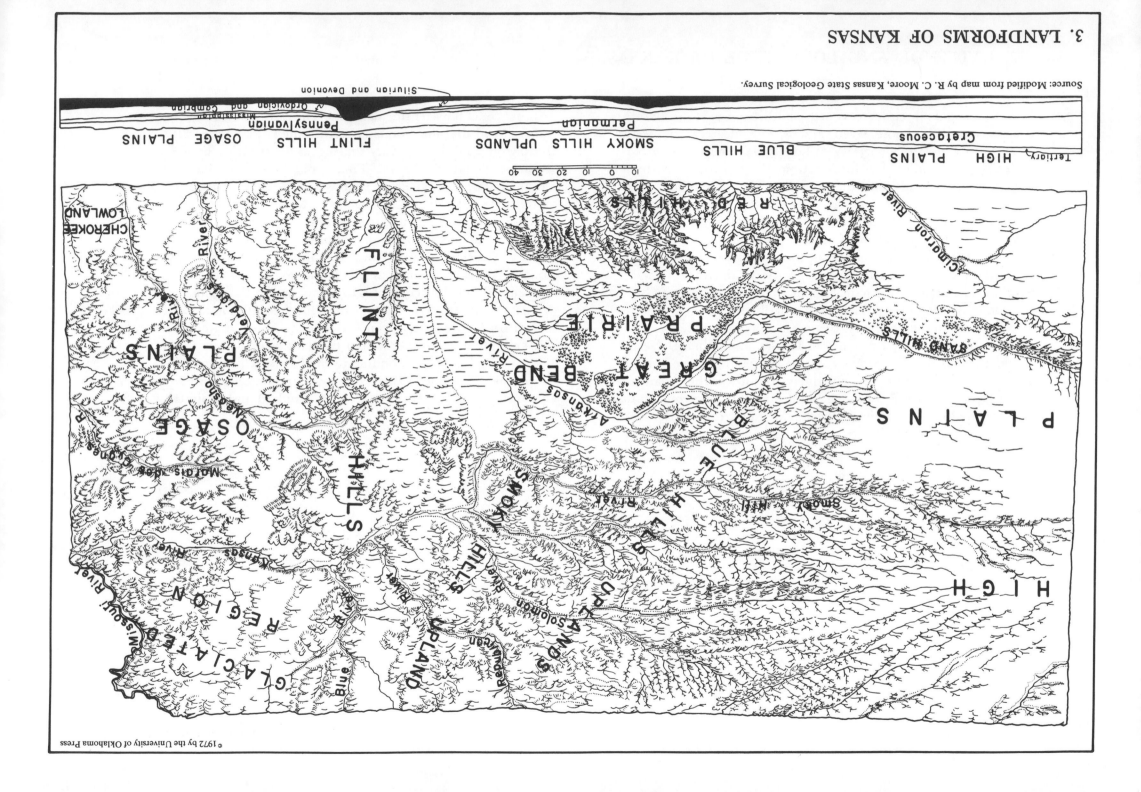

Source: Modified from map by R. C. Moore, Kansas State Geological Survey.

3. LANDFORMS OF KANSAS

ELEVATIONS IN KANSAS range from about 700 feet above sea level in the southeastern corner where the Verdigris River enters Oklahoma to 4,025.5 feet in northwestern Kansas, adjoining the Colorado line. The 400 miles between these low and high places suggests an average change in elevation of 8 to 9 feet per mile. Such a terrain offers vast areas that are relatively level, yet the landscape is seldom flat and featureless. Picturesque hills and valleys abound in the Kansas scene.

The western two-thirds of the state is in the Great Plains region which extends for thousands of miles along the east side of the Rocky Mountains. Smaller portions of this region are identified as the High Plains, the Blue Hills Upland, the Smoky Hills Upland, the Great Bend Prairie, and, along the southern border, the Red Hills. The Great Plains region has a more even surface as it rises gradually westward to the Rockies. When first settled this area was used for grazing livestock and for growing small grains. Farmers in this region later concentrated on production of cattle, wheat, and sorghum.

The more varied landscape of the eastern third of the state is in the Central Lowlands region, with the extreme southeast portion of the Cherokee Lowland in the Ozark Plateau. The Central Lowlands includes the Flint Hills, an extensive well-watered pasture country, the Glaciated Region, and the Osage Plains. First settlements in Kansas were made in this area, later devoted to a more diversified agriculture featuring corn, soybeans, small grains, and livestock. The largest urban communities in the state are in this region or along the eastern border of the Great Plains.

Ninety-six per cent of the land area of Kansas is devoted to farming, with about 59 per cent of that area in cropland. Kansas ranks third nationally for land in farms and second for the acreage devoted to crop production.

The soils of Kansas are among the best in the world. These soils have evolved from decomposition of underlying rock formations or have been transported into the region by water, wind, or ice. Rock strata near the surface in eastern Kansas were laid down by shallow, ancient seas, while those in western Kansas were deposited by streams from the Rocky Mountains. Below these strata are more ancient rock layers associated with the early geologic eras of the earth's development. Kansas' mineral resources, such as oil and gas, come from the rock strata associated with the formation of shallow, ancient seas; while coal deposits were formed from vegetation deposited in ancient swamps during a time when the land was above sea level.

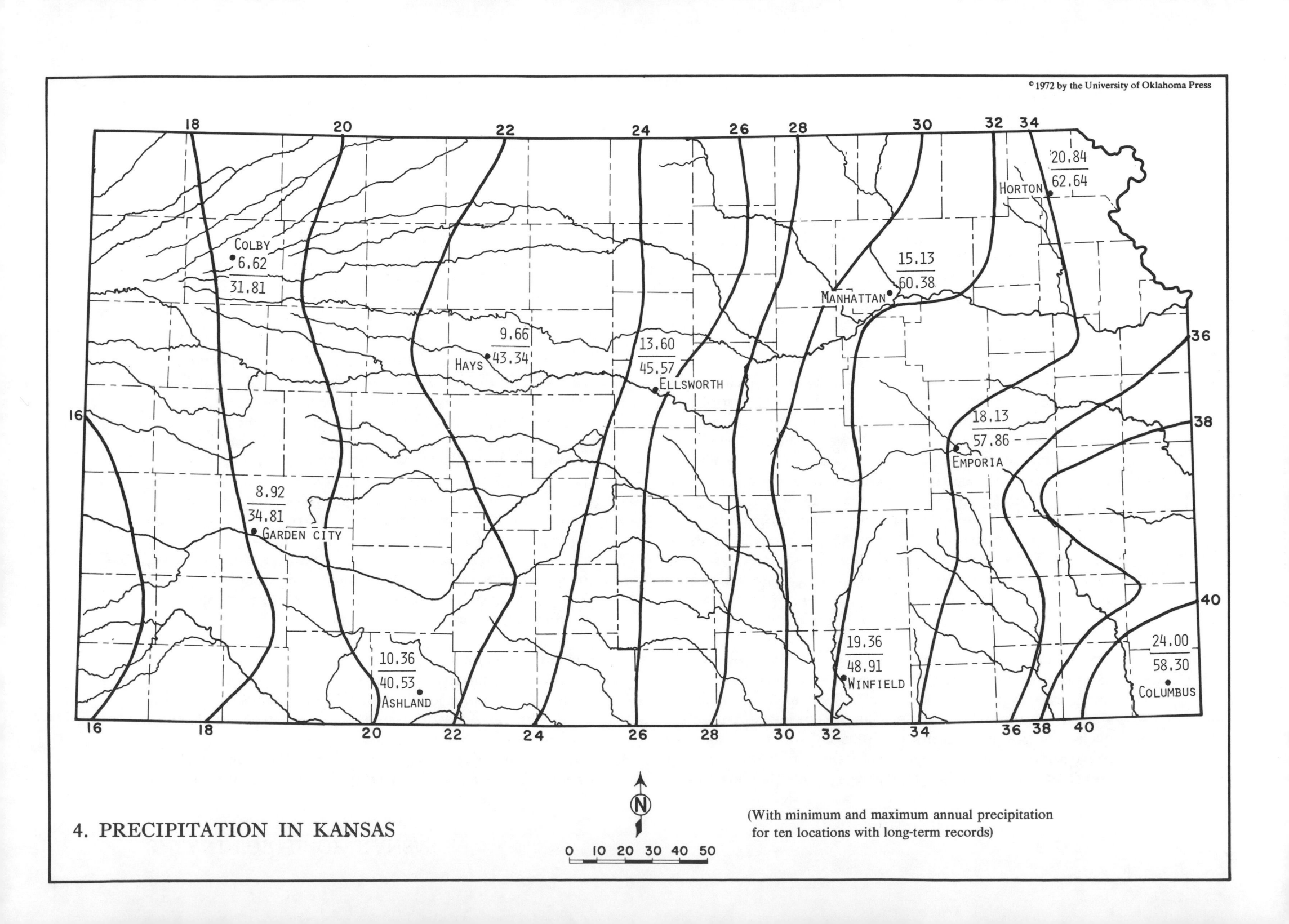

COLBY
• 6.62
——
31.81

HORTON
20.84
——
62.64

15.13
——
60.38
MANHATTAN

9.66
——
43.34
HAYS •

13.60
——
45.57
• ELLSWORTH

18.13
——
57.86
EMPORIA •

8.92
——
34.81
• GARDEN CITY

10.36
——
40.53 •
ASHLAND

19.36
——
48.91
• WINFIELD

24.00
——
58.30
COLUMBUS •

N

0 10 20 30 40 50

4. PRECIPITATION IN KANSAS

(With minimum and maximum annual precipitation
for ten locations with long-term records)

4. PRECIPITATION IN KANSAS

THE AVERAGE ANNUAL PRECIPITATION in Kansas is twenty-six and a half inches. During an average year the total moisture will vary from forty-five inches in the southeast corner to fifteen inches along the western border. Precipitation decreases from east to west about one inch for each 17 miles. Fortunately for the Kansas farmer, most of the moisture comes during the months of April through September, the growing season for Kansas crops. Snow provides a relatively small part of the average total precipitation.

The drier western part of Kansas receives a larger portion of its annual precipitation during the growing season than is the case in the eastern part of the state, but more variance from the normal averages is also found there. The accompanying map shows precipitation records based on a thirty-year moving average. The minimum and maximum figures for ten selected stations are based on long-time records, some taken for more than 110 years. Four of these stations posted their highest precipitation in 1951, when the statewide average was 41.57 inches. Other high rainfall years for two western stations were 1915, the year 1922 for two other stations, and individual peaks of 1895 and 1949 for the other two. Driest years on record find even less consistency for the large area of Kansas. The year 1954 was low for two stations, and each of the other locations had a different low year: 1860, 1893, 1901, 1910, 1911, 1936, 1939, and 1952.

Also important in precipitation figures is the increasing variability in the west as illustrated by Colby, where the low record was 36 per cent of the average and only 21 per cent of the highest recorded. Columbus, on the other hand, had a low record of 57 per cent of average and 41 per cent of the highest recorded. The higher wind velocities in western Kansas, the lower humidity, and the fact that much of the precipitation comes in hard rains, influences the availability of moisture for crop production.

Because of its location, most of Kansas is a part of both the humid continental and middle latitude semi-arid climatic zones. The humid continental area, including most of the eastern three-fourths of Kansas, is characterized by adequate precipitation for cropland agriculture; it has warm summers and in the coldest month the average temperatures are below freezing. The middle latitude semi-arid zone, including the western fourth of Kansas, has less reliable precipitation and the possibility of frequent droughts. Relative humidity is much lower than in the zone to the east, and while daytime summer temperatures may be high, the nights are cool and pleasant. Farmers must compensate for the moisture deficiency by the use of dry-land farming practices, or by the use of irrigation where practical.

Rainfall totals provide some indication of the climate of Kansas, but its latitude, its continental location and distance from large bodies of water, its large number of clear days, its high evaporation factor, and its altitude also have some influence. The natural vegetation of the area reflects the rainfall pattern and is also influenced by the distribution of the precipitation through the year.

The state's greatest annual precipitation, 65.87 inches, was recorded in 1951 at Mound City. The least was at Colby in 1910, with a reported 6.62 inches. Temperature extremes are the 121° F. reported at Fredonia and at Alton in 1936 and the −40° F. recorded at Lebanon in 1905.

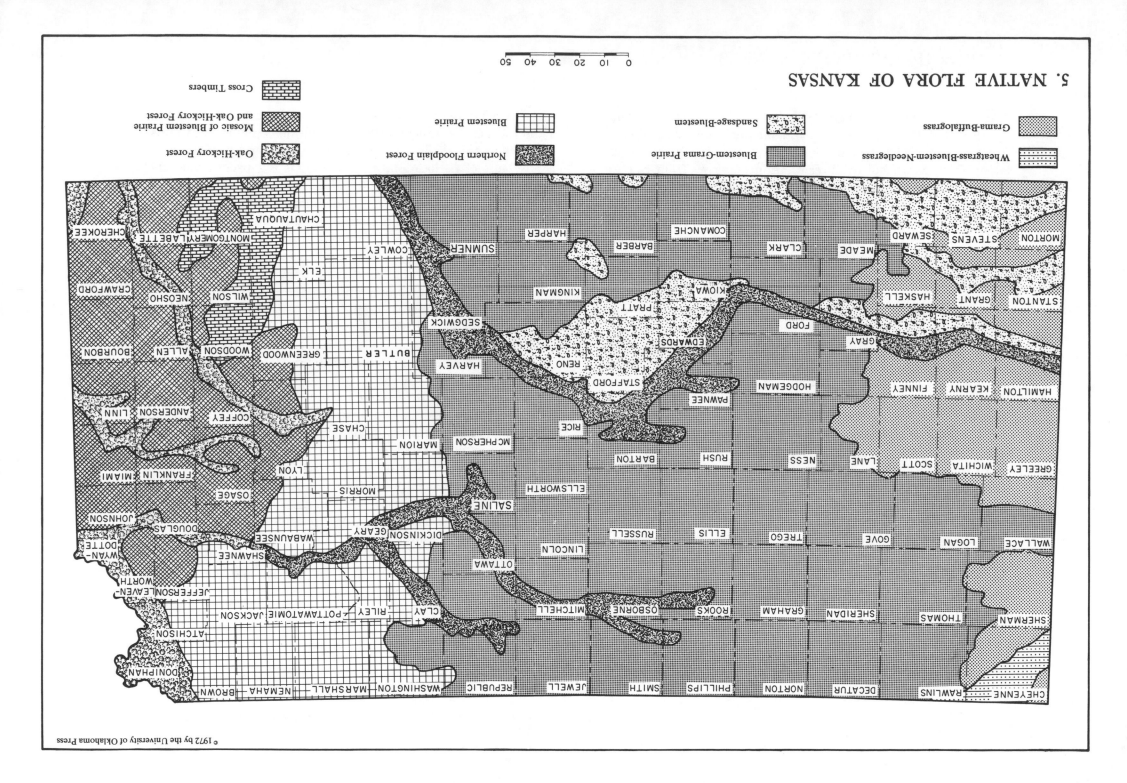

5. NATIVE FLORA OF KANSAS

Cross Timbers

Mosaic of Bluestem Prairie and Oak-Hickory Forest

Oak-Hickory Forest

Bluestem Prairie

Northern Floodplain Forest

Sandsage-Bluestem

Bluestem-Grama Prairie

Grama-Buffalograss

Wheatgrass-Bluestem-Needlegrass

5. NATIVE FLORA OF KANSAS

EXPLORERS PIKE, FRÉMONT, AND NUTTALL took limited notes of the native Kansas vegetation on their trips through the area in the early nineteenth century. Based on this material and their own researches, several botanists and geographers have compiled maps showing the native vegetation of Kansas. The detailed map shown here was prepared by A. W. Küchler in 1964 and republished in 1969.

The fact that previous authors did not precisely agree is probably due to the fluctuations in the general climate of the state, where an increase or decrease in annual precipitation would produce a change in native vegetation. For instance, abnormally dry years would show a migration eastward of short grasses while tall grass dominance would move westward during a series of wet years. Geologic variety and soil types are also influential on native vegetation.

The vegetation of Kansas, except for the oak-hickory forest, the cross timbers, and the northern floodplain forest, was principally a prairie vegetation. In the eastern third of the state the tall bluestem grasses were dominant. A short buffalo and grama grass prairie was the primary vegetation in most western counties. In between was a mixed prairie with a somewhat unstable border due to annual changes in precipitation. Other smaller regions shown on this map, such as the floodplain forests and the sand prairies, were a relatively stable feature of the Kansas landscape. The area of heavy corn production in the state, before the advent of irrigation, was in the region where tall bluestem was the dominant grass. The mixed prairie became the primary region of the later heavy wheat production in Kansas.

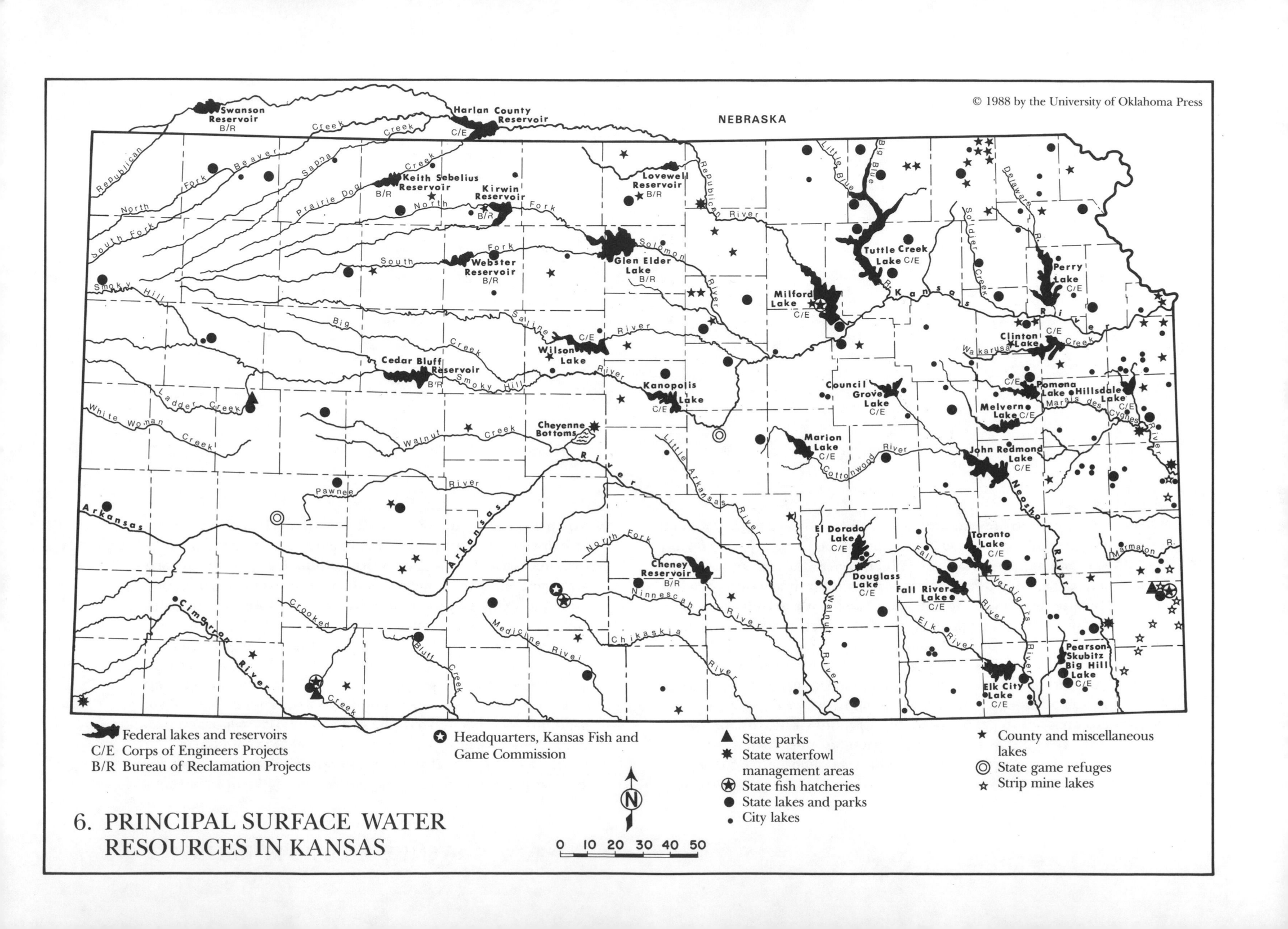

© 1988 by the University of Oklahoma Press

NEBRASKA

Swanson Reservoir B/R

Harlan County Reservoir C/E

Lovewell Reservoir B/R

Keith Sebelius Reservoir B/R

Kirwin Reservoir B/R

Webster Reservoir B/R

Glen Elder Lake B/R

Tuttle Creek Lake C/E

Perry Lake C/E

Milford Lake C/E

Clinton Lake C/E

Wilson Lake

Cedar Bluff Reservoir B/R

Kanopolis Lake C/E

Council Grove Lake C/E

Pomona Lake C/E

Hillsdale Lake

Melvern Lake C/E

Cheyenne Bottoms

Marion Lake C/E

John Redmond Lake C/E

El Dorado Lake C/E

Toronto Lake C/E

Douglass Lake C/E

Cheney Reservoir B/R

Fall River Lake C/E

Pearson Skubitz Big Hill Lake C/E

Elk City Lake C/E

Republican River · North Fork · South Fork · Beaver Creek · Sappa Creek · Prairie Dog Creek · North Fork · South Fork · Smoky Hill · Ladder Creek · White Woman Creek · Walnut Creek · Pawnee River · Arkansas River · Cimarron River · Crooked Creek · Bluff Creek · Medicine River · Ninnescah River · Chikaskia River · North Fork · Little Arkansas River · Cottonwood River · Walnut River · Fall River · Elk River · Verdigris River · Neosho River · Marmaton R. · Marais des Cygnes River · Wakarusa · Solomon River · Saline River · Big Creek · Smoky Hill River · Solomon · Kansas River · Little Blue · Big Blue · Delaware R. · Soldier Creek

Legend

⬛ Federal lakes and reservoirs
C/E Corps of Engineers Projects
B/R Bureau of Reclamation Projects

✪ Headquarters, Kansas Fish and Game Commission

▲ State parks
✳ State waterfowl management areas
✪ State fish hatcheries
● State lakes and parks
• City lakes

★ County and miscellaneous lakes
◎ State game refuges
☆ Strip mine lakes

6. PRINCIPAL SURFACE WATER RESOURCES IN KANSAS

N

0 10 20 30 40 50

6. PRINCIPAL SURFACE WATER RESOURCES IN KANSAS

THE FACE OF KANSAS is changing. With few natural lakes in the state, the water surface for many years meant flowing streams. Most artificial impoundments have been developed since World War II. By 1985 the active farm ponds numbered more than 70,000, covering 100,000 surface acres. They are easily visible to passengers in high-flying aircraft. An additional several hundred local government and water district reservoirs have a combined water surface area of nearly 21,000 acres. State fishing lakes and other state-administered areas, including the huge Cheyenne Bottoms, account for more than 25,000 water acres. Large federal reservoirs, all constructed since World War II, cover more than 120,000 surface acres. More than 400 square miles of the Kansas area is covered by water, and the total storage in all of these lakes and ponds is in excess of 3 million acre-feet. These waters are used for irrigation, for municipal and industrial water supply, for recreation, and for many other purposes. To help control water runoff, many miles of levees and embankments have been built. The federal reservoirs, especially, were constructed for an additional reason—flood control. Those built by the Corps of Engineers have been designated lakes, while the Bureau of Reclamation still calls these water areas reservoirs.

The surface water resource of Kansas is largely the product of falling precipitation with about 1 per cent added by streamflow coming from neighboring states. Most of this water evaporates or is consumed by plants; perhaps 10 to 15 per cent runs off to form streams in the state; and a small portion moves downward to become groundwater. Irrigation demands the largest withdrawal of this water, with municipalities and industries together using almost as much water as irrigation. Limits on irrigation use in the future will likely increase the proportion going to cities and industry.

The expanded Kansas water surface has attracted widespread recreational activity. The Kansas Fish and Game Commission and the State Park and Resources Authority are the agencies primarily responsible for supervision of water recreational sites within the state.

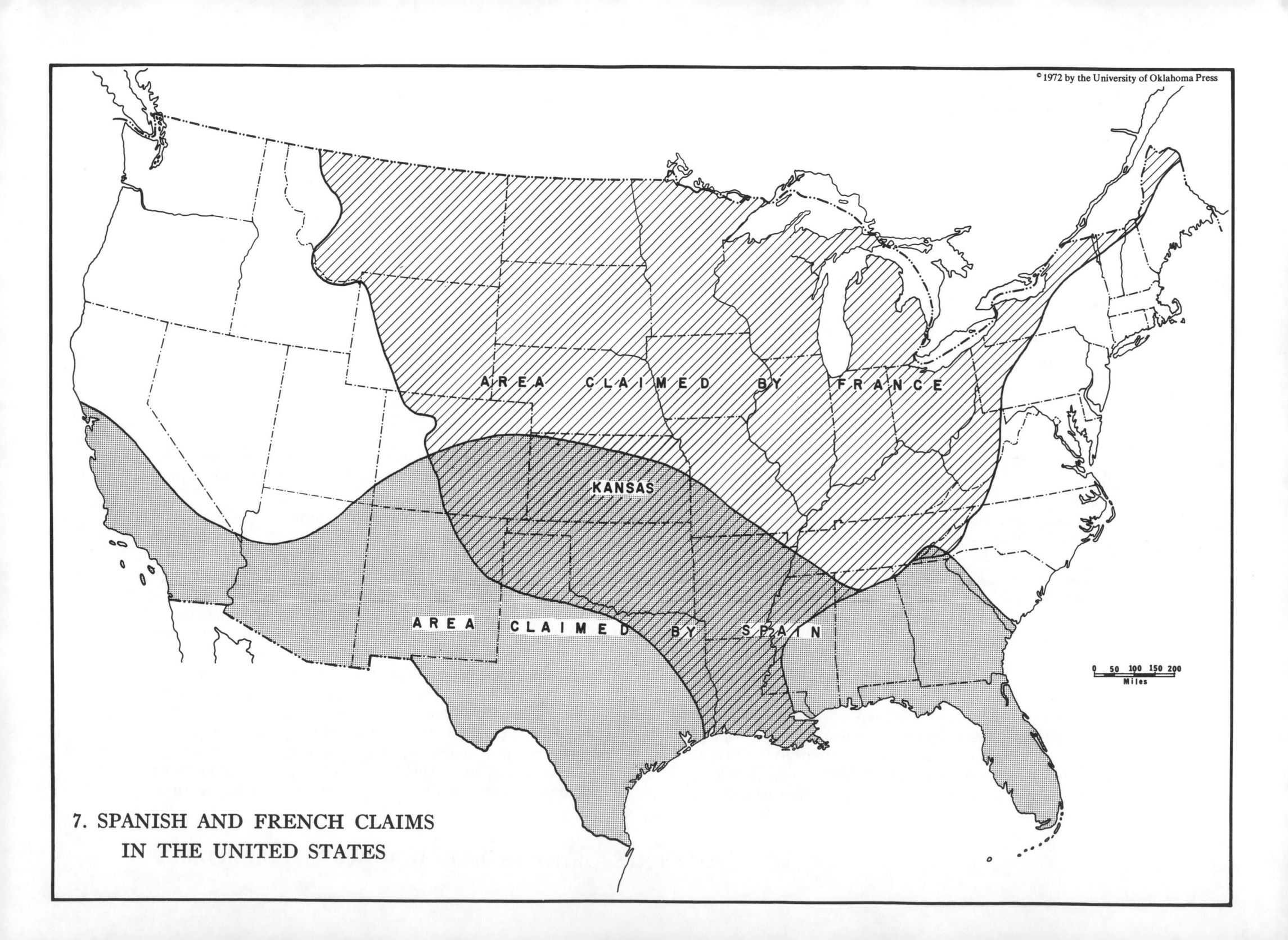

AREA CLAIMED BY FRANCE

KANSAS

AREA CLAIMED BY SPAIN

0 50 100 150 200
Miles

7. SPANISH AND FRENCH CLAIMS
IN THE UNITED STATES

7. SPANISH AND FRENCH CLAIMS IN THE UNITED STATES

WITHIN FIFTY YEARS after the first voyage of Columbus to America, Spain had laid claim, by right of geographical discovery, to the southern part of the region which was later to become the United States. Expeditions of discovery, led by military leaders such as Francisco Vásquez de Coronado and Hernando De Soto, marked out the earliest claims to the land that became Kansas. Later expeditions led by Juan de Oñate and others established Spanish colonies in the Río Grande valley in New Mexico and in parts of Texas, while the Kansas region was left untouched.

The soil of the Kansas area visited by Coronado was regarded as fertile and well-watered, but the lack of precious metals and of a docile, numerous, hard-working, native population, which would be needed for the exploitation of the visible agricultural resources, caused the Spanish to turn their interests elsewhere. Spanish colonization did not take place within the borders of the Kansas area.

English colonization along the Atlantic coast was accompanied by grandiose claims from sea to sea, unsupported by either exploration or colonization. More significant for the Kansas region were the French voyages of discovery down the Mississippi River in 1673, led by missionary Jacques Marquette and trader Louis Joliet, and by the nobleman Robert Cavelier, Sieur de la Salle, in 1682. These journeys and subsequent settlement along the Mississippi River established French claims to all of the territory drained by the Mississippi, a region including Kansas. For much of the next century there were conflicting territorial claims for the area by European powers England, France, and Spain.

Near the end of the French and Indian War, in the secret Treaty of Fontainebleau of November 3, 1762, France ceded to her ally, Spain, all of her territory west of the Mississippi River and the city of New Orleans. In the Treaty of Paris of February 10, 1763, France gave up to England her other claims to mainland North America.

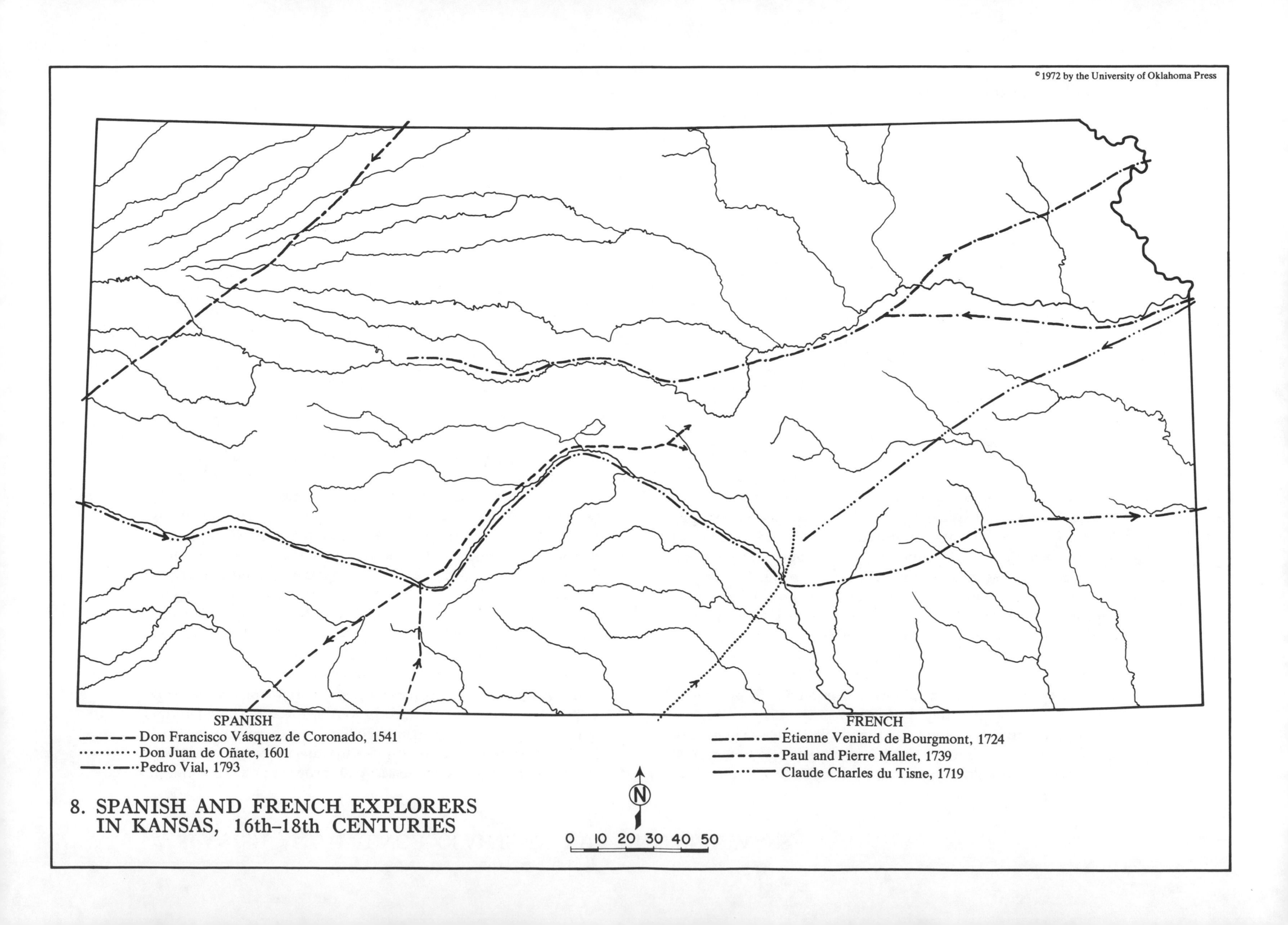

SPANISH

— — — Don Francisco Vásquez de Coronado, 1541
··········· Don Juan de Oñate, 1601
—·—·— Pedro Vial, 1793

FRENCH

—··—··— Étienne Veniard de Bourgmont, 1724
— — — Paul and Pierre Mallet, 1739
—···—··· Claude Charles du Tisne, 1719

8. SPANISH AND FRENCH EXPLORERS IN KANSAS, 16th–18th CENTURIES

N

0 10 20 30 40 50

8. SPANISH AND FRENCH EXPLORERS IN KANSAS, 16th–18th CENTURIES

SINCE THERE WERE FEW IDENTIFIABLE geographical locations in the grasslands of early-day Kansas, the route of the expedition of Francisco Vásquez de Coronado can be given only on the basis of the best of available reconstructions. It is generally assumed that Coronado crossed the Arkansas River on June 29, 1541, at the much-used ford (present-day town of Ford) about which one of his chroniclers wrote "on Saint Peter and Paul's day we reached the river. . . . We crossed it there and went up the other side on the north, the direction turning toward the northeast, and after marching three days we found some Indians who were going hunting." Further descriptions in the chronicle tie the Quivira region visited by the expedition to central Kansas. On his return trip, a month or so later, Coronado took "a more direct route" back to the Río Grande. The next Spanish expedition in the area was led by Juan de Oñate in 1601. He probably struck the Arkansas River below the place visited by Coronado.

French explorers, coming into the region from the direction of the Mississippi River in the eighteenth century, visited Indians in the area. Like those of the Spanish explorers before them, the descriptions given by the French lack the precision required for complete identification. The routes shown are based on the location of Indian tribes they were presumed to have seen.

The French-Canadian brothers, Paul and Pierre Mallet, led a trading expedition to Santa Fe in 1739. They ascended the Missouri and the Platte rivers. Somewhere they left the Platte and went cross-country to Santa Fe. Some map descriptions have them taking the route shown here, while others place their trek west of present-day Kansas. The route of Pedro Vial from Santa Fe to St. Louis is known with more precision. Vial took trading goods over this long trail at a time when Spain's eastern territorial border was the Mississippi River, so he crossed no international boundary. A portion of Vial's route was later followed by the Santa Fe Trail.

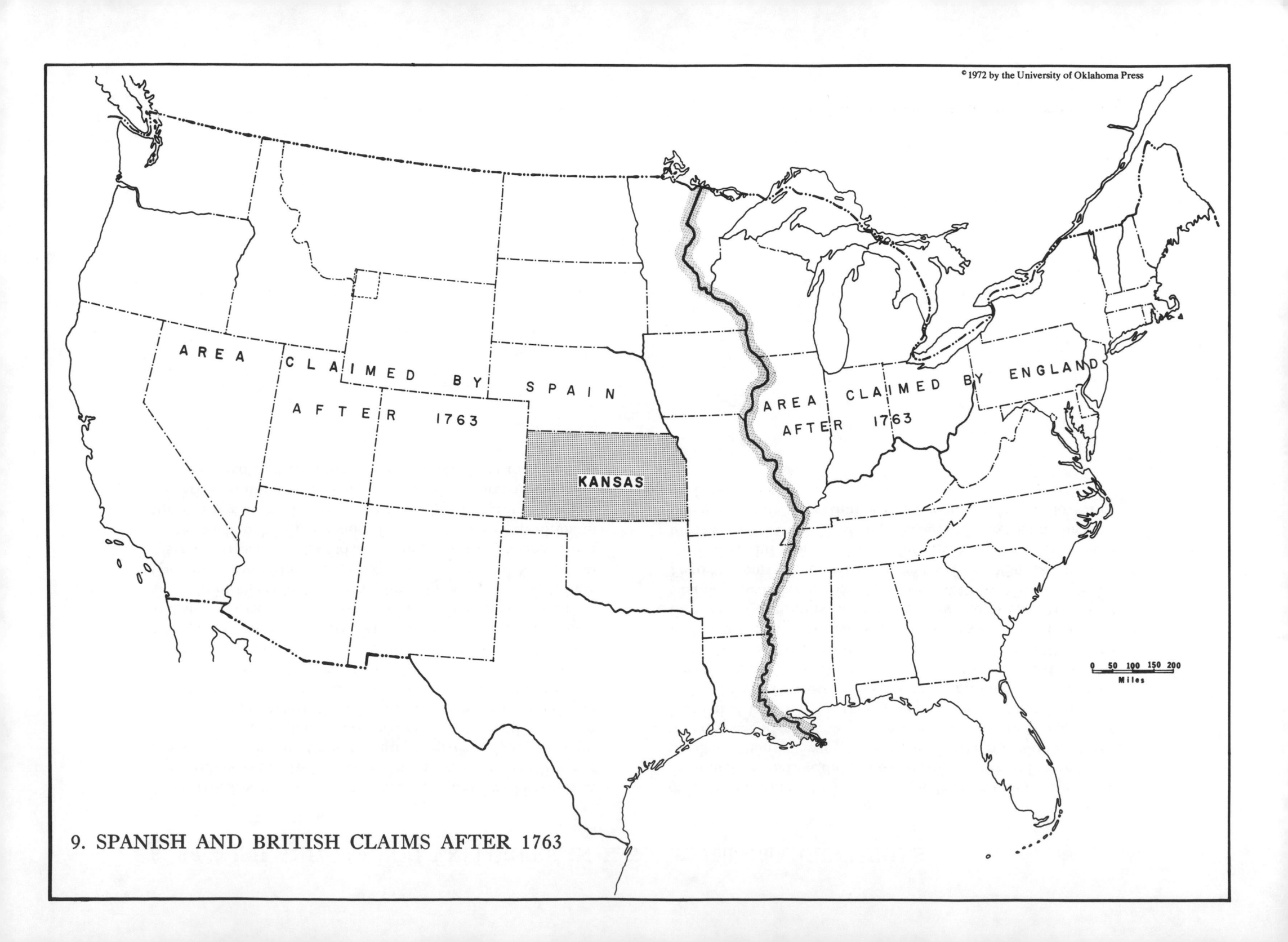

© 1972 by the University of Oklahoma Press

AREA CLAIMED BY SPAIN AFTER 1763

AREA CLAIMED BY ENGLAND AFTER 1763

KANSAS

0 50 100 150 200
Miles

9. SPANISH AND BRITISH CLAIMS AFTER 1763

9. SPANISH AND BRITISH CLAIMS AFTER 1763

WITH FRANCE REMOVED from the continent of North America after the end of the French and Indian War, the international border between Spanish and English territory was the Mississippi River. Except for a small region around New Orleans, England gained control of all territory east of the Mississippi including East and West Florida. The English and Spanish land frontiers were in direct contact more than they had ever been before, and Spain made efforts to strengthen the defenses of her new acquisitions from New Orleans to St. Louis.

The outbreak of the American Revolution brought Spanish indications of sympathy for the rebels even before the Declaration of Independence. When France formally allied with the United States against Britain on February 6, 1778, Spain indicated her interest but stayed out of the war until June 21, 1779, when she formally declared war against Britain. Consequently,

Spain had a hand in the treaty negotiations ending the war and she regained Florida from England.

The Kansas region was under Spanish authority during this period, but the native Indians remained virtually untouched and did not understand the European claims to their land. Fur-trading activities originating in St. Louis and minor trading expeditions traversing the area between St. Louis and Santa Fe provided infrequent incursions into the region by outsiders.

With the Treaty of Paris (1783), the newly independent United States of America became the owner of a vast tract of western land located north of Florida and east of the Mississippi River. By the end of the eighteenth century American settlers and investors, who had rapidly occupied choice lands in the Mississippi Valley, were eagerly pressing for expansion into the region west of the great river.

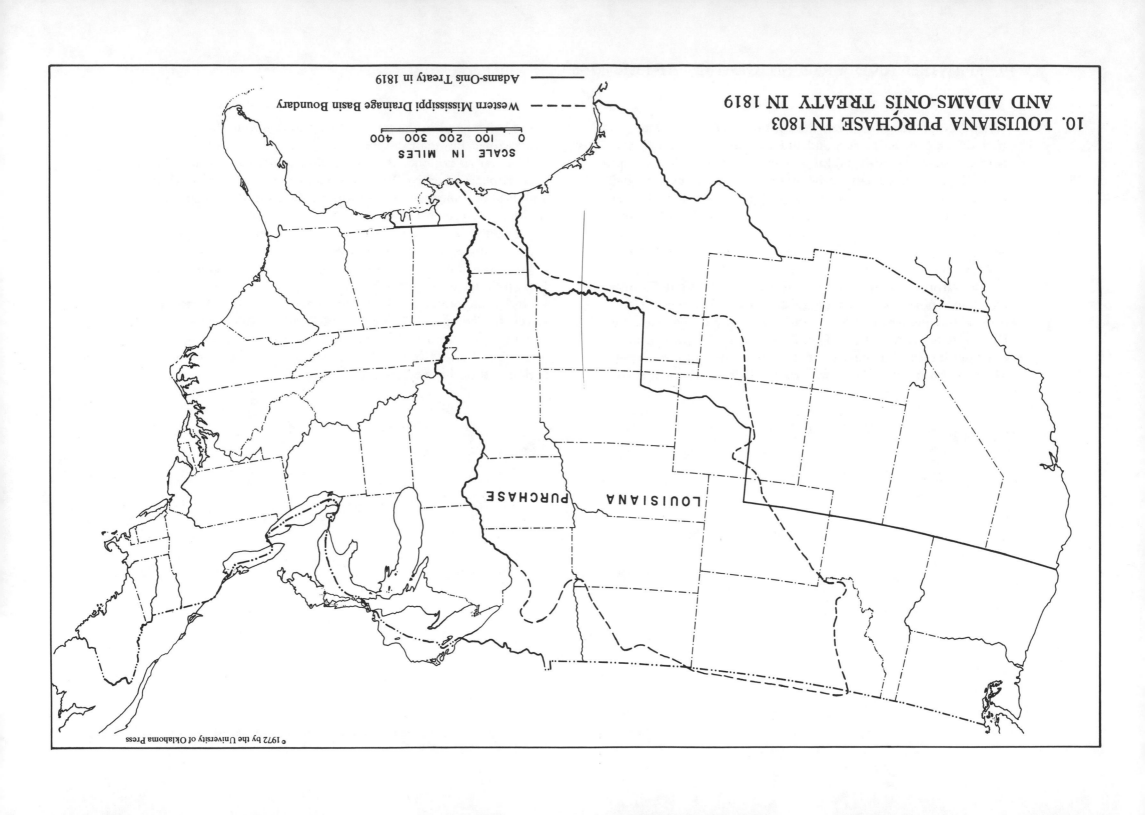

10. LOUISIANA PURCHASE IN 1803
AND ADAMS-ONIS TREATY IN 1819

— Adams-Onís Treaty in 1819

--- Western Mississippi Drainage Basin Boundary

SCALE IN MILES

0 100 200 300 400

LOUISIANA PURCHASE

© 1972 by the University of Oklahoma Press

10. LOUISIANA PURCHASE IN 1803 AND ADAMS-ONÍS TREATY IN 1819

THE EXPANSION OF AMERICAN SETTLERS into the Mississippi and Ohio river valleys resulted in the production of surplus agricultural products which were marketed after being transported by river through the port of New Orleans. Spanish colonial policy handicapped commercial activity carried on by Americans through Spanish territory, but some trade was permitted. News that Spain had been forced to return the province of Louisiana and New Orleans to France leaked out after the secret Treaty of San Ildefonso, October 1, 1800, and confirmation of the treaty in 1801. The territorial ambitions of France under Napoleon were an alarming threat to American security. President Jefferson soon instructed the American minister to France, Robert R. Livingston, to obtain an "irrevocable guarantee of free navigation and the right of deposit" at New Orleans. Plans were later made to negotiate the purchase of New Orleans and West Florida.

Through a set of circumstances fortuitous for the United States, Napoleon abandoned his imperial ambitions for Louisiana and agreed to sell the entire area for sixty million francs, an equivalent of approximately $15,000,000. In the twentieth century this figure seems incredibly small, but the young, poor, United States in the early nineteenth century had an annual federal budget that was about half the amount paid for the Louisiana territory, and most of the money paid France had to be borrowed.

The Louisiana Purchase treaty was ratified by the Senate on October 20, 1803, and the United States took formal possession of the territory at New Orleans on December 20, 1803. Transfer of authority was made at St. Louis the next year. President Jefferson was perplexed by the constitutional questions involved in the purchase and acquisition of territory, but the results promised by these actions made him a broad constructionist on this issue.

With the Louisiana Purchase the United States got rid of Napoleon as a neighbor, it doubled the territorial area of the country, and it gained control of the Mississippi River as a commercial outlet. The boundaries of Louisiana as acquired from France were indefinite. An initial claim was made to the western Mississippi drainage basin. Claims were later effected to the West Florida area, which afterward became part of the states of Mississippi and Alabama.

In a convention signed with Great Britain in 1818, the northern boundary of Louisiana was established at the forty-ninth parallel between Lake of the Woods and the Rocky Mountains. In a treaty with Spain, signed February 22, 1819, the United States acquired Florida. Of significance to the Kansas area, was the compromise border between Spanish territories and the Louisiana territory negotiated by Secretary of State John Quincy Adams and the Spanish minister, Luis Onís. The Adams-Onís treaty set the Sabine River, the Red River, the 100th meridian, the Arkansas River, and a line from the source of the Arkansas River to the forty-second parallel as principal parts of the boundary. About 7,500 square miles of the future state of Kansas again became Spanish territory through that action.

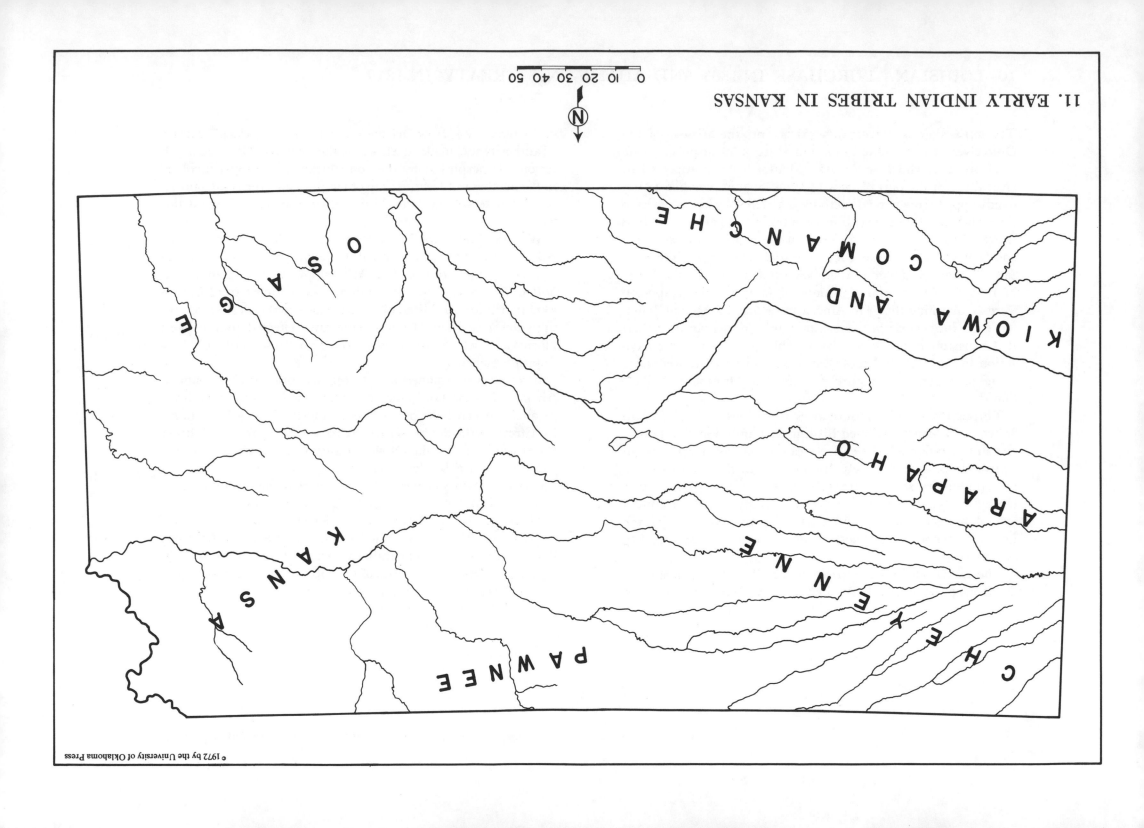

11. EARLY INDIAN TRIBES IN KANSAS

11. EARLY INDIAN TRIBES IN KANSAS

THE NATIVE PEOPLES FOUND in the Kansas region by Coronado and by later explorers included the Indians of Quivira, most likely the Wichitas of a later day. Except for a brief time during the Civil War, when the Wichita Indians were located on the site of the present city of Wichita, this Indian nation called the region of southwestern Oklahoma and adjacent parts of Texas their home.

The Kansa and Osage Indians, native to the area of eastern Kansas, were of Siouan linguistic stock. These closely-related tribes had permanent villages, corn fields, and gardens along some of the principal rivers of Kansas. To supplement their diet they went on seasonal hunting expeditions to the buffalo range located west of their traditional hunting grounds.

Typically, the Kansas and Osages were enemies of the Pawnees, who were Indians of Caddoan linguistic stock like the Wichitas. Their primary villages were located along the Platte River in Nebraska, but their hunting grounds extended as far south as the Smoky Hill River and as far east as the Blue River. At various times they had small villages on the banks of the lower Republican River or farther upstream in present-day Republic County. The name Pawnee Republic, used in reference to these Indians, is the source of the river and county name.

Indians of the High Plains, because of their roving life and dependence on the buffalo, were known as nomadic or wild Indians, in contrast to the more sedentary village tribes located along the eastern fringe of the plains. The Cheyennes and Arapahoes were tribes of Algonquian speaking Indians and were allies against encroachment on their hunting grounds in the central Great Plains. They had village locations in the valleys in the Rockies but they spent a good part of each year living in skin tipis which they frequently moved to new locations in search of the buffalo herds of the grasslands.

Relatively late arrivals to the Kansas area were the Shoshonispeaking Comanches and the Kiowas. After many years of conflict these tribes allied against their enemies and dominated the southern plains, including parts of Kansas. The tipi-dwelling, nomadic Indians of the western half of Kansas were among the earliest tribes to acquire the horse, and they became skilled horsemen.

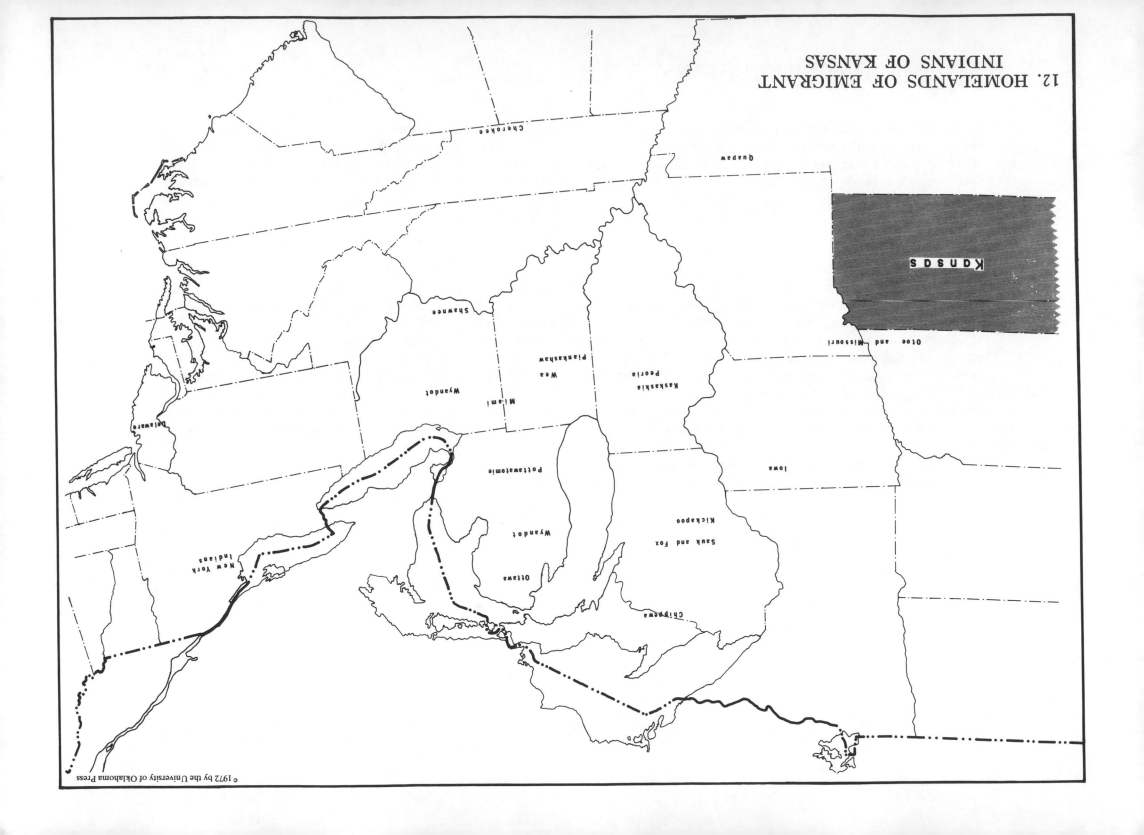

Kansas

Otoe and Missouri

Quapaw

Cherokee

Shawnee

Wyandot

Miami

Wea

Piankashaw

Kaskaskia

Peoria

Delaware

Pottawatomie

Wyandot

Kickapoo

Sauk and Fox

Iowa

Ottawa

Chippewa

New York Indians

12. HOMELANDS OF EMIGRANT INDIANS OF KANSAS

By the mid-1820's a plan for the removal of Indians from areas east of the Mississippi River to vacant lands in the west was being formulated for both humanitarian and political reasons. In 1825 the Kansa and Osage nations agreed to treaties restricting their territory, and similar arrangements were made with native Indians north and south of the region that became Kansas. As a consequence of defining boundaries and restricting reservations of Indians native to the area, large tracts of unclaimed land lay west of the Missouri River, the state of Missouri, and the territory of Arkansas.

President Jackson's Indian policy, which proposed voluntary emigration of eastern Indians to lands west of the Mississippi, was implemented by Congress in the act of May 28, 1830. Indians were to be removed from their eastern lands to tracts in the west set aside for permanent occupancy.

The Indians whose ancestral home was north of the Ohio River were relocated on reservations in what became territorial Kansas and Nebraska. For the most part, Indians from south of the Ohio were assigned lands in the area that became Oklahoma. The Quapaws and Cherokees, for instance, were assigned reservations whose northern boundaries were barely within the territory of Kansas.

Some movement of the emigrant tribes to Kansas got under way even before congressional action in 1830. Most tribes made the trek in the 1830's but some did not move west until the 1840's. The collectively identified New York Indians comprised representatives of the following tribes: Seneca, Onondaga, Cayuga, Tuscarora, Oneida, St. Regis, Stockbridge, Munsee, and Brothertown. Altogether, some twenty-seven tribes or fractions of tribes made up the emigrant Indians offered land in Kansas. Most of the removal program was completed before 1846, only a short time before strong pressures began to build up for further removal of all the Indian tribes to the Indian territory located south of Kansas.

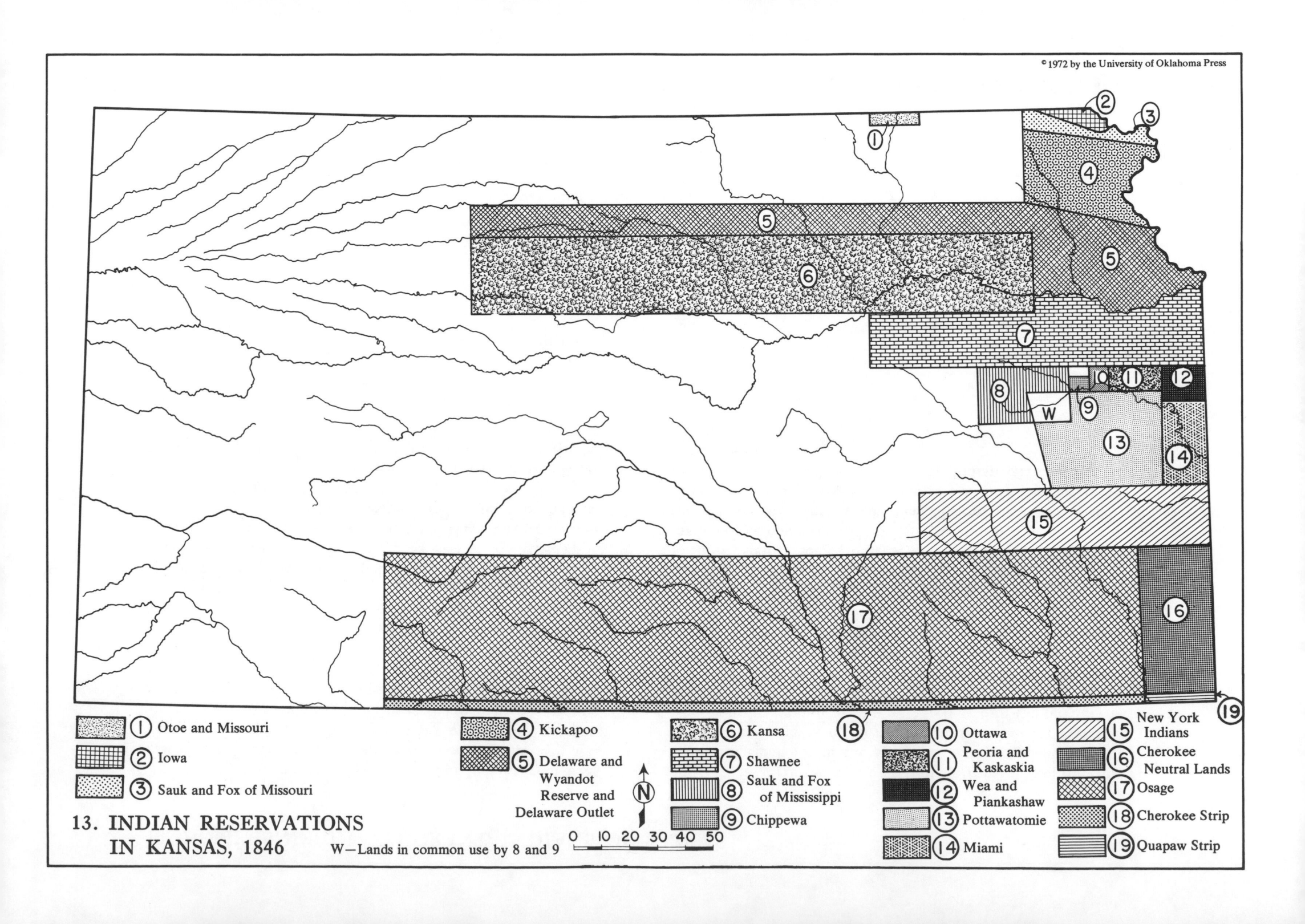

© 1972 by the University of Oklahoma Press

13. INDIAN RESERVATIONS
IN KANSAS, 1846

W—Lands in common use by 8 and 9

0 10 20 30 40 50

N

① Otoe and Missouri
② Iowa
③ Sauk and Fox of Missouri
④ Kickapoo
⑤ Delaware and Wyandot Reserve and Delaware Outlet
⑥ Kansa
⑦ Shawnee
⑧ Sauk and Fox of Mississippi
⑨ Chippewa
⑩ Ottawa
⑪ Peoria and Kaskaskia
⑫ Wea and Piankashaw
⑬ Pottawatomie
⑭ Miami
⑮ New York Indians
⑯ Cherokee Neutral Lands
⑰ Osage
⑱ Cherokee Strip
⑲ Quapaw Strip

13. INDIAN RESERVATIONS IN KANSAS, 1846

INDIANS FROM THE OHIO VALLEY and the Great Lakes region who were relocated on reservations in the area that became eastern Kansas were recipients of high-quality land that was often better than the land they had ceded to the federal government. In general they received an amount of land, carved from the former Kansa and Osage domain, that was as large an acreage as the possessions they had left. But these factors did not make removal any easier. The Indians, like any other people, were reluctant to leave their ancestral homes and embark on the long journey to reservations marked out for them in the West.

The Wyandot tribe was one of the last to remove to Kansas. Objecting to the lands originally assigned to them because they thought the promised reservation was too far from civilization, the Wyandots acquired thirty-nine sections from the Delaware tribe located on the easternmost tip of the Delaware reservation.

The Kansa nation occupied two distinct reservations: the large tract on the Kansas River, shown on this map, and, after 1847, another reservation located on unclaimed land near Council Grove. The various Pottawatomie bands, shown here on a reserve in east central Kansas, were then relocated on the eastern portion of the ceded Kansa reserve. In later years the Pottawatomie Indian Reservation was decreased to an eleven-mile square in Jackson County. Two other smaller reservations which lasted into the twentieth century were the Kickapoo reserve in Brown County, and the Iowa, Sauk and Fox reserve located in northern Brown and Doniphan counties and on adjacent lands in Nebraska.

Most of the Indian reservations described as permanent in 1846 were the homes of the various emigrant tribes for about a generation before they were again moved, this time to Indian Territory, the present state of Oklahoma. Even the Kansa and Osage tribes, with historic attachments to the region of eastern Kansas, were forced to sell their reservations and move in the 1870's to new locations just south of the Kansas border in Indian Territory.

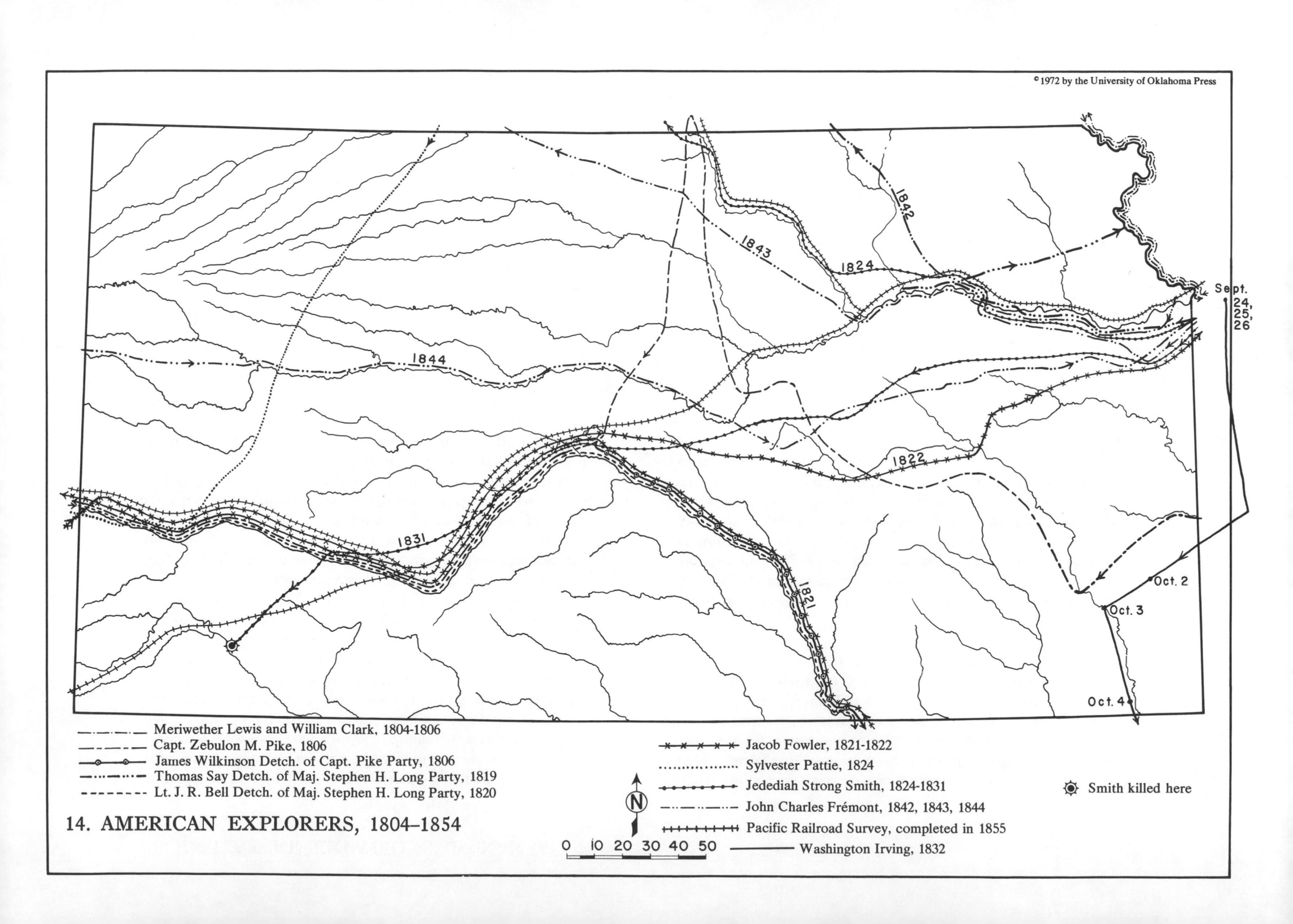

© 1972 by the University of Oklahoma Press

1843

1842

1824

1844

1822

1831

1821

Sept. 24, 25, 26

Oct. 2

Oct. 3

Oct. 4

————·—·—— Meriwether Lewis and William Clark, 1804-1806
———·——·—— Capt. Zebulon M. Pike, 1806
——o——o—— James Wilkinson Detch. of Capt. Pike Party, 1806
——··——··—— Thomas Say Detch. of Maj. Stephen H. Long Party, 1819
———————— Lt. J. R. Bell Detch. of Maj. Stephen H. Long Party, 1820

—x——x——x—— Jacob Fowler, 1821-1822
·················· Sylvester Pattie, 1824
——•—•—•—— Jedediah Strong Smith, 1824-1831
——···——···—— John Charles Frémont, 1842, 1843, 1844
+++++++++++ Pacific Railroad Survey, completed in 1855
———————— Washington Irving, 1832

⊙ Smith killed here

14. AMERICAN EXPLORERS, 1804–1854

N

0 10 20 30 40 50

14. AMERICAN EXPLORERS, 1804–1854

IN THE HALF-CENTURY before the creation of the territory of Kansas, official and unofficial American explorers helped the nation to become acquainted with the area. Early official explorers, such as Lewis and Clark, visited only the well-traveled Missouri River portion of the future state. Zebulon Pike led an exploring party completely across the future state, and he visited a Pawnee village located just across the northern border. When his party reached the Arkansas River, Pike sent a small detachment downstream under the leadership of Lieutenant James Wilkinson.

The next official exploration of the region, led by Major Stephen H. Long in 1819–20, followed a route which completely circled the future state but did not visit the interior. However, detachments from the Long expedition aided in a more complete understanding of the area. One, led by Thomas Say, visited a Kansa village on the Blue River in 1819, and the other, under the command of Lieutenant John R. Bell, descended the Arkansas River in 1820. Long, and to some extent Pike before him, contributed to the idea that the western part of the future state of Kansas was a portion of the Great American Desert.

The fur trappers, as unofficial explorers of the West, were often the first outsiders to move through a new land. Jacob Fowler, Sylvester Pattie, and Jedediah Strong Smith are outstanding examples of this group. Fowler recorded interesting descriptions of the territory through which he traveled in 1821–22. Pattie, better known for his exploits in the Spanish Southwest, traveled across the area in 1824. Another early visitor was the outstanding fur trader–map maker, Jedediah Strong Smith, who wintered in a Pawnee village in 1824. He encountered many dangers on his significant journeys of discovery in the Rockies and the Far West. While escorting a caravan over the relatively safe trail to Santa Fe in 1831, Smith was killed by Comanche warriors at Wagon Body Springs in Seward County.

Other visitors to the area in later years who recorded their impressions included Washington Irving and John C. Frémont. Irving, on his 1832 journey, which became the basis for his *Tour of the Prairies*, spent several days traveling through the southeastern part of future Kansas. Frémont, the noted "Pathfinder" of the West, traversed the Kansas region as head of several official explorations. By his time the area was well known, so that Frémont's reports pass quickly over the grasslands and concentrate on his activities in the mountains and Far West. A final look at the Kansas region before the area was established as a territory was made under the auspices of the War Department, whose Pacific railroad surveys, published in 1855, provided suggested routes for future railroads.

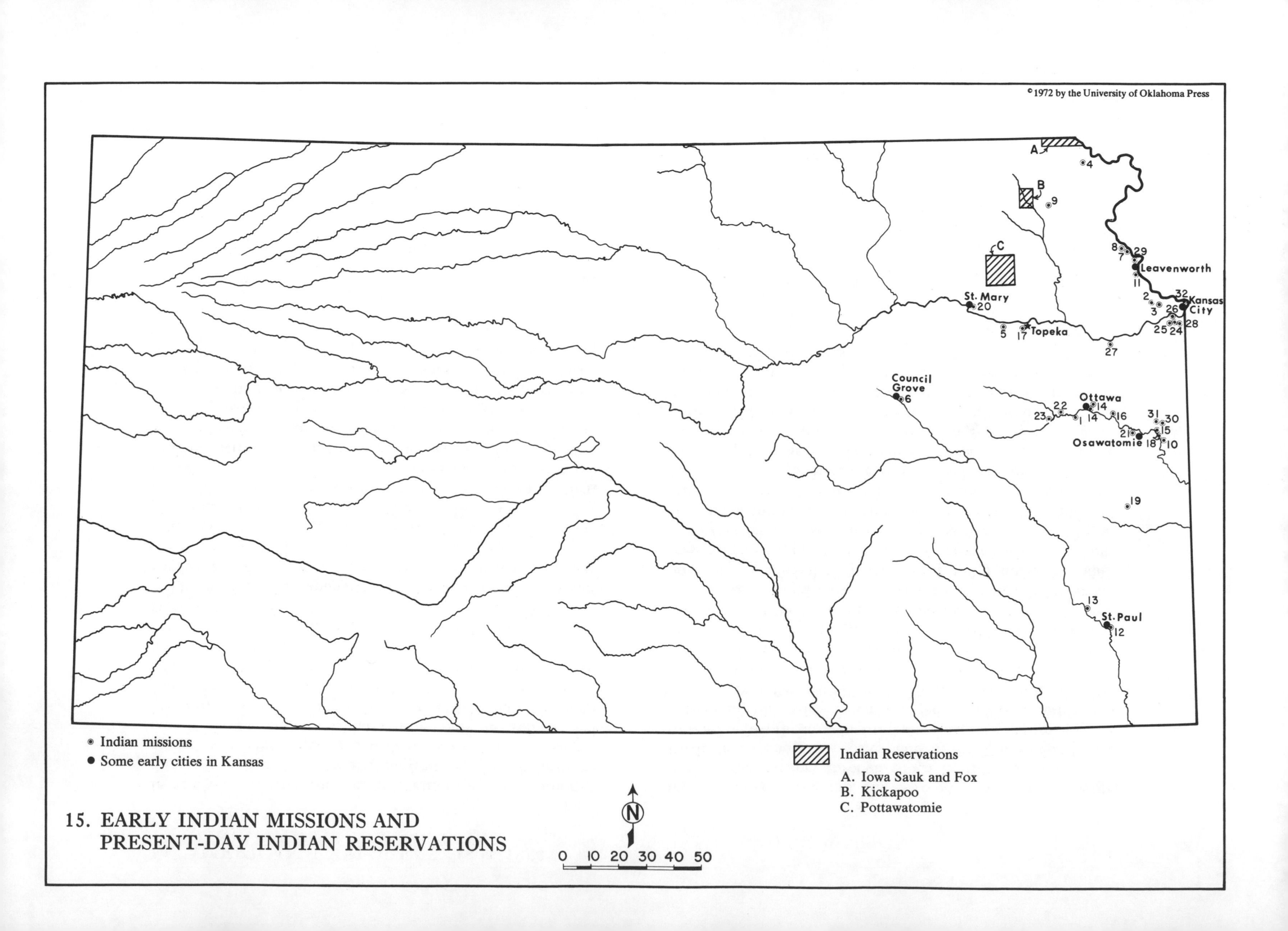

© 1972 by the University of Oklahoma Press

A
⊙ 4
B
⊙ 9
8 ⊙ 29
7 ⊙
Leavenworth
11
32
2 ⊙ 26 Kansas
3 ⊙ City
25 24 28
St. Mary
20
5 ⊙ 17 ★ Topeka
27

Council
Grove
⊙ 6
22 Ottawa
23 ⊙ 14
1 14 ⊙ 16 31 30
2 ⊙ 15
Osawatomie 18 10

⊙ 19

13
St. Paul
12

⊙ Indian missions
● Some early cities in Kansas

▨ Indian Reservations

A. Iowa Sauk and Fox
B. Kickapoo
C. Pottawatomie

15. EARLY INDIAN MISSIONS AND
PRESENT-DAY INDIAN RESERVATIONS

Ⓝ
0 10 20 30 40 50

15. EARLY INDIAN MISSIONS AND PRESENT-DAY INDIAN RESERVATIONS

MISSIONS AND MISSION SCHOOLS were established in early-day Kansas to assist Indians in the transformation from their tribal culture to American citizenship. No missions were provided in the region of Kansas for the nomadic or "wild" Indians of the High Plains, and the accompanying map shows that the Council Grove location for the Kansa mission was the westernmost Indian mission in the state.

Some of the mission schools provided academic training for Indian youth, but more frequently the instruction was vocational and the term "manual labor school" was often used. Well-known missionaries in the region included Benton Pixley, Isaac McCoy, Jotham Meeker, Dr. Johnston Lykins, Thomas Johnson, Samuel Irvin, and John Schoenmakers. Indian assistants like the Delaware, Charles Journeycake, or the Kickapoo prophet, Kennekuk, had outstanding influence upon fellow tribesmen at their missions.

The following list provides the names, locations, and years of activity of Indian missions shown on the accompanying map:

1. Chippewa and Munsee Moravian (1862–1905), Franklin County.
2. Delaware Baptist on two adjacent sites (1832–67), Wyandotte County.
3. Delaware Methodist (1832–44), Wyandotte County.
4. Iowa, Sauk and Fox Presbyterian (1837–63), Doniphan County.
5. and 6. Kansa Methodist on two sites (1835–45), Shawnee County and (1850–54), Morris County.
7. Kickapoo Catholic (1836–41), Leavenworth County.
8. Kickapoo Methodist (1833–59), Leavenworth County.
9. Kickapoo Presbyterian (1856–68), Brown County.
10. Miami Catholic (1850–?), Miami County.
11. Munsee Moravian (1845–60), Leavenworth County.
12. Osage Catholic (1847–70), Neosho County.
13. Mission Neosho [United Foreign Missionary Society: Presbyterian, Reformed Dutch, and Associated Reformed Churches] to the Osage (1824–29), Neosho County.
14. Ottawa Baptist on two adjacent sites (1837–55), Franklin County.
15. Peoria and Kaskaskia Methodist (1833–43), Miami County.
16. and 17. Pottawatomie Baptist on two sites (1837–55), Franklin County and Shawnee County.
18., 19., and 20. Pottawatomie Catholic on three sites (1836–69), Miami, Linn, and Pottawatomie counties.
21. Pottawatomie Methodist (1838–48), Miami County.
22. and 23. Sauk and Fox Methodist on two sites (1860–66), Franklin and Osage counties.
24. Shawnee Baptist (1831–55), Johnson County.
25. Shawnee Friends (1837–69), Johnson County.
26., 27., and 28. Shawnee Methodist on three sites (1830–62), Wyandotte, Douglas, and Johnson counties.
29. Stockbridge Baptist (1844–48), Leavenworth County.
30. Wea Baptist (c1840–56), Miami County.
31. Wea and Piankashaw Presbyterian (1834–35), Miami County.
32. Wyandot Methodist (1843–55), Wyandotte County.

Three Indian reservations remained in Kansas in 1988: the Iowa, Sac [Sauk] and Fox reservation northeast of Reserve, the Kickapoo reservation west of Horton, and the Pottawatomie reservation west of Mayetta.

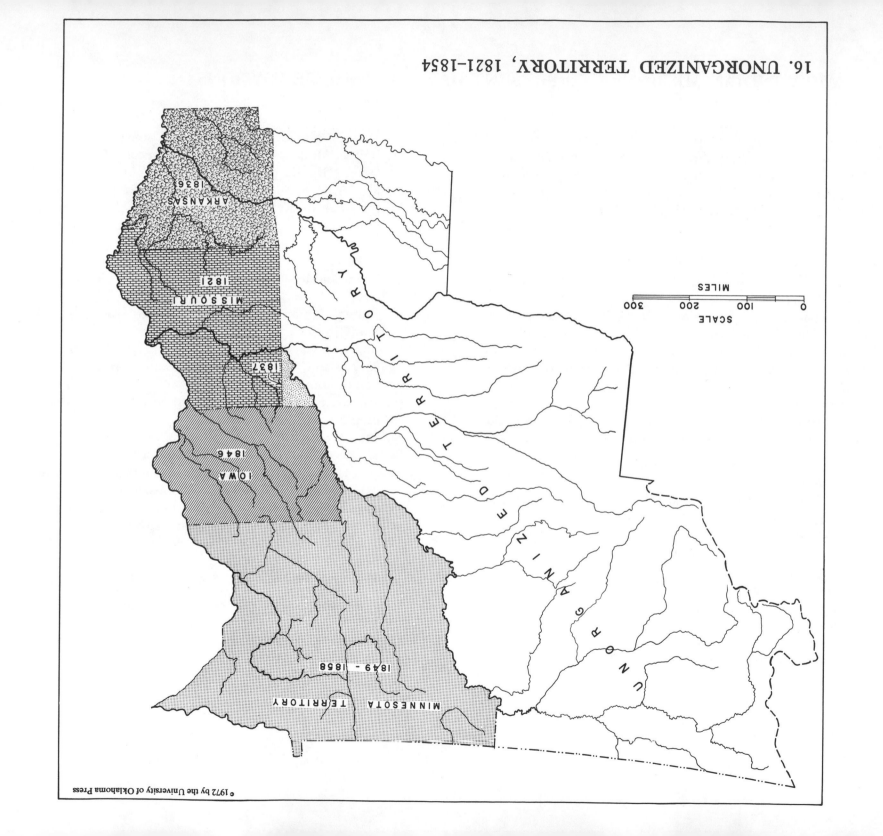

SCALE
0   100   200   300
MILES

ARKANSAS
1836

MISSOURI
1821

1837

IOWA
1846

MINNESOTA TERRITORY
1849 – 1858

UNORGANIZED TERRITORY

16. UNORGANIZED TERRITORY, 1821–1854

THE VAST AREA of the Louisiana Purchase was initially governed from New Orleans and St. Louis as the Louisiana Territory. In 1812 Louisiana gained statehood and the region outside the state became the Missouri Territory. Missouri gained statehood in 1821, and her western border was extended to the Missouri River with the Platte Purchase. From 1819 to 1824 the territory of Arkansas provided the governing authority for that portion of the Louisiana Purchase located west of Arkansas.

The area north of Missouri and east of the Missouri River was known as Iowa Territory from 1838 to 1846, when Iowa became a state. Minnesota Territory was a very large area having control of that part of Iowa Territory that did not gain statehood and also a part of the former Wisconsin Territory.

The creation of states and territories just to the west of the Mississippi River brought no congressional action for territorial government for the region which lay still farther west of those areas. This remaining part of the Louisiana Purchase was therefore identified as "Unorganized Territory." Into this vast land of the Indian there was some penetration by fur trappers, missionaries, army personnel and infrequent travelers, but there was no official provision for local government. This unorganized territory was considered Indian country, and non-Indians were granted permission to pass through the area but they could not settle permanently nor own land there.

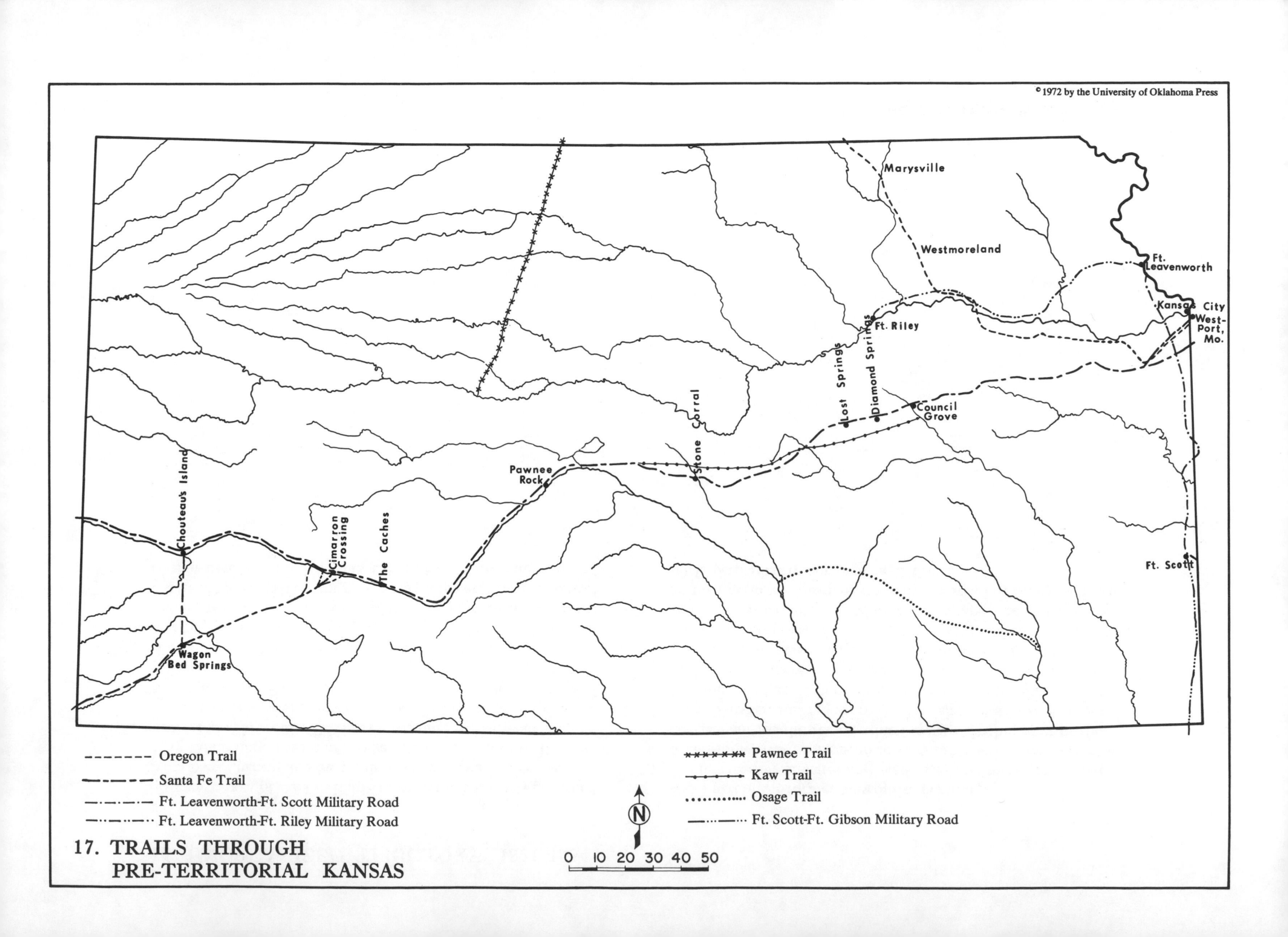

Marysville

Westmoreland

Ft. Leavenworth

Kansas City
West-
Port,
Mo.

Ft. Riley

Lost Springs

Diamond Springs

Council Grove

Stone Corral

Chouteau's Island

Pawnee Rock

Ft. Scott

Cimarron Crossing

The Caches

Wagon Bed Springs

- - - - Oregon Trail

- · - Santa Fe Trail

- · - · - Ft. Leavenworth-Ft. Scott Military Road

- · · - Ft. Leavenworth-Ft. Riley Military Road

✗✗✗✗✗✗ Pawnee Trail

· · · · Kaw Trail

· · · · · · · Osage Trail

— · · · — Ft. Scott-Ft. Gibson Military Road

N

0 10 20 30 40 50

17. TRAILS THROUGH PRE-TERRITORIAL KANSAS

17. TRAILS THROUGH PRE-TERRITORIAL KANSAS

BEFORE THE TERRITORY OF KANSAS was created in 1854 the region was known as a place to cross in order to reach Santa Fe, Oregon, or California. The Santa Fe Trail was an ancient passageway used regularly after 1821 by merchant-traders from Missouri who took manufactured goods to Santa Fe to exchange for furs and other items available there. Mexican traders also provided caravans going to western Missouri in this international trade. The region from Council Grove to near Santa Fe was the most hazardous part of the trail, which was about eight hundred miles long when Westport or Independence, Missouri, were the jumping-off places. Important locations along the trail in Kansas included Diamond Springs, Lost Springs, Stone Corral, Pawnee Rock, The Caches, Cimarron Crossing, Chouteau's Island, and Wagon Bed Springs. In western Kansas a Santa Fe-bound caravan had the choice of two routes, the more dangerous dry, or desert, route southwest from Cimarron Crossing and other Arkansas River crossings, or the mountain route which followed the river into Colorado before turning south. An official survey in 1825 provided an alternate, little-used route south from Chouteau's Island, but travelers preferred the route blazed earlier, even though they were without water for two or more days.

The long road for fur trading expeditions or for Oregon-bound emigrants resulted in many trails west from the Missouri. The route shown from Westport, up the Kansas River valley, northwest through present Westmoreland and across the Blue River near Marysville was most heavily traveled.

Indian trails to buffalo-hunting grounds were also a feature of the preterritorial period. The Pawnee Trail extended from villages along the Platte toward the Smoky Hill River. The Kaw Trail, blazed by Kansa Indians from their reservation near Council Grove, paralleled the Santa Fe Trail. The Osage Trail leading to the present-day site of Wichita provided this southeastern Kansas tribe with an easy route to buffalo country.

Three army posts antedated Kansas territory, and roads connecting Fort Leavenworth with Fort Scott and with Fort Riley provided additional access to the area.

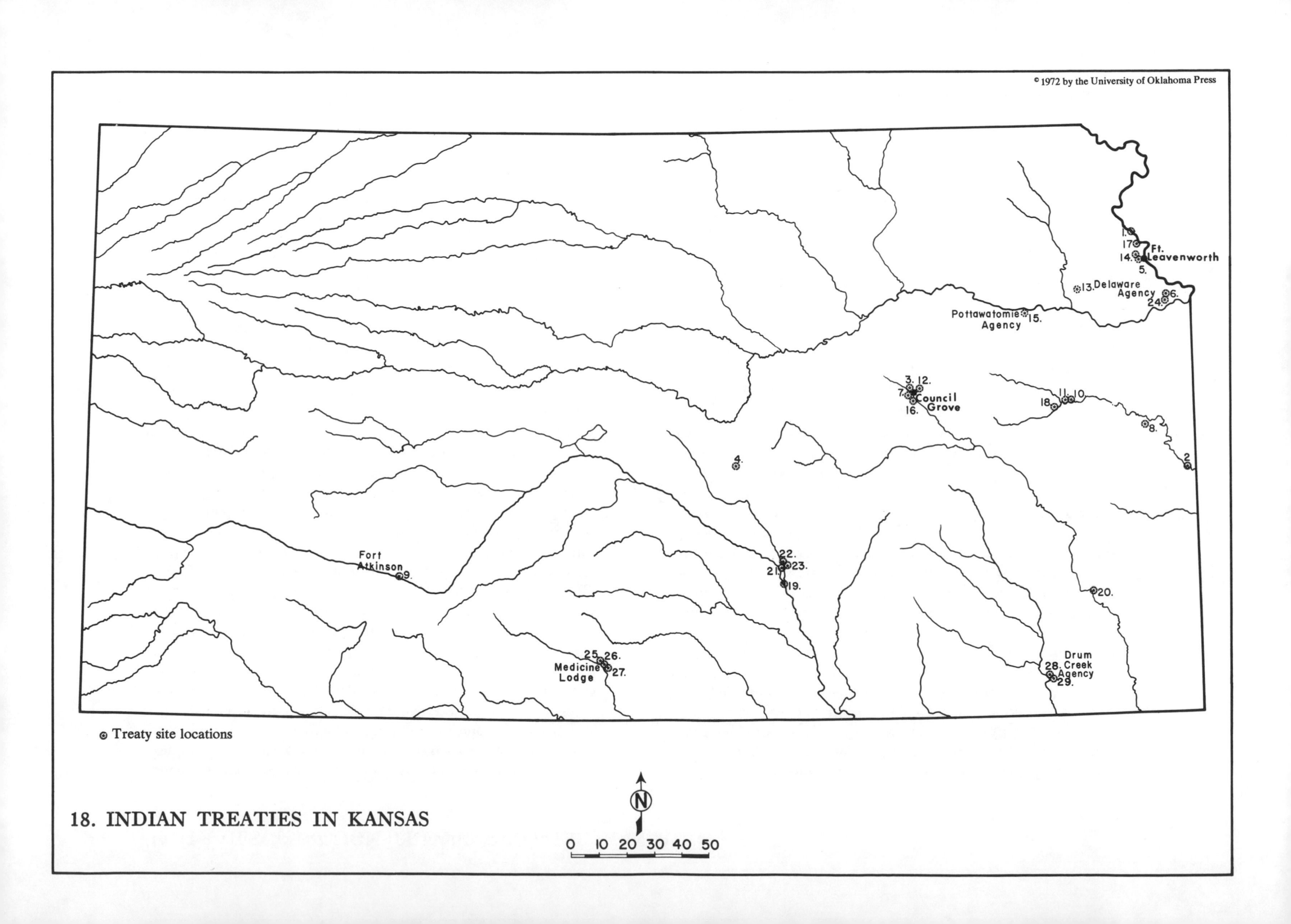

1.
17.
14. Ft.
Leavenworth
5.
13. Delaware
Agency 6.
24. 6.
Pottawatomie 15.
Agency

3. 12.
7. Council
Grove
16.
18. 11. 10.

8.

2.

4.

Fort
Atkinson 9.

22.
21. 23.
19.

20.

25. 26.
Medicine 27.
Lodge

Drum
28. Creek
Agency
29.

⊚ Treaty site locations

18. INDIAN TREATIES IN KANSAS

N

0 10 20 30 40 50

18. INDIAN TREATIES IN KANSAS

TWENTY-NINE TREATIES between Indians and the United States government or between two or more Indian tribes under the watchful eye of the federal government were drawn up in Kansas. They were:

1. Kansa and Osage in council with Major Stephen H. Long, on Isle au Vache in Missouri River, Atchison County, August 24, 1819.
2. Osage at the United States factory on the Marais des Cygnes River, with United States Commissioner Richard Graham, August 31, 1822.
3. Great and Little Osage at Council Grove with United States Commissioners Benj. H. Reeves, George C. Sibley, and Thomas Mather, August 10, 1825.
4. Kansa at Sora Creek [Dry Turkey Creek], McPherson County, with same commissioners meeting Osage in 3., above, August 16, 1825.
5. Iowa, Sauk and Fox of Missouri at Fort Leavenworth with United States Commissioner William Clark, September 17, 1836.
6. At Delaware agency between Delaware and Wyandot tribes, December 14, 1843.
7. Kansa near Council Grove with United States Commissioners Thomas H. Harvey and Richard W. Cummins, January 14, 1846.
8. Pottawatomie [of the Prairie, of the Wabash, and of Indiana] and including Chippewa and Ottawa, at Pottawatomie Creek near the Marais des Cygnes with United States Commissioners T. P. Andrews, Thomas H. Harvey, and Gideon C. Matlock, June 17, 1846.
9. Comanche, Kiowa, and Kiowa-Apache at Fort Atkinson, Ford County, with United States Commissioner Thomas Fitzpatrick, July 27, 1853.
10. Chippewa and Munsee at Sauk and Fox agency with United States Commissioner David Crawford, July 16, 1859.
11. Sauk and Fox at Sauk and Fox agency with United States Commissioner Alfred B. Greenwood, October 1, 1859.
12. Kansa at Kansa agency, Council Grove, with United States Commissioner Alfred B. Greenwood, October 5, 1859.
13. Delaware at Sarcoxie on Delaware reservation with United States Commissioner Thomas B. Sykes, May 30, 1860.
14. Delaware at Leavenworth with United States Commissioner William P. Dole, July 2, 1861.
15. Pottawatomi [Mission, Prairie, and Woods bands] at their agency with United States Commissioner William W. Ross, November 15, 1861.
16. Kansa at their agency near Council Grove with United States Commissioner H. W. Farnsworth, March 13, 1862.
17. Kickapoo at Kickapoo agency with United States Commissioner Charles B. Keith, June 28, 1862.
18. Sauk and Fox (and representatives of thirteen other tribes refugee from Indian territory) at Sauk and Fox agency near Quenemo, Osage County, with Superintendent of Indian Affairs W. G. Coffin, October 8, 1864.
19. Comanche, Kiowa, Arapaho, and Kiowa-Apache at mouth of the Little Arkansas, August 15, 1865.
20. Osage at Canville Trading Post, Neosho County, with D. N. Cooley, United States Commissioner, September 29, 1865.
21. Cheyenne and Arapaho at camp on the Little Arkansas with United States Commissioners John B. Sanborn, William S. Harney, Thomas Murphy, Kit Carson, William W. Bent, Jesse H. Leavenworth, and James Steele, October 14, 1865.
22. [Kiowa-]Apache, Cheyenne, and Arapaho at Council Grounds on Little Arkansas with United States commissioners listed in 21., above, October 17, 1865.
23. Kiowa and Comanche at Council Grounds on Little Arkansas with United States commissioners listed in 21., above, October 18, 1865.
24. Delaware at Delaware agency with Superintendent of Indian Affairs Thomas Murphy, July 4, 1866.
25. Kiowa and Comanche at council camp on Medicine Lodge Creek with United States Commissioners Nathaniel G. Taylor, William

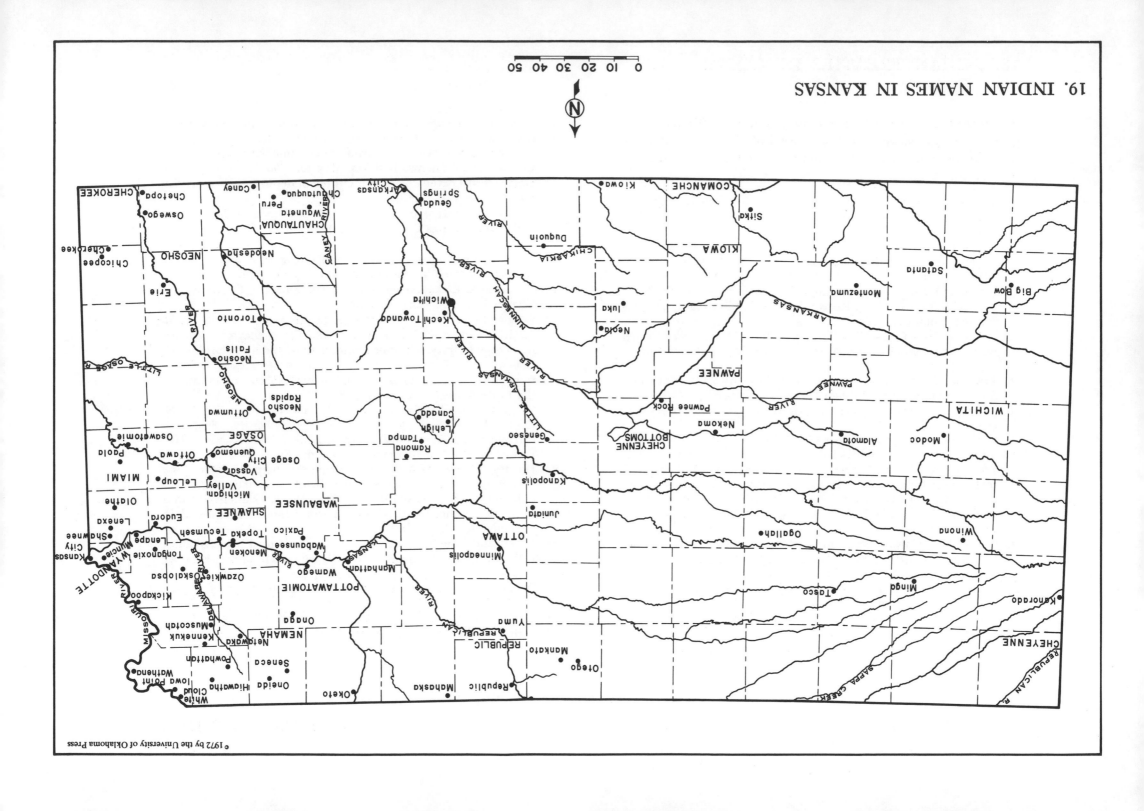

19. INDIAN NAMES IN KANSAS

S. Harney, C. C. Augur, Alfred S. H. Terry, John B. Sanborn, Samuel F. Tappan, and John B. Henderson, October 21, 1867.

26. Kiowa, Comanche, and [Kiowa-]Apache with United States commissioners listed in 25., above, October 21, 1867.

27. Cheyenne and Arapaho at council camp on Medicine Lodge Creek with United States commissioners listed in 25., above, October 28, 1867.

28. Osage at Drum Creek agency, Montgomery County, with United States Commissioner N. G. Taylor, May 27, 1868.

29. Osage at Drum Creek agency, Montgomery County, with United States Commissioners J. D. Lang, John V. Farwell, and Vincent Colyer, September 10, 1870.

Almost a hundred other treaties involving Indians who were resident at some time in Kansas occurred outside the Kansas region. After 1871, treaties were no longer made with Indian nations. Instead, following negotiation, laws affecting Indians were passed by Congress.

19. INDIAN NAMES IN KANSAS

THE FACE OF THE MAP of the state of Kansas is filled with names of Indian origin. The state name came from the Kansas River, which was in turn named for the tribe inhabiting its banks. Kansas City, Kanopolis, and Kanorado are other examples of the use of this word, and at one time there was a Kansas County in the southwestern part of the state. Seventeen other present-day counties have Indian names, mostly for tribes who were resident in the area at one time. The names of Arapahoe, Sequoyah, Otoe, and Peketon were attached to earlier counties.

Also of Indian origin were the names of the largest rivers in the state, the Missouri, the Kansas, the Arkansas, and many other streams as well. Other river names, such as the Smoky Hill, were translations of Indian names for these waterways.

The three largest cities in Kansas have Indian names: Wichita, for the tribe living on the site during the Civil War; Kansas City, for the state and, indirectly, for the tribe; and Topeka, a name given the area by the Kansa tribe because it was a good place to dig wild potatoes.

Other town names are of diverse Indian origin. Osawatomie, for instance, is a combination of Osage and Pottawatomie. Iowa Point, Osage City, and Pawnee Rock are examples of a combination of Indian and English words, and Minneapolis combines an Indian and a Greek word.

In general, the Indian names used in Kansas that did not have a local connection were drawn from names already in use in various parts of the United States to the northeast of Kansas. Oneida, Hiawatha, Powhattan, Manhattan, and Ottumwa are examples. Indian names of southeastern United States origin include Tampa, Cherokee, and Iuka. On the other hand, Ramona, Modoc, and Yuma have a far western origin; Sitka comes from Alaska; and Montezuma and Tasco supposedly came from Mexico.

An examination of names of townships and of creeks and other natural features in Kansas discloses many more Indian names. While their numbers are no longer great in the state, the Indians as a people have made an indelible impression through the names that are tied to the Kansas landscape.

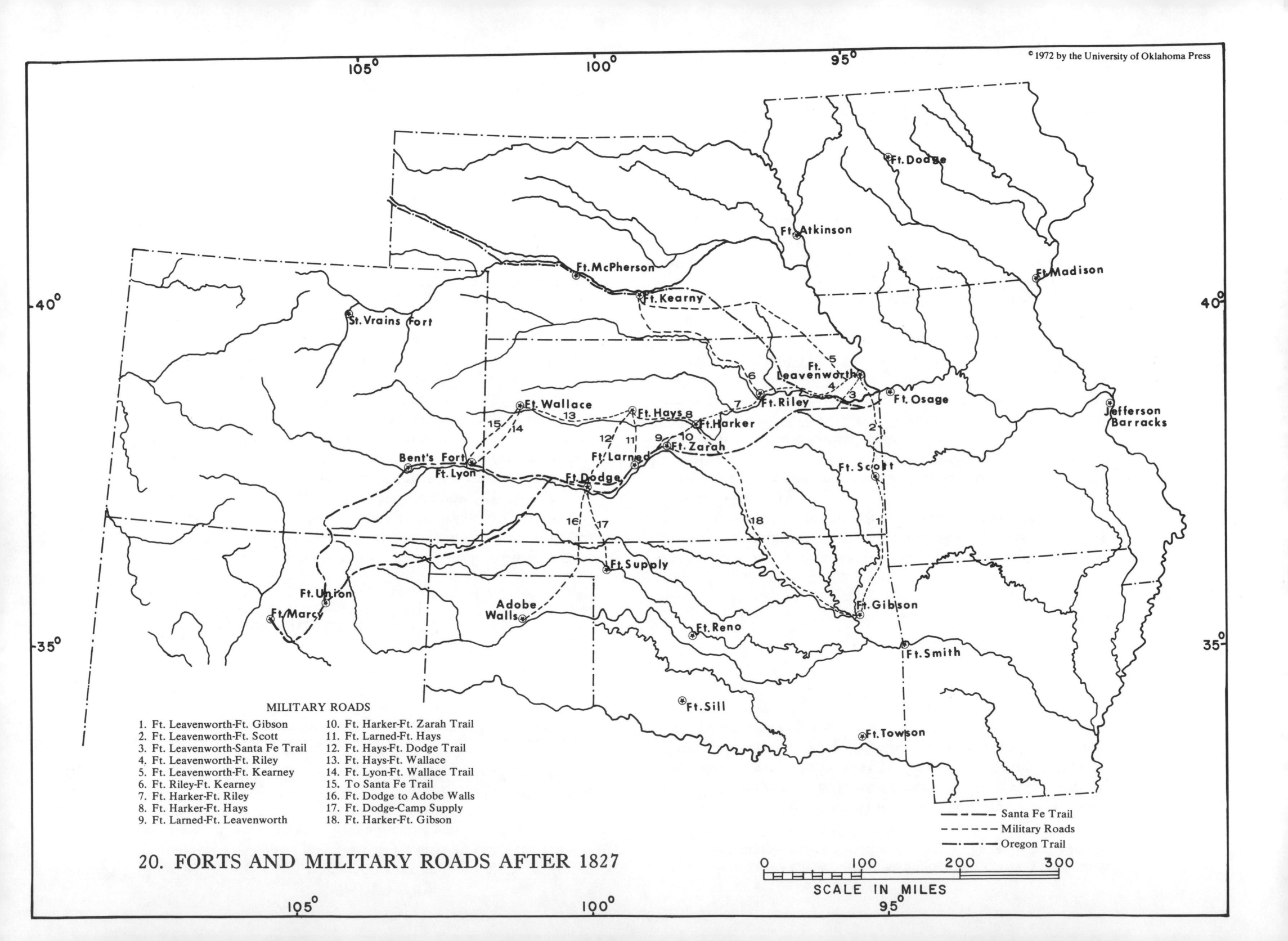

© 1972 by the University of Oklahoma Press

105°   100°   95°

40°   40°

Ft. Dodge

Ft. Atkinson

Ft. McPherson

Ft. Madison

Ft. Kearny

St. Vrains Fort

5

6   Ft.
Leavenworth
4
3   Ft. Osage

Ft. Wallace   7   Ft. Riley
13   Ft. Hays 8
Jefferson
Barracks
15   14   Ft. Harker
12   11   9   10
Bent's Fort   Ft. Larned   Ft. Zarah   2
Ft. Lyon   Ft. Dodge   Ft. Scott

1

16   17   18

Ft. Union   Ft. Supply

Ft. Marcy   Adobe
Walls   Ft. Gibson

35°   Ft. Reno   35°
Ft. Smith

MILITARY ROADS

1. Ft. Leavenworth-Ft. Gibson   10. Ft. Harker-Ft. Zarah Trail
2. Ft. Leavenworth-Ft. Scott   11. Ft. Larned-Ft. Hays
3. Ft. Leavenworth-Santa Fe Trail   12. Ft. Hays-Ft. Dodge Trail
4. Ft. Leavenworth-Ft. Riley   13. Ft. Hays-Ft. Wallace
5. Ft. Leavenworth-Ft. Kearney   14. Ft. Lyon-Ft. Wallace Trail
6. Ft. Riley-Ft. Kearney   15. To Santa Fe Trail
7. Ft. Harker-Ft. Riley   16. Ft. Dodge to Adobe Walls
8. Ft. Harker-Ft. Hays   17. Ft. Dodge-Camp Supply
9. Ft. Larned-Ft. Leavenworth   18. Ft. Harker-Ft. Gibson

Ft. Sill

Ft. Towson

20. FORTS AND MILITARY ROADS AFTER 1827

— — — Santa Fe Trail
- - - - Military Roads
—·—·— Oregon Trail

0   100   200   300
SCALE IN MILES

105°   100°   95°

20. FORTS AND MILITARY ROADS AFTER 1827

THE UNITED STATES ARMY established Fort Leavenworth in 1827 (as Cantonment Leavenworth), the oldest permanent United States military post west of the Missouri River. An important link in the military road system leading south from Fort Leavenworth was Fort Scott (1842–65). Fort Riley (1853–), established in 1852 as Camp Centre, was located between the Oregon and Santa Fe trails to provide protection for travelers on overland routes. Four nonpermanent forts operating at short intervals along the Santa Fe Trail in western Kansas were Mann (1845–48), Atkinson (1850–54), Mackay (1850–51), and Aubrey (1865–66). Forts of more permanent construction which were built along the projected route of the first railroad from Kansas City to Denver were Harker (1864–73), Hays (1865–89), and Wallace (1865–82). Farther south along the Santa Fe Trail and the future route of the Santa Fe railroad were Forts Zarah (1864–69), Larned (1859–82), and Dodge (1864–82).

Numerous local camps, forts, or fortifications, inspired by fear of Indians or developed briefly as a stopping place for army personnel, were located in other parts of Kansas. Abandonment of most of these military posts came after the Indian tribes were firmly established on reservations. Only Fort Leavenworth and Fort Riley remained in the twentieth century as important training centers for the army.

The military roads which connected these posts were as important to the people of Kansas as the army forts. Some improvement, such as bridges and culverts, was made on these roads, and civilian traffic soon learned to use the military roads for cross-country travel. Widely used during the territorial period were the military roads from Fort Leavenworth to Fort Scott and Fort Riley and to the Santa Fe Trail. After the Civil War the roads marked out to other forts generally followed the easiest cross-country paths.

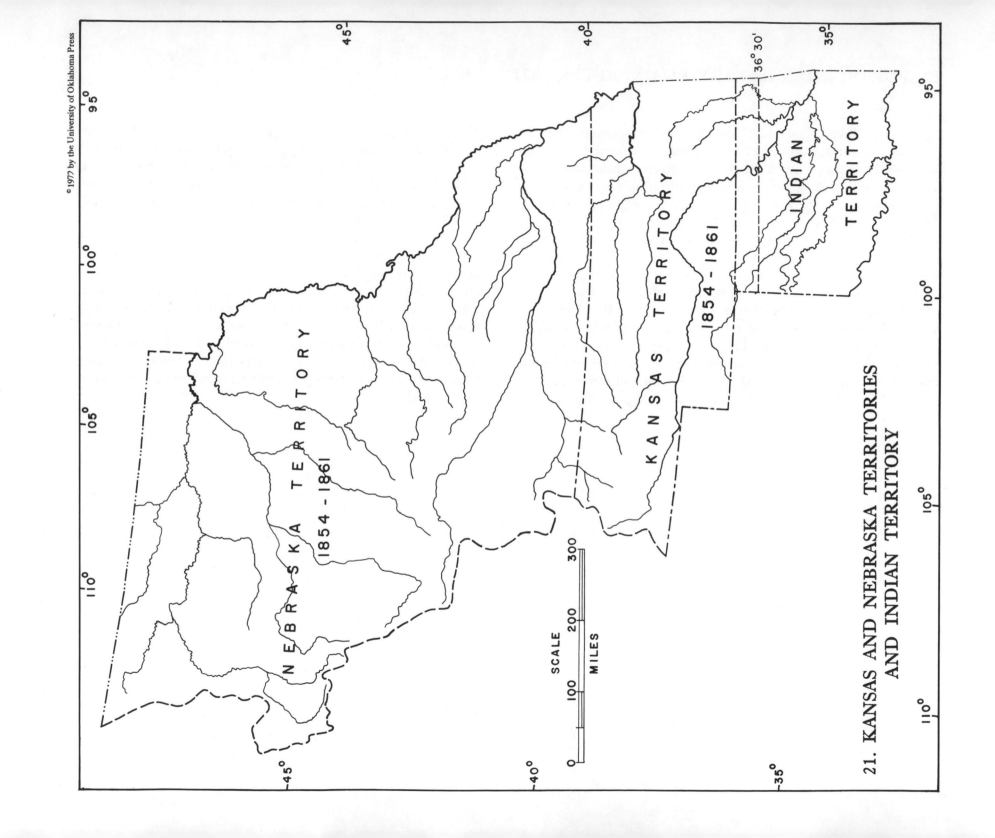

NEBRASKA TERRITORY
1854 – 1861

KANSAS TERRITORY
1854 – 1861

INDIAN
TERRITORY

SCALE

MILES

0   100   200   300

21. KANSAS AND NEBRASKA TERRITORIES
AND INDIAN TERRITORY

21. KANSAS AND NEBRASKA TERRITORIES AND INDIAN TERRITORY

THE PASSAGE of the Kansas–Nebraska Act, May 30, 1854, created the twin territories of Kansas and Nebraska out of Unorganized Territory. The only portion of the Louisiana Purchase acquired from France in 1803 which still remained unorganized was the Indian Territory to the south of 37° North Latitude.

The provision of the Missouri Compromise of 1820 that had divided the area of the United States west of Missouri between free and slave territory at 36°30′ was repealed by the Kansas-Nebraska Act. This re-opening of the slavery question in Kansas and Nebraska Territories was to find a solution, in the words of Senator Stephen A. Douglas, through "popular sovereignty." By popular sovereignty he meant that the people in the territories would decide the future status of slavery, rather than having the decision made by Congress. The southern boundary of Kansas was placed at 37° rather than 36°30′ because it was erroneously believed that the northern boundary of the Cherokee lands was lo-

cated at the thirty-seventh parallel.

The act creating Kansas Territory defined its boundaries as follows. "Beginning at a point on the western boundary of the State of Missouri, where the thirty-seventh parallel of north latitude crosses the same; thence west on said parallel to the eastern boundary of New Mexico; thence north on said boundary to latitude thirty-eight; thence following said boundary westward to the east boundary of the Territory of Utah, on the summit of the Rocky Mountains; thence northward on said summit to the fortieth parallel of latitude; thence east on said parallel to the western boundary of the State of Missouri; thence south with the western boundary of said State to the place of beginning." The area enclosed within these boundaries was 126,283 square miles, or 50 per cent more land than was later included in the state of Kansas. Nebraska Territory covered a huge area more than twice as large as Kansas Territory.

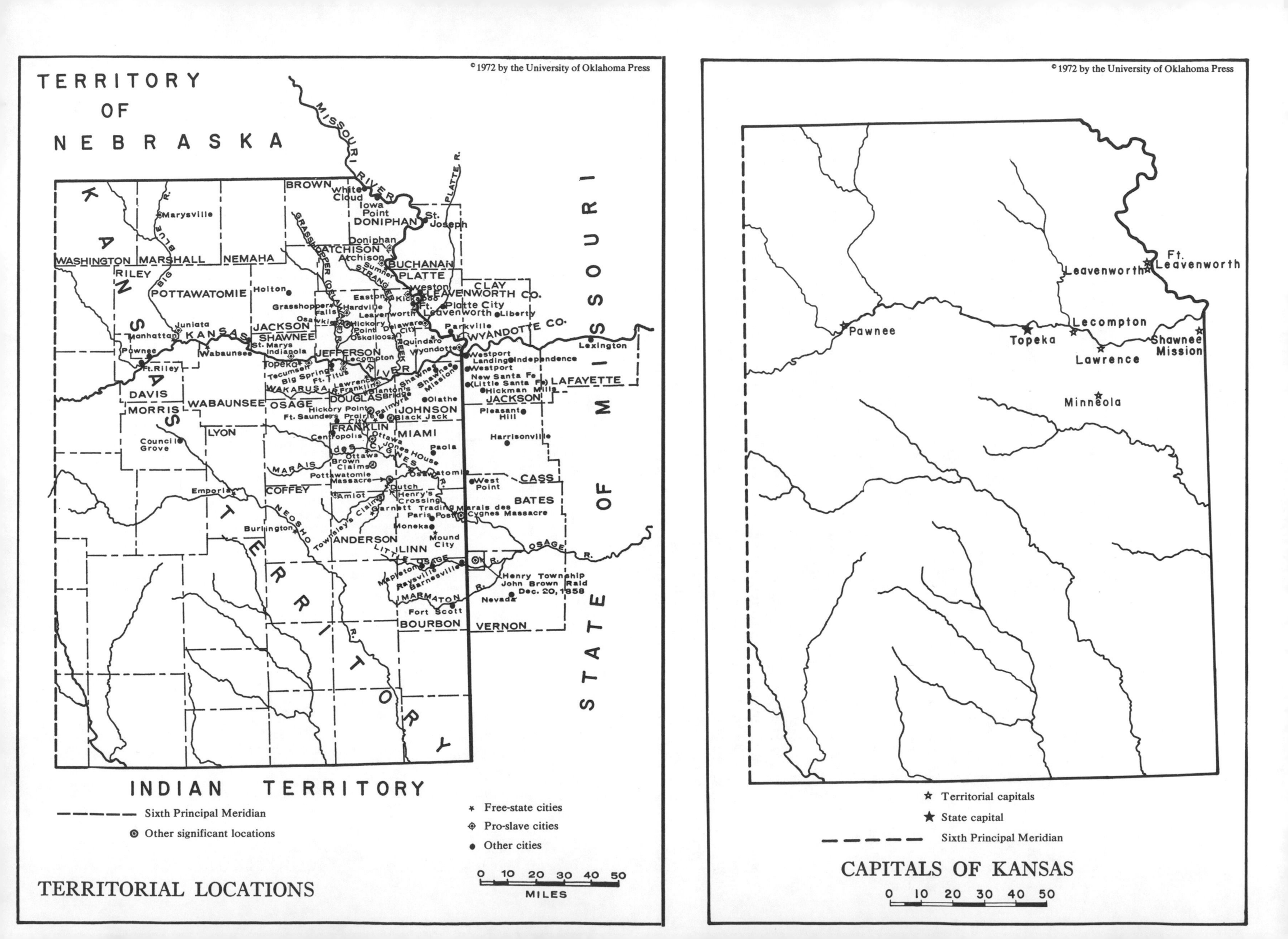

TERRITORY
OF
N E B R A S K A

BROWN
White
Cloud
Iowa
Point
DONIPHAN St. Joseph

Marysville

WASHINGTON MARSHALL NEMAHA
RILEY
Doniphan
ATCHISON
Atchison
Sumner BUCHANAN
PLATTE
POTTAWATOMIE Holton Weston CLAY
Easton Kickapoo LEAVENWORTH CO. Platte City
Grasshopper Hardville
Falls Leavenworth Leavenworth Liberty
Osawkie Hickory
Juniata Point Delaware
Manhattan KANSAS JACKSON St. Marys Point City Parkville
Pawnee SHAWNEE Indianola Oskaloosa Quindaro WYANDOTTE CO.
Wabaunsee Topeka Lecompton Wyandotte Lexington
Ft. Riley JEFFERSON Westport
Tecumseh Landing Independence
DAVIS Big Springs Ft. Titus RIVER Westport
WAKARUSA Lawrence Shawnee New Santa Fe LAFAYETTE
MORRIS WABAUNSEE OSAGE N.Franklin Blanton's Mission (Little Santa Fe)
Franklin Bridge Hickman Mills JACKSON
DOUGLAS Shawnee
Council MORRIS Hickory Point Olathe Pleasant
LYON Ft. Saunders Palmyra JOHNSON Hill
Grove Black Jack
FRANKLIN MIAMI Harrisonville
Centropolis Ottawa
des Jones House Paola
Emporia Brown Ottawa CYGNES Osawatomie CASS
Claims West
COFFEY Pottawatomie Dutch Point
Massacre Henry's BATES
Amlot Crossing Marais des
Garnett Trading Cygnes Massacre
Burlington Paris Post
NEOSHO Monekae
Towsley's Claim
ANDERSON Mound
LITTLE City
LINN
Mapleton OSAGE
Raysville Osage R. Henry Township
Barnesville John Brown Raid
Dec. 20, 1858
MARMATON Nevada
Fort Scott
BOURBON VERNON

K A N S A S
T E R R I T O R Y

S T A T E   O F   M I S S O U R I

INDIAN   TERRITORY

- - - - Sixth Principal Meridian
⊙ Other significant locations

✳ Free-state cities
⊕ Pro-slave cities
● Other cities

0 10 20 30 40 50
MILES

TERRITORIAL LOCATIONS

Ft.
Leavenworth
Leavenworth
Pawnee Lecompton
Topeka Shawnee
Lawrence Mission
Minneola

✳ Territorial capitals
★ State capital
- - - - Sixth Principal Meridian

CAPITALS OF KANSAS

0 10 20 30 40 50

Territory Locations

THE OPENING OF THE TERRITORY of Kansas in 1854 attracted widespread national attention because of the issue of "popular sovereignty" and the fact that Missouri, a slave state, had a common border with the new territory. Missourians, on their own and with the political support of the national administration of President Franklin Pierce, quickly occupied strategic locations. In the early days of the territory most of the Missouri River towns were largely populated by former Missourians and were supporters of the proslavery cause. At a greater distance from the eastern border of the territory were the primary locations of "Free State" settlers, Lawrence and Topeka. Most of the supporters of the Free State cause came from the older states along the Ohio River; some were Missourians; and one small, influential group came all the way from New England under the sponsorship of the New England Emigrant Aid Company.

By 1856, the violence that erupted in territorial Kansas between proslavery and Free State factions was described in national newspapers as "Bleeding Kansas." Men went heavily armed to their voting precinct and about their daily business. Support for Kansas came from other parts of the nation in direct proportion to local feelings on the institution of slavery. A sizable demonstration against Lawrence, known as the "Wakarusa War," was a stand-off, with large bodies of armed men on opposing sides. But on May 21, 1856, the Lawrence community was surrounded by a proslavery posse and the Free State Hotel was burned. In response to this action abolitionist John Brown led a small party to Pottawatomie Creek and "executed" five proslavery settlers on the night of May 24, 1856. Additional violence brought terror to the countryside and raids were made

into neighboring counties in Missouri. Brown became an abolitionist hero in the North with plans to free the slaves in all of the southern states by first capturing Harpers Ferry, Virginia. In order to divert attention from this plan, Brown led his only raid into Missouri on December 20, 1858, where he "liberated" a few slaves. The Marais des Cygnes Massacre on May 19, 1858, in which eleven Free State men were lined up by a proslave band and five were killed, came after Free State dominance in Kansas elections was already evident.

Capitals of Kansas

Governor Andrew Reeder arrived in territorial Kansas October 4, 1854, and he lived and maintained his office at Fort Leavenworth for about fifty days. From November 24, 1854, to June, 1855, the Shawnee Methodist Mission served as his headquarters. Then he moved to Pawnee, a town located near the Fort Riley reservation. There he convened the first territorial legislature on July 2, only to have the legislature adjourn, over the governor's veto, to Shawnee Mission on July 6, 1855. A week later the governor returned to Shawnee Mission, and the last official act of the territorial government there was on December 11, 1855. In the meantime, the legislature, on August 18, 1855, identified Lecompton as the territorial capital, and the government was established there by April 20, 1856. The third territorial legislature met in Lecompton December 7, 1857, and adjourned to Lawrence on January 5, 1858, where the session met from January 8 to February 13, 1858.

Minneola was discussed as a possible capital, and an act locating the territorial capital in this Franklin County community was passed by the legislature, vetoed by the governor, and passed by

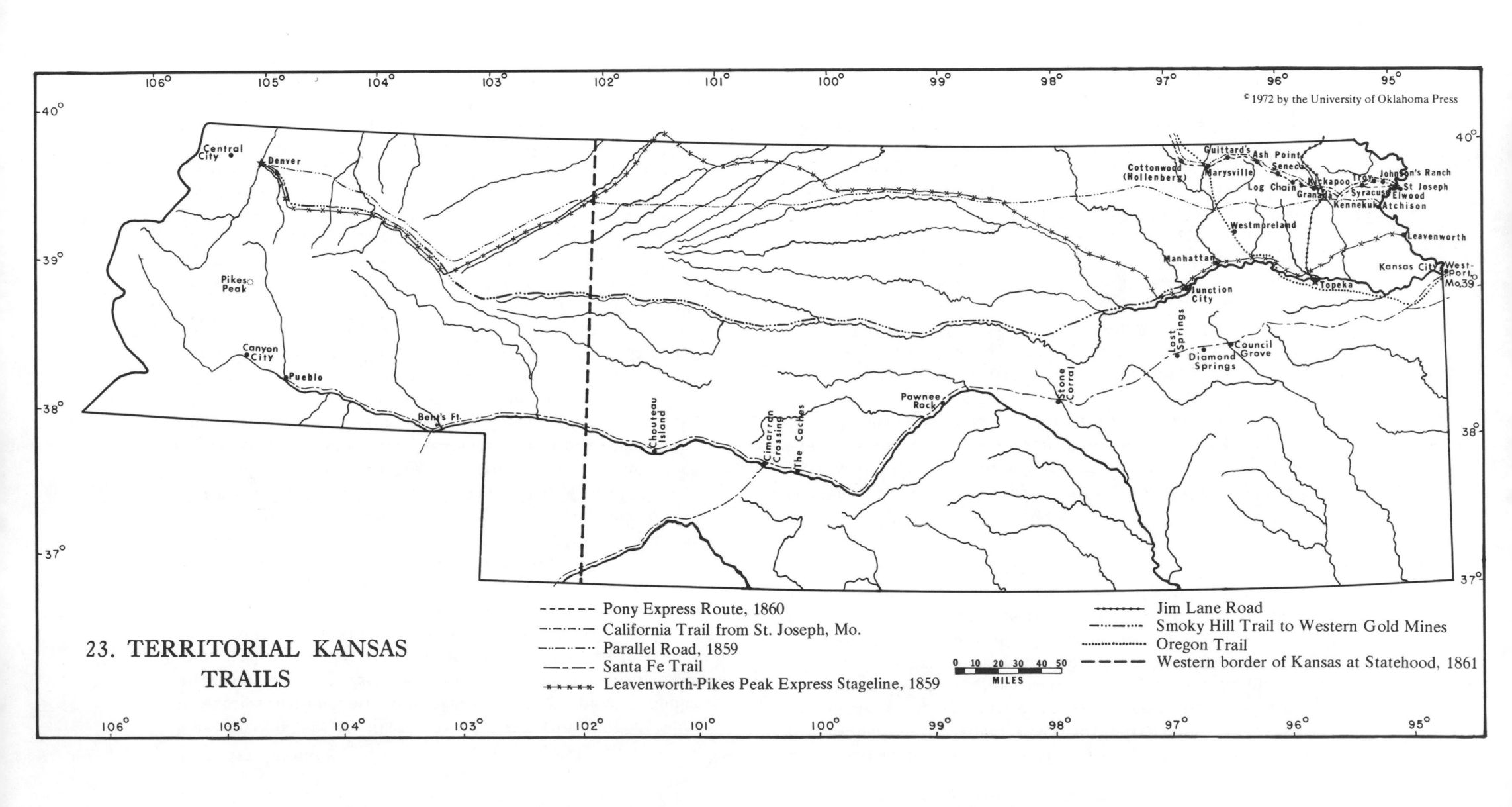

23. TERRITORIAL KANSAS TRAILS

- - - - - Pony Express Route, 1860
-·-·- California Trail from St. Joseph, Mo.
-··-··- Parallel Road, 1859
-·-·- Santa Fe Trail
★★★★★ Leavenworth-Pikes Peak Express Stageline, 1859

++++++ Jim Lane Road
·-·-·- Smoky Hill Trail to Western Gold Mines
············ Oregon Trail
- - - - Western border of Kansas at Statehood, 1861

0 10 20 30 40 50
MILES

Central City
Denver
Pikes Peak
Canyon City
Pueblo
Bent's Ft.
Chouteau Island
Cimarron Crossing
The Caches
Pawnee Rock
Stone Corral
Lost Springs
Diamond Springs
Council Grove
Junction City
Manhattan
Westmoreland
Cottonwood (Hollenberg)
Marysville
Guittard's
Ash Point
Seneca
Log Chain
Granada
Nickapoo
Syracuse
Kennekuk
Elwood
Atchison
St. Joseph
Johnson's Ranch
Leavenworth
Kansas City
West-Port Mo.39
Topeka

the legislature over the veto. Although the United States attorney general ruled that removal of the capital to Minneola was a violation of the organic act of the territory, the third constitutional convention met there on March 23, 1858, and then adjourned to Leavenworth.

The fourth territorial legislature set the pattern for the remaining years of the territory of Kansas. The legislature assembled at Lecompton on January 3, 1859, and adjourned to Lawrence on January 5, with the session lasting from January 7 to February 11, 1859. The fifth territorial legislature convened at Lecompton January 2, 1860, and adjourned to Lawrence over the governor's veto for a session lasting from January 7 to 18,

1860. Similarly, the sixth territorial legislature met in Lecompton on January 7, 1861, and adjourned to Lawrence the following day, to be adjourned permanently with the creation of the new state.

Topeka was initially the temporary capital, and soon became the permanent capital of the state. Topeka's location in the northeast corner of the state brought occasional agitation for removal to a more central location. One example was the resolution of a convention meeting at Abilene in 1888. Another was an action of the angry Populist portion of the House of Representatives during the "legislative war" of 1893, advocating removal of the capital to Kanopolis.

23. TERRITORIAL KANSAS TRAILS

THE INCREASE IN POPULATION in territorial Kansas and the desire of westward-bound travelers to cross this immense territory led to the development of additional roads to augment the Indian trails and military roads already in use. By 1854 the Santa Fe and the Oregon trails had served travelers for almost a generation and their routes were well-defined. After 1849 the impact of gold discoveries in California caused the Oregon Trail to be labeled the California Trail by California-bound travelers. The California Trail from St. Joseph, Missouri, shown here in the northeast corner of the territory, joined the main stem of the Oregon or California Trail just west of Marysville. The Jim Lane Road or Lane's Trail was a route through free territory in Iowa and Nebraska, over which Free State settlers, often attracted to Kansas by the speeches of ardent Free Stater James H.

Lane, could travel without having to go through the proslave state of Missouri.

Three roads shown on this map were prompted by the discovery of gold near Denver and the rush to the Rockies in 1859. They were the Parallel Road, so-called because it ran about thirty miles south of the northern Kansas border in the vicinity of the First Standard Parallel which was being determined by federal land surveys; the Smoky Hill Trail to western gold mines; and the stage line operated by the Leavenworth–Pikes Peak Express. All of these routes were hazardous. Good water and food supplies were usually inadequate for the unprepared traveler, who had to cross about five hundred miles of unsettled country before he arrived in Denver. Both the Parallel Road and the Smoky Hill Trail were used by persons bound for the mines who

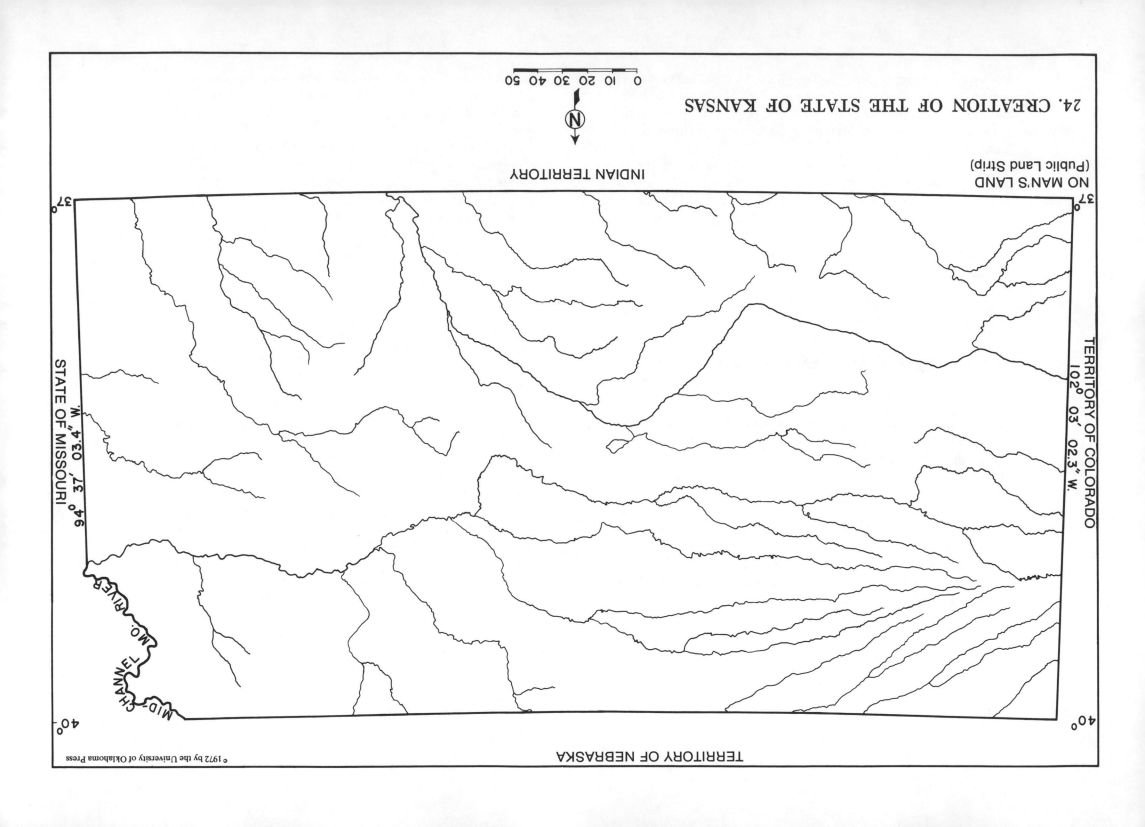

NO MAN'S LAND
(Public Land Strip)

INDIAN TERRITORY

TERRITORY OF COLORADO

102° 03′ 02.3″ W.

STATE OF MISSOURI

94° 37′ 03.4″ W.

MO. RIVER

MID-CHANNEL

TERRITORY OF NEBRASKA

37°

37°

40°

40°

0 10 20 30 40 50

N

walked or had their own transportation. By paying a fare of $125, a person could ride the stage of the Leavenworth–Pikes Peak Express, which had twenty-five stations between Leavenworth and Denver. The stations were located about twenty-five miles apart, with six men and extra livestock at each station.

Because of its effort to speedily deliver mail over great distances the Pony Express has gained a glamorous and romantic history, even though it operated less than a year and a half. During the winter of 1859–60, W. H. Russell, of the firm of Russell, Majors and Waddell, completed plans for the two-thousand-mile Pony Express between St. Joseph, Missouri, and Sacramento, California. Each rider rode about thirty-three miles, changing horses twice, about every eleven miles, after leaving his home station. The entire one-way trip required ten days. Slightly more than 125 miles of the eastern end of the Pony Express was in Kansas, and the twice-a-week deliveries each way found the riders on this section carrying the mail at an average speed of ten miles an hour.

24. CREATION OF THE STATE OF KANSAS

THE EASTERN BOUNDARY of the state of Kansas was established long before the territory of Kansas was organized, by the act of Congress of March 6, 1820, which created the state of Missouri and the survey made in 1823 of the "meridian line passing through the middle of the mouth of the Kansas river, where the same empties into the Missouri river." This line was found to be 94°37′03.4″ West Longitude. Through the "Platte Purchase" treaty of September 17, 1836, the northwest counties were added to the state of Missouri February 15, 1837, and the mid-channel of the Missouri River became the boundary in that region.

The northern and southern boundaries, at 40° and 37°, were a product of the Kansas-Nebraska Act of May 30, 1854. At the time Kansas became a state the territory of Nebraska was the neighbor on the north and the Public Land Strip, later called "No Man's Land," and Indian Territory were located across the southern border.

The western boundary, determined by the Wyandotte Constitutional Convention in July, 1859, and accepted by the people of Kansas and the Congress, was set at 25° west of the zero meridian in Washington. When the United States reverted to the use of the Greenwich meridian in London this boundary was found to be located a few miles west of the 102nd meridian at 102°03′02.3″ West Longitude.

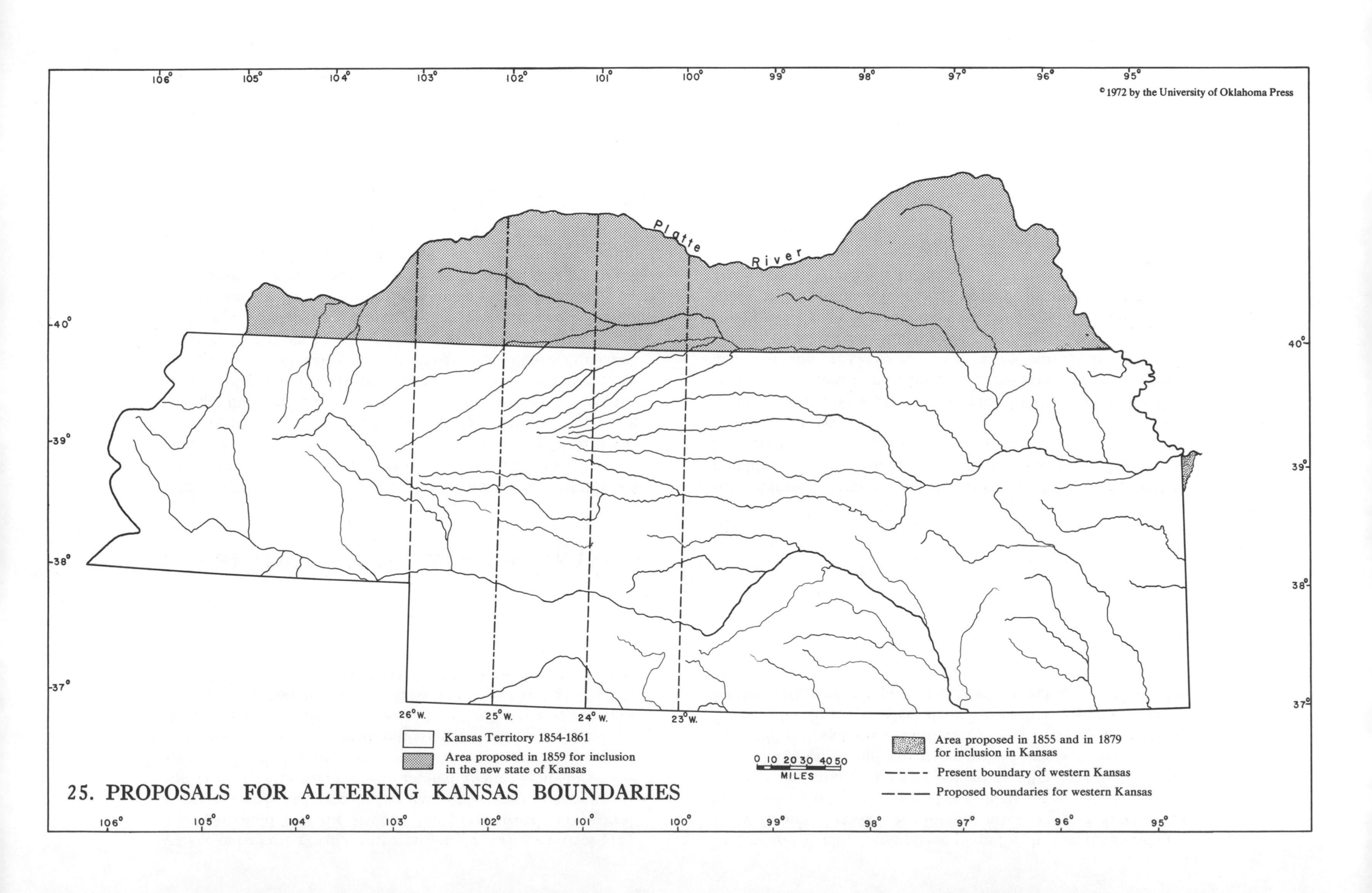

Platte River

25. PROPOSALS FOR ALTERING KANSAS BOUNDARIES

Kansas Territory 1854-1861

Area proposed in 1859 for inclusion
in the new state of Kansas

Area proposed in 1855 and in 1879
for inclusion in Kansas

0 10 20 30 40 50
MILES

Present boundary of western Kansas

Proposed boundaries for western Kansas

25. PROPOSALS FOR ALTERING KANSAS BOUNDARIES

THE FIRST THREE Kansas constitutional conventions, meeting at Topeka in 1855, at Lecompton in 1857, and Leavenworth in 1858, made no changes in the proposed state boundaries from those already existing for the territory. However, when the first territorial legislature was sitting at Shawnee Mission in 1855 there were serious proposals there and also in the Missouri legislature at Jefferson City in favor of transferring to the territory of Kansas some sixty square miles between the Big Blue River, located in present-day metropolitan Kansas City, and the Kansas border. Again in 1879 there was interest in the transfer of that territory expressed by some Kansas City, Missouri, citizens, and the Kansas legislature passed a concurrent resolution backing the move. Little support was provided from Jefferson City.

The primary concern and action for altering the Kansas boundaries came at the session of the Kansas constitutional convention meeting at Wyandotte from July 5 to 29, 1859. Arriving at the convention several days after it had convened, a party of Nebraskans sought seats for the purpose of getting the northern boundary of the future state of Kansas established at the Platte River. No doubt there were internal disputes in Nebraska regarding the location of the capital and the use of territorial funds. The Nebraska delegates were denied seats, but they were permitted to voice their proposal to the convention. One of their number, a Mr. Reeves, stated that the "Platte river is the natural northern boundary of Kansas while our present boundary is only an imaginary one. It is a wild turbulent and almost impassable stream; it is not navigable even for flatboats." Strong support was expressed by Samuel D. Houston of Riley County, one of the westernmost delegates, but a resolution asking Congress to establish the northern boundary on the Platte River was defeated twenty-nine to nineteen.

Discussion about the location of the western boundary consumed much of the convention's time. Delegate Houston asked that the territorial boundary be retained, no doubt, because it would place his area, around Manhattan, in a more advantageous position in a new, large state. The delegates to the convention came from the northeast counties of Kansas, and as far as most of them were concerned the future state should have a limited expanse. Most of the proposals for a western boundary were for the twenty-third, twenty-fourth, twenty-fifth or twenty-sixth meridian west of Washington, although the twenty-seventh meridian was mentioned, also. (Between 1850 and 1912 the zero meridian for astronomic purposes in the United States was the Naval Observatory at Washington.) The decision of the constitutional convention to locate the Kansas western boundary at the 25° West Longitude was the product of an amendment replacing 23° on the next-to-last day of the convention. On the final day of the session an effort to replace 25° with 26° failed. After the United States began use of the Greenwich Observatory in London as the zero meridian, the western Kansas border was found to be about 2.8 miles west of 102°, and it assumed the strange figure of 102°03′02.3″ West Longitude.

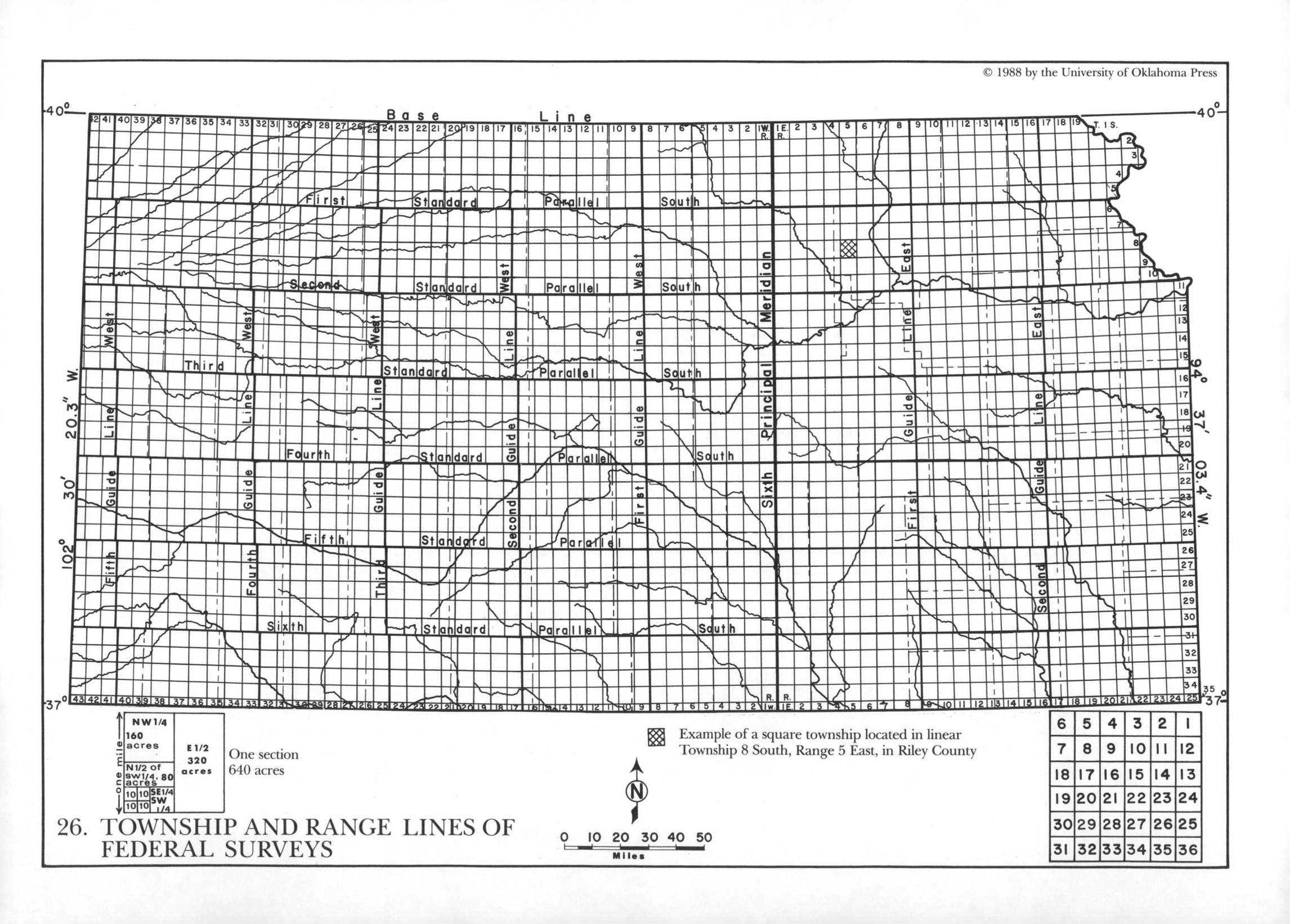

NW 1/4
160
acres

E 1/2
320
acres

One section
640 acres

N 1/2 of
sw 1/4, 80
acres

SE 1/4
SW
1/4

10 10

10 10

one mile

one mile

Example of a square township located in linear
Township 8 South, Range 5 East, in Riley County

6	5	4	3	2	1
7	8	9	10	11	12
18	17	16	15	14	13
19	20	21	22	23	24
30	29	28	27	26	25
31	32	33	34	35	36

26. TOWNSHIP AND RANGE LINES OF FEDERAL SURVEYS

0 10 20 30 40 50

Miles

N

MOST OF THE FEDERAL SURVEYS in Kansas were carried out by private surveyors operating under contract and supervised by one of the various surveyors general. The first surveys were completed in the northeast part of the territory, where early settlement took place, and generally the work proceeded from east to west.

Until July 1, 1867, Nebraska and Kansas were united under one surveyor general. Holders of that office to that time were John Calhoun, who located his office successively at Fort Leavenworth, Leavenworth, Wyandotte, Lecompton, and at Nebraska City, Nebraska; Ward B. Burnett, who followed him on July 3, 1858; Mark W. Delahay, his replacement in April, 1861, who a short time later established his office in Leavenworth; Daniel W. Wilder, who became surveyor general on October 8, 1863; and Hiram S. Sleeper, appointed March 15, 1865. The last person to hold the office was Carmi W. Babcock, appointed April 3, 1869. His headquarters was located in Lawrence. The original surveys were completed and the office was closed on June 30, 1876.

Instructions from the General Land Office in Washington provided for a survey of the Kansas-Nebraska border (40° North Latitude) to be used as the Base Line from which survey lines would run. The initial point of the Sixth Principal Meridian was located on the Base Line 108 miles west of the Missouri River, to serve as the controlling line for east-west range lines. The Sixth Principal Meridian and its base line serves as the control for the public surveys in Kansas and Nebraska, most of the land surveyed in Colorado and Wyoming, and a small area in South Dakota.

To correct for expected inaccuracies in the surveys, the earliest surveys used Township 8 East of the Sixth Principal Meridian with its oversize sections. Elsewhere, the standard practice, based on instructions from Washington, provided for east-west standard parallels located thirty miles apart in Kansas; in Nebraska they were twenty-four miles apart. North-south guide lines (or meridians) were located forty-eight miles apart. All of Kansas is located in townships that are south of the base line, and all townships along the southern boundary are designated Township 35 South. Range lines, the east-west designation for each township, begin at the Sixth Principal Meridian. In the southeastern corner of the state the township is Range 25 East, while the southwestern corner township is Range 43 West. Systematic numbering of the thirty-six sections within each six-mile square township provides a simple way for a unique description of each piece of land in the state. Standardized designation of smaller pieces of land within a section simplify land descriptions.

Passengers in high-flying aircraft can easily see that Kansas was a public land state. The historic federal surveys initially marked the land and subsequent territorial and state legislation provided roads at the section boundaries of these surveys.

CHEYENNE RAWLINS DECATUR NORTON PHILLIPS SMITH JEWELL REPUBLIC WASHINGTON MARSHALL NEMAHA BROWN

DONIPHAN

Oberlin 1881

Kirwin 1875

SHERMAN THOMAS SHERIDAN GRAHAM ROOKS OSBORNE

CLOUD

ATCHISON Doniphan 1857

Atchison 1861

Colby 1894

MITCHELL Cawker City 1872

Concordia 1870

CLAY RILEY POTTAWATOMIE JACKSON

JEFFERSON LEAVEN-WORTH Kickapoo 1857

OTTAWA

SHAWNEE

WALLACE LOGAN GOVE TREGO ELLIS RUSSELL

LINCOLN

DICKINSON GEARY 1857 Ogden WABAUNSEE

1854 Lecompton DOUGLAS

WYAN-DOTTE

WaKeeney 1879

Junction City 1859

Topeka 1861

JOHNSON

SALINE

OSAGE

GREELEY WICHITA SCOTT LANE NESS

Hays City 1874

ELLSWORTH

Salina 1871

MORRIS LYON

FRANKLIN MIAMI

RUSH BARTON

MCPHERSON MARION

RICE

CHASE

COFFEY

ANDERSON LINN

PAWNEE

STAFFORD

HAMILTON KEARNY FINNEY HODGEMAN

Garden City 1883

Larned 1874

RENO HARVEY

BUTLER GREENWOOD WOODSON ALLEN BOURBON Mapleton 1861

GRAY EDWARDS

SEDGWICK

1861 & Humboldt 1862

1857 Fort Scott

FORD PRATT

STANTON GRANT HASKELL

Dodge City 1894

KIOWA

KINGMAN

Wichita 1872

Augusta 1870

ELK

WILSON NEOSHO

CRAWFORD

MORTON STEVENS SEWARD MEADE CLARK

COMANCHE

BARBER

SUMNER COWLEY

Neodesha 1870

MONTGOMERY LABETTE CHEROKEE

HARPER

CHAUTAUQUA

Independence 1871

⊗ Federal Land Office locations
The date is the year established

Kansas National Forest, 1905-1915

27. FEDERAL LAND OFFICES IN KANSAS

0 10 20 30 40 50

27. FEDERAL LAND OFFICES IN KANSAS

TWENTY-FIVE DIFFERENT Kansas communities have served as the headquarters for federal land offices in Kansas. Because each office had an annual budget, considered substantial in its day, and because visitors from a distance would come to file claim for their land, acquisition of the office for a town or city was regarded as a great boon to community development. The Register and the Receiver and their clerks were important men in each of their communities.

During the territorial period four land offices were opened at Lecompton, Doniphan, Fort Scott, and Ogden. The Doniphan office was relocated at Kickapoo and the Ogden office moved to Junction City. A listing of all of the federal land offices in Kansas is as follows:

Lecompton: established July 22, 1854; open May, 1856; removed to Topeka.

Doniphan: established March 3, 1857; open October 15, 1857; removed to Kickapoo.

Fort Scott: established March 3, 1857; open July, 1857; removed to Humboldt.

Ogden: established March 3, 1857; open October 12, 1857; removed to Junction City.

Kickapoo: established December 3, 1857; removed to Atchison.

Junction City: established October 6, 1859; removed to Salina.

Atchison: established September 6, 1861; records to Topeka, December 26, 1863.

Topeka: established September 10, 1861; office closed April 30, 1925.

Humboldt: established September 16, 1861; open September 23, 1861; removed to Mapleton.

Mapleton: established November 1, 1861; removed to Humboldt.

Humboldt: established May 15, 1862; removed to Neodesha.

Augusta: established July 7, 1870; removed to Wichita.

Concordia: established July 7, 1870; open January 16, 1871; records to Topeka, February 28, 1889.

Neodesha: established December 15, 1870; open December 8, 1871; removed to Independence.

Salina: established May 1, 1871; records to Topeka, December 21, 1893.

Independence: established October 3, 1871; open March 26, 1872; records to Topeka, February 28, 1889.

Wichita: established February 20, 1872; open March, 1872; records to Topeka and Garden City, February 28, 1889.

Cawker City: established May 28, 1872; open June 23, 1872; removed to Kirwin.

Hays (City): established June 20, 1874; open August 7, 1874; removed to WaKeeney.

Larned: established June 20, 1874; open August 7, 1874; records to Garden City, January 25, 1894.

Kirwin: established January 4, 1875; records to Oberlin, September 11, 1893.

WaKeeney: established October 20, 1879; records to Colby, November 28, 1904.

Oberlin: established May, 1881; removed to Colby.

Garden City: established May, 1883; open October 1, 1883; removed to Dodge City.

Colby: established February 5, 1894; records to Topeka, April 1, 1909.

Dodge City: established February 10, 1894; records to Topeka, September 1, 1919.

The years of large-scale land disposal by the federal government, the 1870's and 1880's, saw the number of land offices increase from five to eight and then nine. Only three offices re-

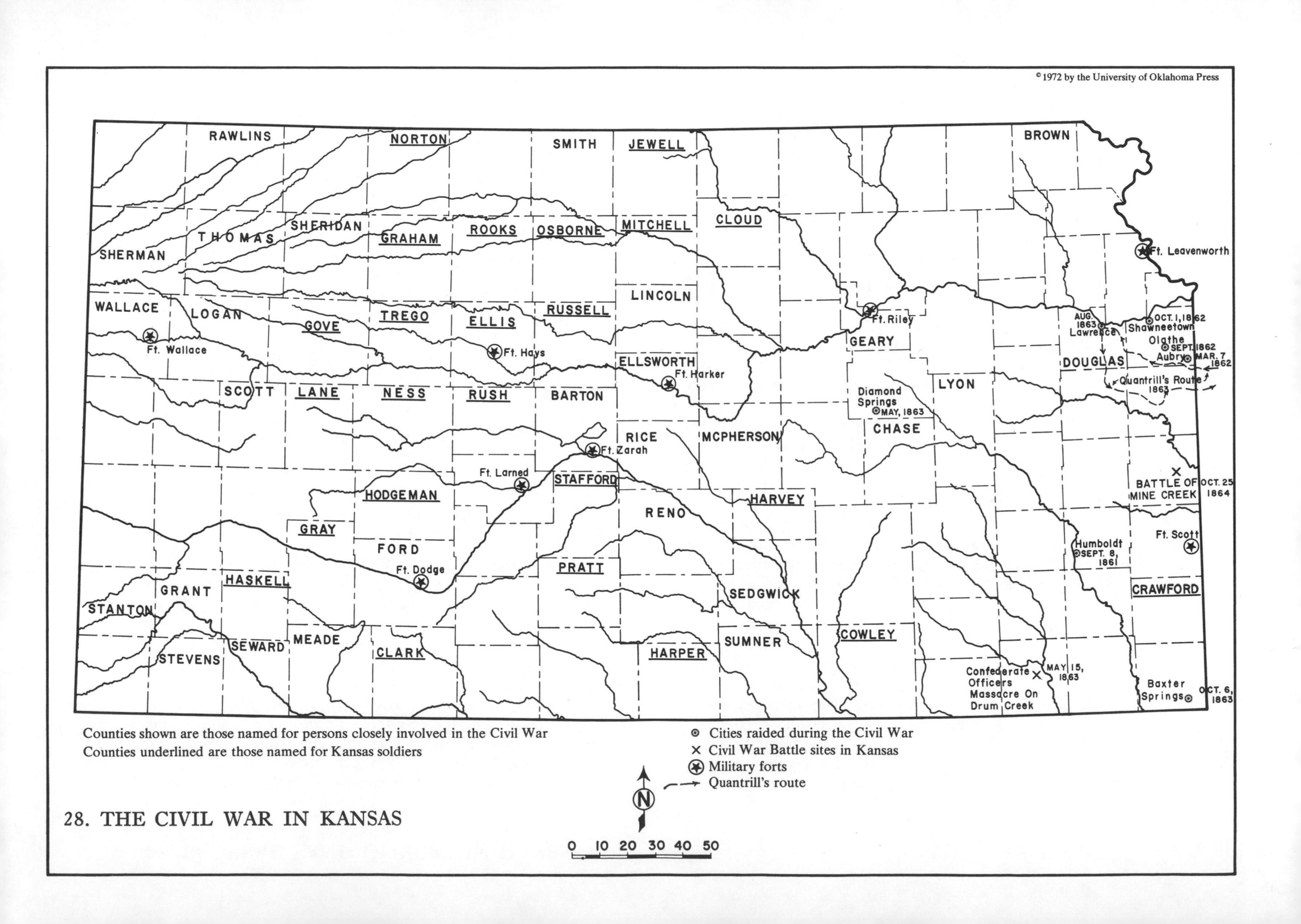

RAWLINS NORTON SMITH JEWELL BROWN

THOMAS SHERIDAN GRAHAM ROOKS OSBORNE MITCHELL CLOUD

SHERMAN ⊛ Ft. Leavenworth

WALLACE LOGAN LINCOLN

GOVE TREGO ELLIS RUSSELL ⊛ Ft. Riley GEARY

⊛ Ft. Wallace ⊛ Ft. Hays AUG. 1863 ⊙ OCT. 1, 1862
Lawrence Shawneetown
Olathe
ELLSWORTH ⊙ SEPT. 1862
SCOTT LANE NESS RUSH BARTON ⊛ Ft. Harker Aubry⊙ MAR. 7
1862
DOUGLAS
⟶ Quantrill's Route
1863
RICE LYON
Diamond MCPHERSON
⊛ Ft. Zarah Springs
⊙ MAY, 1863 CHASE

Ft. Larned
HODGEMAN ⊛ STAFFORD HARVEY × OCT. 25
BATTLE OF 1864
MINE CREEK

GRAY RENO
Humboldt Ft. Scott
FORD ⊙ SEPT. 8, ⊛
PRATT 1861

GRANT HASKELL ⊛ Ft. Dodge SEDGWICK CRAWFORD
STANTON

STEVENS SEWARD MEADE CLARK COWLEY
HARPER SUMNER
Confederate MAY 15,
Officers × 1863 Baxter
Massacre On Springs⊙ ⊙ OCT. 6,
Drum Creek 1863

Counties shown are those named for persons closely involved in the Civil War ⊙ Cities raided during the Civil War
Counties underlined are those named for Kansas soldiers × Civil War Battle sites in Kansas
⊛ Military forts
N ⟶ Quantrill's route

28. THE CIVIL WAR IN KANSAS

0 10 20 30 40 50

mained open in the 1900's. All Kansas records were gathered eventually at Topeka, and that office closed April 30, 1925, and the records were transferred to Washington, D.C.

Another federal agency operating in Kansas from 1905 to 1915 was the Kansas National Forest. Trees were planted in large numbers on designated land south and west of Garden City. In 1908 there were 302,287 acres within the borders of this artificial national forest. During some years more than a million trees were planted, but few survived. Except for 3,021.20 acres which were reserved for the Kansas State Game Preserve, all of this land was restored to homestead entry on December 1, 1915.

28. THE CIVIL WAR IN KANSAS

To SOME KANSANS the Civil War began in Kansas, because the violence of "Bleeding Kansas" of the early territorial period arose over issues that brought on the conflict between North and South. This claim would be difficult to verify, but the fact remains that more than twenty thousand Kansans were recruited to fight for the Union during the Civil War, and the 3,106 casualties suffered by these troops was the highest rate for any state in the Union. (The population in 1860 was 107,206.) After the Civil War the influx of settlers into Kansas brought the number of veterans to about 100,000, so that the Civil War was never far from the minds of Kansas citizens of the nineteenth century.

Four Kansas forts were established before the firing on Fort Sumter, and all of the other semi-permanent forts in the state came into being during the war years. Most of the military action was far removed from Kansas. The Battle of Mine Creek of October 25, 1864, involved a total of about 25,000 men and was the most important Civil War battle fought in Kansas. Other action within the state included the raids of Confederate or guerrilla forces and the massacre of Confederate officers by Osage Indians.

The most widely known Civil War raid was that directed against Lawrence by William C. Quantrill, who gathered together about 450 men, "the largest such force ever assembled under one command during the entire Civil War." Quantrill's purpose was to kill prominent Kansans and to destroy Lawrence in revenge for the burning of Osceola, Missouri. Perhaps he succeeded beyond his expectations, for 150 townsmen were killed, another 30 wounded, some fatally, the business center was gutted, and 200 homes were burned out or severely damaged.

With the rapid development of Kansas after the Civil War the names of many persons prominently connected with the war were used as names for fifty Kansas counties. These county names include fifteen persons who were members of Kansas military units and died of wounds or were killed in action. Their names are Cowley, Ellis, Gove, Graham, Harper, Hodgeman, Jewell, Mitchell, Ness, Pratt, Rooks, Rush, Russell, Stafford, and Trego. Five others in Kansas units for whom counties were named survived the war, although one was killed while still in service in late 1865. Other members of the Union army for whom Kansas counties were named include Generals Lyon, McPherson, Sedgwick, and Wallace, all killed in battle, and such national leaders as President Lincoln, congressmen, senators, and members of the cabinet. Also remembered were Generals Grant, Logan, Scott, Thomas, Sheridan, Rawlins, and Sherman, and Clara Barton, the only woman recognized in the permanent naming of a Kansas county. Brown County, for United States Senator A. G. Browne from Mississippi, was named before Browne served in the Confederate army. Davis County, named for Jefferson Davis, later President of the Confederacy, was renamed Geary County in 1889. Howard County, named for General O. O. Howard, was divided in 1875 into Elk and Chautauqua counties.

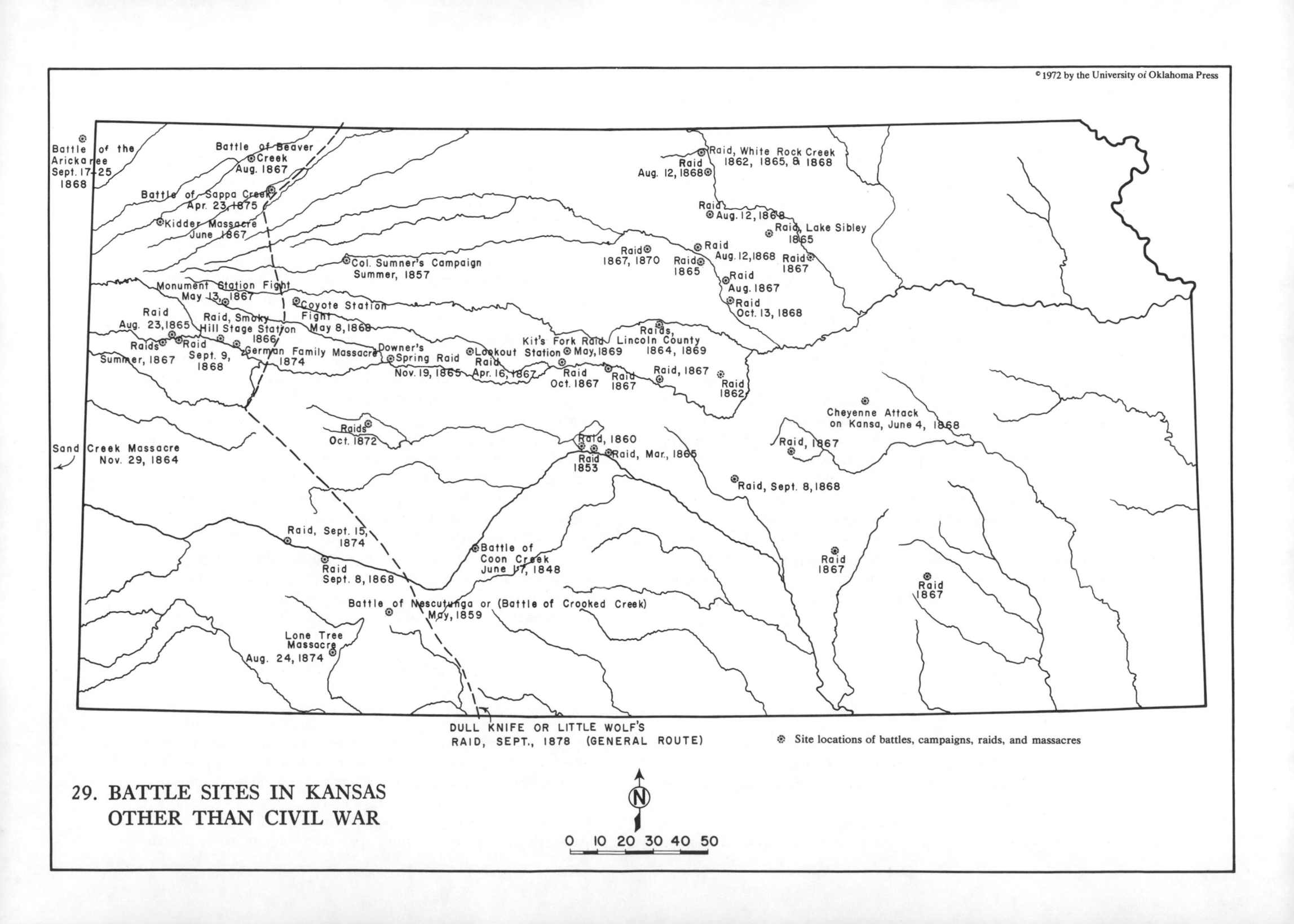

© 1972 by the University of Oklahoma Press

Battle of the
Arickaree
Sept. 17-25
1868

Battle of Beaver
Creek
Aug. 1867

Raid, White Rock Creek
1862, 1865, & 1868

Raid
Aug. 12, 1868

Battle of Sappa Creek
Apr. 23, 1875

Kidder Massacre
June 1867

Raid
Aug. 12, 1868

Raid, Lake Sibley
1865

Col. Sumner's Campaign
Summer, 1857

Raid
1867, 1870

Raid
1865

Raid
Aug. 12, 1868

Raid
1867

Monument Station Fight
May 13, 1867

Raid
Aug. 1867

Raid
Aug. 23, 1865

Coyote Station
Fight
May 8, 1868

Raid
Oct. 13, 1868

Raid, Smoky
Hill Stage Station
1866

Raids,
Lincoln County
1864, 1869

Raids
Summer, 1867

Raid
Sept. 9,
1868

German Family Massacre
1874

Downer's
Spring Raid
Nov. 19, 1865

Lookout Station
Raid
Apr. 16, 1867

Kit's Fork Raid
May, 1869

Raid, 1867

Raid
1862

Raid
Oct. 1867

Raid
1867

Raids
Oct. 1872

Cheyenne Attack
on Kansa, June 4, 1868

Raid, 1867

Sand Creek Massacre
Nov. 29, 1864

Raid, 1860

Raid, Mar., 1865

Raid
1853

Raid, Sept. 8, 1868

Raid, Sept. 15,
1874

Raid
1867

Raid
Sept. 8, 1868

Battle of
Coon Creek
June 17, 1848

Raid
1867

Battle of Nescutunga or (Battle of Crooked Creek)
May, 1859

Lone Tree
Massacre
Aug. 24, 1874

DULL KNIFE OR LITTLE WOLF'S
RAID, SEPT., 1878 (GENERAL ROUTE)

⊛ Site locations of battles, campaigns, raids, and massacres

29. BATTLE SITES IN KANSAS OTHER THAN CIVIL WAR

N

0 10 20 30 40 50

29. BATTLE SITES IN KANSAS OTHER THAN CIVIL WAR

ALMOST ALL OF THE BATTLES in Kansas other than the violence of the territorial period or the Civil War were conflicts between Indians and whites or between Indian tribes. Local histories for the region often identify these conflicts as Indian depredations, and most contemporary assessments of responsibility place the entire blame for such action on the Indians involved.

One of the earliest engagements shown on the map was the Battle of Coon Creek, June 17, 1848, involving Comanche and Kiowa-Apache warriors, perhaps as many as eight hundred, and seventy-six raw troopers under the command of Lieutenant William B. Royall. Most of the army group had been recruited a short time earlier to serve as replacements for the Santa Fe battalion, then located in Chihuahua. Armed with German-made breech-loading carbines the troopers were more than a match for the excellent Indian horsemen who possessed only lances and bows and arrows. Colonel E. V. Sumner, with about three hundred mounted cavalry in a campaign against Cheyenne Indians, found his prey and had a sharp engagement on July 29, 1857, just east of present-day Hoxie. Two years later Major Earl Van Dorn, with friendly Indians as scouts and four troops of cavalry, attacked a Comanche village located on Crooked Creek, southwest Ford County.

Most of the other actions came in the 1860's and 1870's. The Sand Creek Massacre in eastern Colorado, November 29, 1864, destruction of a supposedly friendly Cheyenne village by Colorado volunteers under Colonel J. M. Chivington, inflamed Indians throughout the plains. In many parts of western and north central Kansas small bands of Indians attacked new settlements, stage stations, or railroad construction workers in an effort to drive the whites from their ancestral hunting grounds. In 1867 and 1868, for example, about two hundred people were killed by Indians in Kansas alone, a figure not much different from the previous two years.

In early September, 1868, Colonel George A. Forsyth, with some fifty scouts, left Fort Wallace to become involved in one of the hardest-fought battles of the late sixties. This Battle of the Arickaree or Battle of Beecher's Island, was in Colorado on the Arickaree, a branch of the Republican River, some five miles west of the northwestern corner of Kansas. The Indians encountered included a large concentration of Cheyennes led by the celebrated war chief Roman Nose, assisted by various bands of Sioux. Casualties were heavy on both sides; Lieutenant Fred H. Beecher, of the regular army, a nephew of Henry Ward Beecher, was one of the first of the scouts to die. Altogether Forsyth's losses were five killed and sixteen wounded, whereas the Indian losses were later discovered to be seventy-five killed and many of their 970 warriors wounded. The Lone Tree Massacre, also, was carried out by Cheyennes, who killed six government surveyors in Meade County.

Two other actions involving conflict between Indians and whites seem to have a close relationship. The first, in 1875, was the Battle of Sappa Creek, also known as the Cheyenne Indian Massacre. A band of seventy-five Northern Cheyennes, who were traveling some forty miles west of settlements on a return flight to their homes in the Black Hills, were intercepted by a cavalry company out of Fort Wallace and most of the Indians were killed. Three years later, Northern Cheyennes on a reservation in Indian Territory broke out in an effort to relocate near the Sioux in the north. Under chiefs Dull Knife and Little Wolf they spent eighteen days moving through hostile country in Kansas, crossing railroad lines, evading troops, and killing some forty settlers at the cost of about ten warriors. Perhaps it was no coincidence that most of the white victims were recent settlers in Rawlins and Decatur counties near the site of the Battle of Sappa Creek.

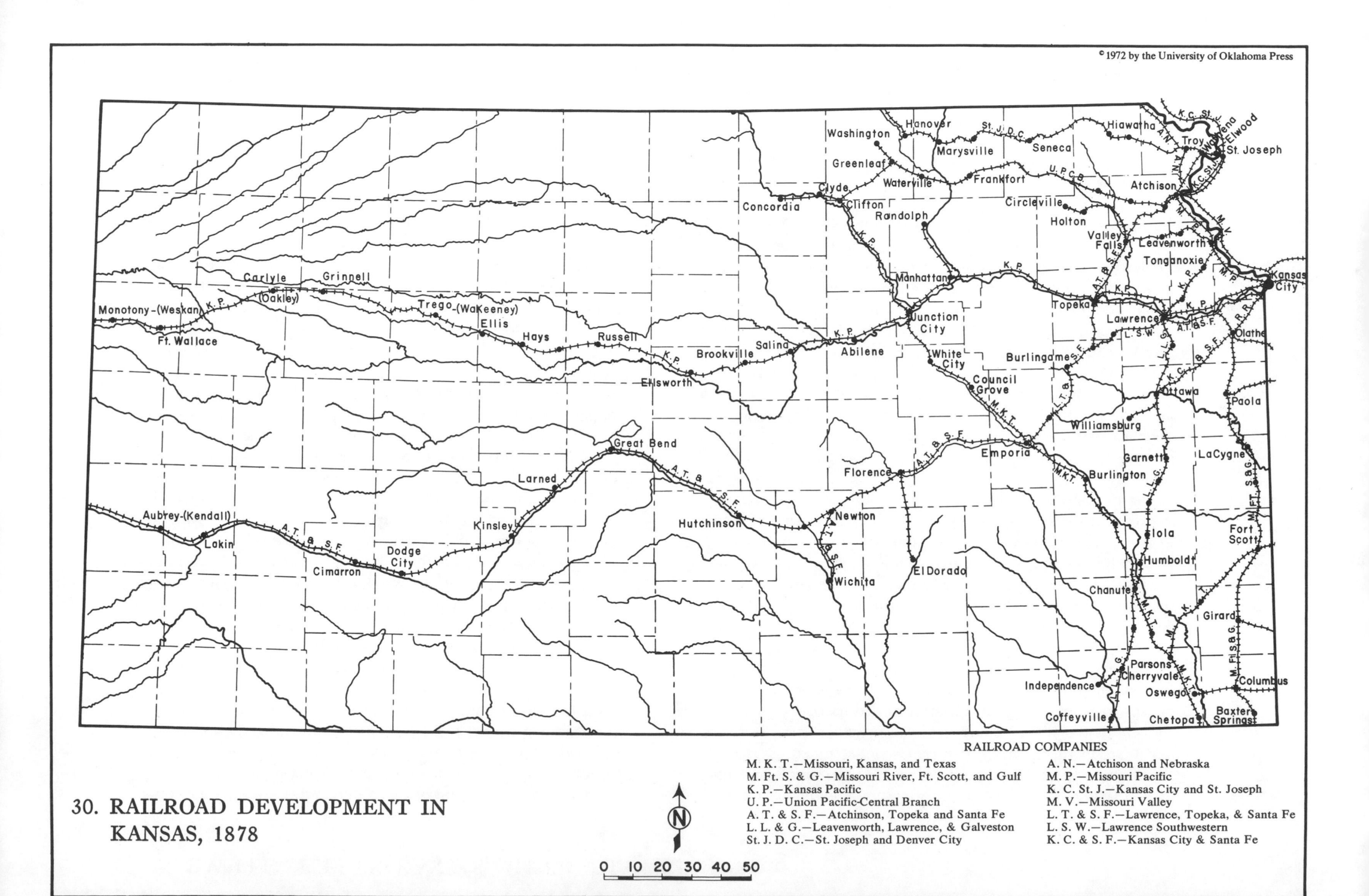

30. RAILROAD DEVELOPMENT IN KANSAS, 1878

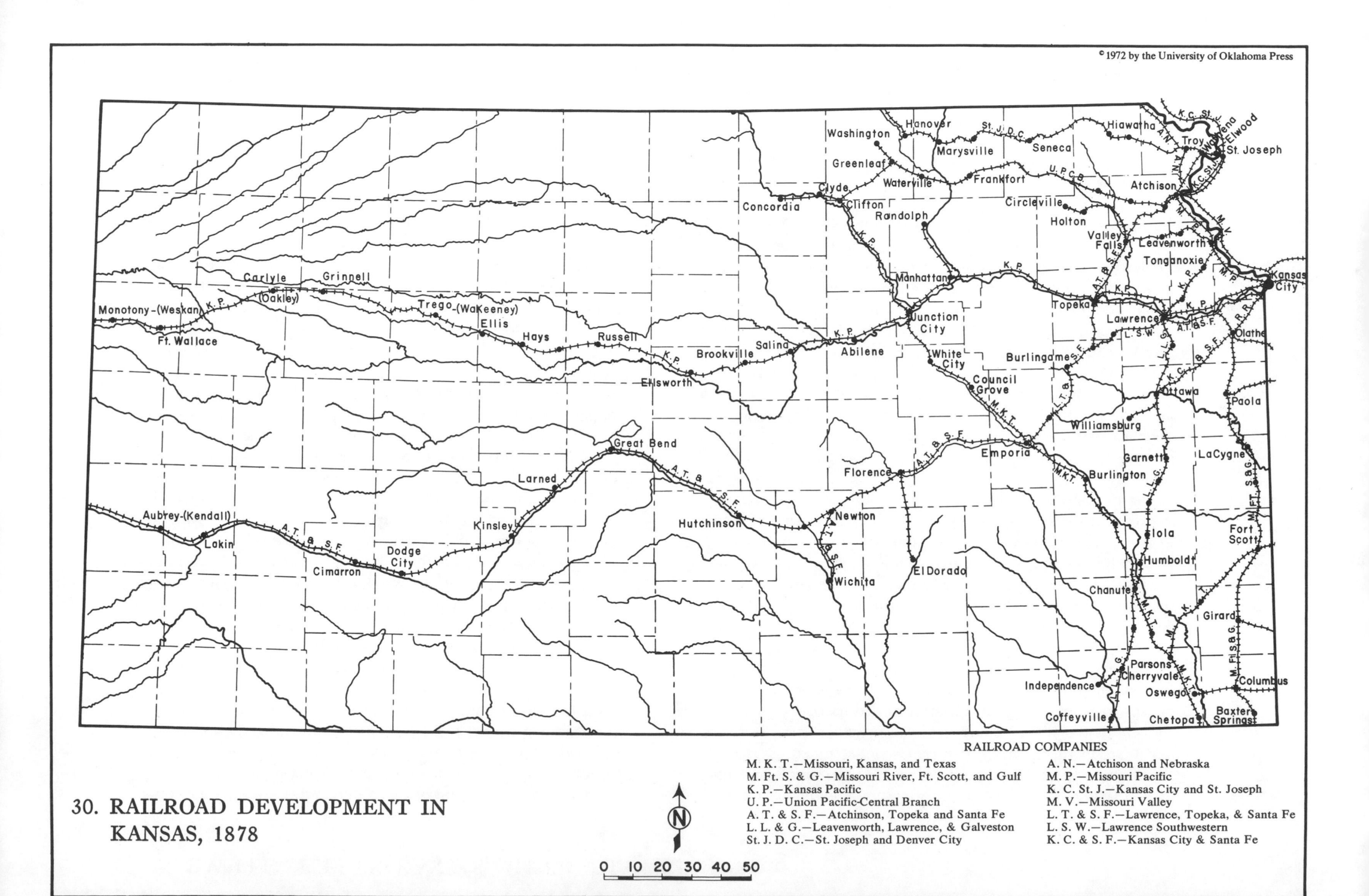

RAILROAD COMPANIES

M. K. T.—Missouri, Kansas, and Texas
M. Ft. S. & G.—Missouri River, Ft. Scott, and Gulf
K. P.—Kansas Pacific
U. P.—Union Pacific-Central Branch
A. T. & S. F.—Atchison, Topeka and Santa Fe
L. L. & G.—Leavenworth, Lawrence, & Galveston
St. J. D. C.—St. Joseph and Denver City

A. N.—Atchison and Nebraska
M. P.—Missouri Pacific
K. C. St. J.—Kansas City and St. Joseph
M. V.—Missouri Valley
L. T. & S. F.—Lawrence, Topeka, & Santa Fe
L. S. W.—Lawrence Southwestern
K. C. & S. F.—Kansas City & Santa Fe

N

0 10 20 30 40 50

30. RAILROAD DEVELOPMENT IN KANSAS, 1878

DURING ITS BRIEF TERRITORIAL EXISTENCE there was much discussion in Kansas about railroad development. Numerous railroads were chartered by the territorial legislature and conventions were organized to promote new railroad projects. Prior to statehood the only track completed was the five miles between Elwood and Wathena.

The Civil War put an end to most railroad construction, but important legislation for transcontinental railroads was the Pacific Railway Act of July 1, 1862. Kansas beneficiaries of this law were the Union Pacific, Eastern Division, renamed the Kansas Pacific, and the Atchison and Pikes Peak, later using the name Union Pacific, Central Branch. Both of these lines received a federal land grant, plus a loan of United States bonds. With such support the U.P.C.B. built to Waterville, while the K.P. built to the 394th-mile post, near the western Kansas line. Later the U.P.C.B. built a few miles west of Waterville, while the K.P., with land grant support, built into Denver. The K.P. was the long-line railroad in the state for two or three years.

Another major land grant railroad was the Atchison, Topeka and Santa Fe, which was to receive its 2,900,000-acre land grant when it reached the western border of Kansas. The Union Pacific, Southern Branch, later known as the Missouri, Kansas and Texas, which started construction south from Junction City, received a portion of the land given to Kansas for internal improvements. Other lines receiving a portion of this land were the Kansas and Neosho Valley, renamed the Missouri River, Fort Scott and Gulf; the Leavenworth, Lawrence and Fort Gibson, which later took the name Leavenworth, Lawrence and Galveston; and the Northern Kansas, which became the St. Joseph and Denver City.

The year 1878 was near the end of severe economic hard times and little construction of railroad track had taken place during the previous five years. However, almost three thousand miles of railroad track was in place in Kansas, and the major outline of a future railroad system had come into being. In the older part of the state the railroads usually built their track between towns already in existence, but in newer areas railroad construction and plans had a vital influence on the economic development of the region.

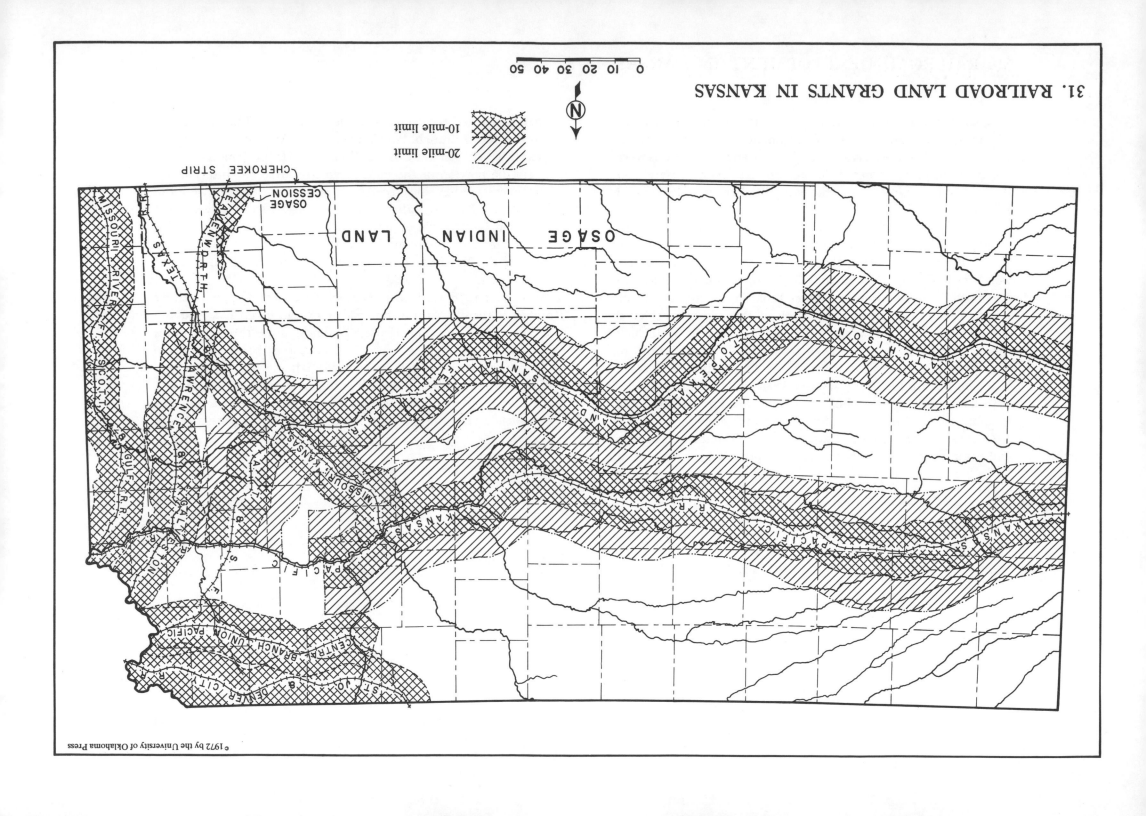

31. RAILROAD LAND GRANTS IN KANSAS

20-mile limit

10-mile limit

31. RAILROAD LAND GRANTS IN KANSAS

GRANTS OF LAND TO RAILROADS to speed construction of track mileage in Kansas amounted to almost one-sixth of the area of the state. Without these land grants, which were usually sold as quickly as possible, railroad construction could not have taken place as soon, nor is it likely that as many miles of track would have been built. The federal government granted more than four million Kansas acres directly to two railroads—the Kansas Pacific, with a grant of 3,925,791 acres, and the Union Pacific, Central Branch, with a grant of 223,141 acres. In addition there were large grants, also in excess of four million acres, made to the state for transfer to railroads. The largest grantee was the Atchison, Topeka and Santa Fe, recipient of 2,944,788 acres. The half-million-acre internal improvement grant supplied to Kansas on gaining statehood was turned over to railroads. Also, railroad companies were able to purchase surplus Indian lands at a reduced cost in order to further acquire assets for railroad construction.

Since railroad grants, historically, were for alternate sections and not made for a solid block of land, one must recognize the meaning of the boundaries of the land grants shown on the map. The Kansas Pacific, for instance, received twenty sections per mile of track, which were located in the western three-fourths of the state. Most all of this land was located within twenty miles of the right-of-way, on alternate sections (all with odd numbers in the township survey). Intervening even-numbered sections, except for two school sections in each township, were retained by the federal government for sale at a higher price, or for home-steading in eighty rather than 160-acre tracts. Very little of the Santa Fe land grant was available to the railroad east of Cottonwood Falls. Between there and Dodge City the Santa Fe grant extended twenty miles from the right-of-way, but west of Dodge City, the railroad was able to fulfill its grant within the ten-mile limits. The route picked by the Santa Fe from Newton to Dodge City was no doubt influenced by the Osage Indian Land, not available to that railroad.

In southeast Kansas the Osage Cession and the Cherokee Neutral Lands were opened for non-Indian use by treaties negotiated in the 1860's. When much of this land was given to railroads, settlers who had come into the area organized a Settlers' Protective Association of the Osage Ceded Lands to protect their claim to the land. Lengthy litigation was ended in 1875 with a decision in favor of the association. In the Cherokee Neutral Lands "The Neutral Land Home-protecting Corps" was organized to fight for the interests of 3,500 pre-emptors who had claimed the land under the Pre-emption Act. After much turmoil and litigation they lost to the railroad in a suit appealed to the United States Supreme Court.

Some railroads sought to gain as much revenue as possible from their land grants by delaying sale until the area had built up. Others sought to encourage settlement by selling land at relatively low rates on easy terms, so that the railroad would have a population to serve. The latter procedure built a more friendly atmosphere for railroad development.

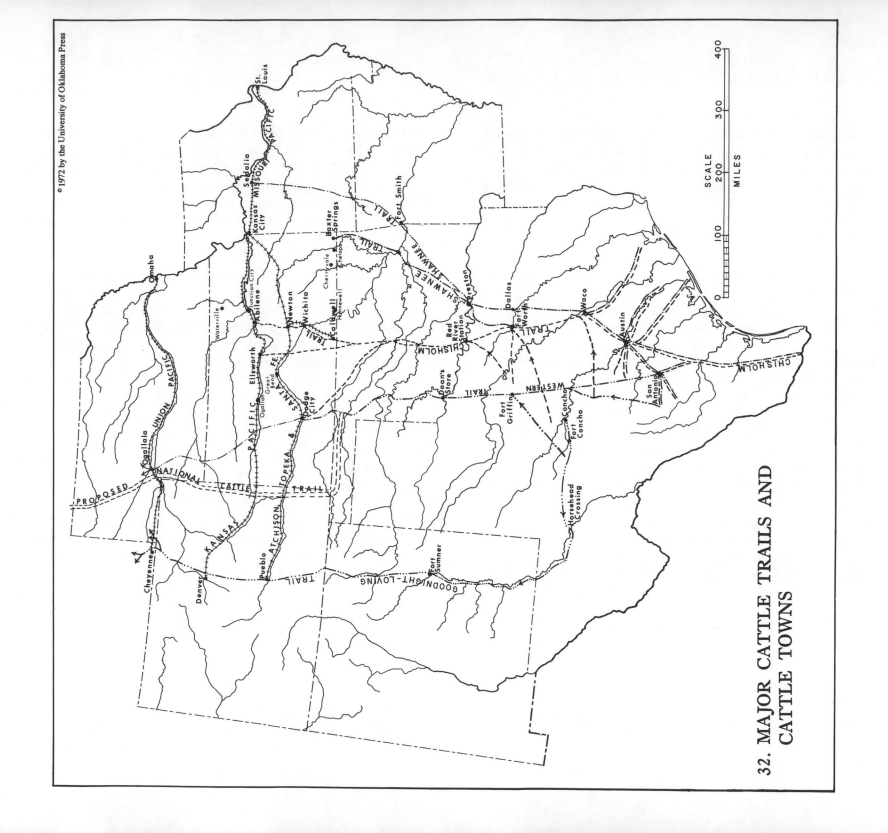

32. MAJOR CATTLE TRAILS AND CATTLE TOWNS

BEFORE THE CIVIL WAR there was some effort to market the longhorn cattle found in large numbers on the range land of south Texas, but no permanent market routes were established. The high prices offered for beef in the North during the post-Civil War years led to the development of the "long drives" to railroad towns, mostly located in Kansas. The period covered by the "long drives" lasted from about 1865 to 1885.

Sedalia, Missouri, at the end of the Missouri Pacific, had been the first objective of the trail drives, but the route through a forested, farming country produced many handicaps for a Texas trail herd. By 1867, under the leadership of Joseph G. McCoy, terminal facilities were developed at Abilene, and this railroad town served as a primary market for Texas longhorns for four years. Originally, the Chisholm Trail had applied to the central portion of this trail from Wichita to the Canadian River, used by Jesse Chisholm, trader to the Indians. By extension, the name Chisholm Trail soon applied to the whole route from south Texas to Abilene. When Abilene ceased operation as a cattle town after the 1871 season, new markets were established at Ellsworth on the Kansas Pacific and at Newton on the Atchison, Topeka and Santa Fe. Newton was a cattle town for a single year, with Wichita taking over as Ellsworth's primary competitor. From about 1875 for ten years thereafter Dodge City, reached by the Western Trail, was the objective of most of the trail herds, although during some of these years Caldwell shipped more cattle than Dodge City did.

Cherryvale, Chetopa, and Baxter Springs at various times served as markets for cattle driven north from Texas. Waterville, on the Union Pacific, Central Branch; Junction City, just east of Abilene; and Hunnewell, just east of Caldwell, received a little of the cattle business. Some herds were loaded onto cattle cars at Great Bend, and at least one herd was shipped east from Ogallah, but the most prominent Kansas cattle towns were Abilene, Newton, Ellsworth, Wichita, Caldwell, and Dodge City.

Perhaps five million longhorns were driven up the trail during the twenty years of the long drive. About half of these cattle were marketed by rail to feed lots near packing houses in the north. The other cattle were sold to ranchers in the Great Plains, who were making use of the grassland after the buffalo had been killed off and the Indians had been restricted to reservations. Ogallala, Nebraska, and Cheyenne, Wyoming, were more significant markets in the northern ranching country, although they also served briefly as the "long drive" cattle town markets for the Union Pacific.

A belated effort to provide a permanent pathway for moving cattle north and south was the proposal in 1884 which asked for congressional support for a National Cattle Trail—but it did not succeed. From 1866 through the 1880's, the Goodnight-Loving Trail provided a relatively safe route for moving longhorn cattle to the Colorado or Wyoming range country.

By the mid-1880's the long drives, subjects of much romantic nostalgia for the Old West, came to an end. Blizzards had killed many cattle which were driven north and wintered in preparation for marketing the following spring. Homesteaders were moving in and taking up much of the land around Dodge City and other cattle towns, and they were stringing barbed wire fences across the trails to protect their crops. Prices for longhorns also declined, and railroads were built into the Texas range country, making the long drives to a distant market no longer necessary.

The end of the long drives caused the cattle business to originate new practices, upgrade their beef animals, enclose their pastures, and develop the "closed range" cattle industry.

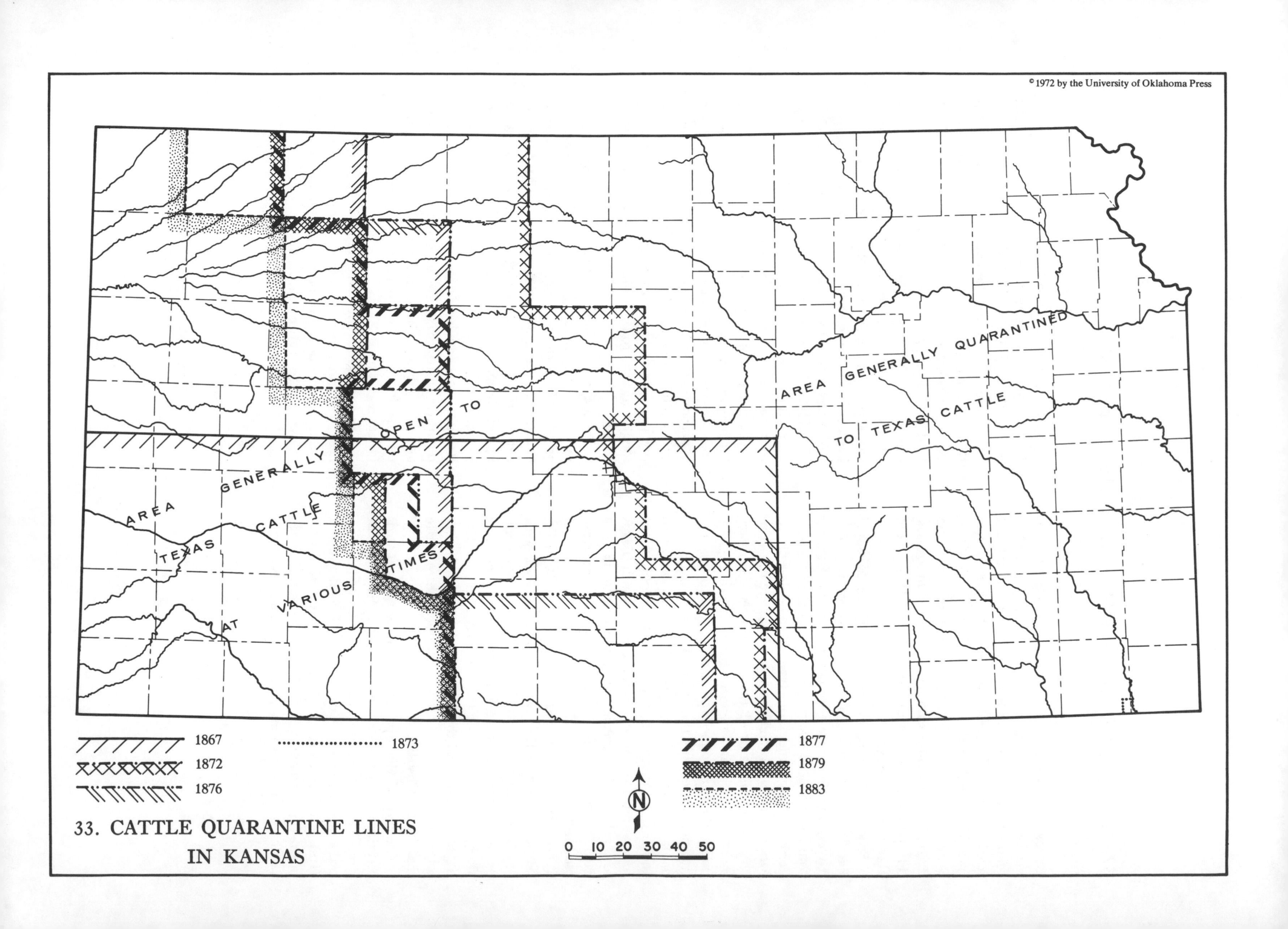

© 1972 by the University of Oklahoma Press

AREA GENERALLY QUARANTINED TO TEXAS CATTLE

AREA GENERALLY OPEN TO TEXAS CATTLE AT VARIOUS TIMES

//////// 1867   ············· 1873   ╱╱╱╱╱╱ 1877

✗✗✗✗✗✗✗ 1872   1879

╲╲╲╲╲╲ 1876   1883

N

33. CATTLE QUARANTINE LINES
IN KANSAS

0 10 20 30 40 50

33. CATTLE QUARANTINE LINES IN KANSAS

WHEN KANSAS BECAME A STATE in 1861 a law was passed barring entry of Texas cattle into the state during the warm-weather months of the year. The purpose of this quarantine action was to avoid contact with cattle which could transmit Texas or Spanish fever to the cattle of Kansas. Actually, the Texas longhorns were immune to the disease, but they carried the tick, which would drop off the longhorns and infect domestic cattle in Missouri or Kansas or other northern states. The tick could not survive freezing weather, so the quarantine line did not apply in cold weather.

In 1867 the Kansas legislature modified the law to permit Texas longhorns to come into Kansas west of the sixth principal meridian and south of a line drawn through the center of the state. Abilene was a short distance inside the quarantined zone, but Joseph G. McCoy received assurances from Governor Samuel J. Crawford that the law would not be prosecuted for the Abilene cattle town. Other modifications were made by the state legislature in subsequent years. Settlers were moving west, they were bringing cattle with them not immune to Texas fever, and their livestock was protected by changes in the quarantine line. One slight change made in the quarantine line in 1873 allowed Texas cattle in a small area around Chetopa. An examination of the quarantine line of 1876 discloses that Dodge City and Caldwell were the only cattle towns not inside the quarantined area. The last quarantine law against Texas cattle, passed by the Kansas legislature, was in 1883, just a few years before the demise of the long drive.

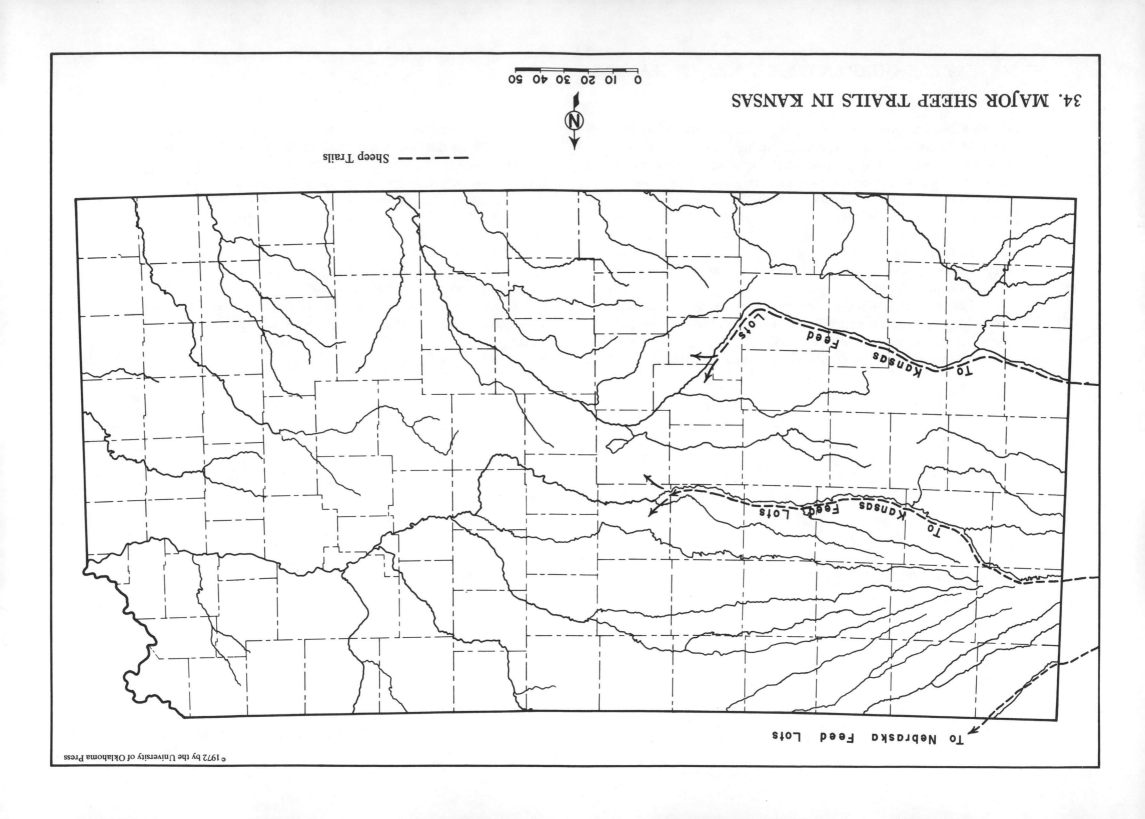

34. MAJOR SHEEP TRAILS IN KANSAS

Sheep Trails – – – –

N

0 10 20 30 40 50

To Kansas Feed Lots

To Kansas Feed Lots

To Nebraska Feed Lots

34. MAJOR SHEEP TRAILS IN KANSAS

DURING THE LAST THIRD of the nineteenth century, sheep were driven long distances to feed lots and railheads in Kansas, Nebraska, and Minnesota, for later shipment to the east. Seeming less romantic than the cattle industry, the sheep industry nonetheless played a prominent role in the economy of the west. Sheep were grazed on the open range just as cattle were, and they often competed for scarce grass and water. Because dogs were frequently used to herd sheep and because the lone herder would walk rather than ride a horse like the cowboy, the herder was subjected to the cattleman's scorn. Cowboys claimed a natural priority of cattle over sheep. Nevertheless, the sheep industry prospered for the same reasons as the cattle industry—high prices for meat, plus the added bonus of good wool prices.

Between 1865 and 1900 some fifteen million sheep were driven from the Rocky Mountain area into feed lots and pastures of the Great Plains. Many of these sheep stayed on farms and ranches in Kansas and provided some of the income for nineteenth-century farm and ranch development in the state.

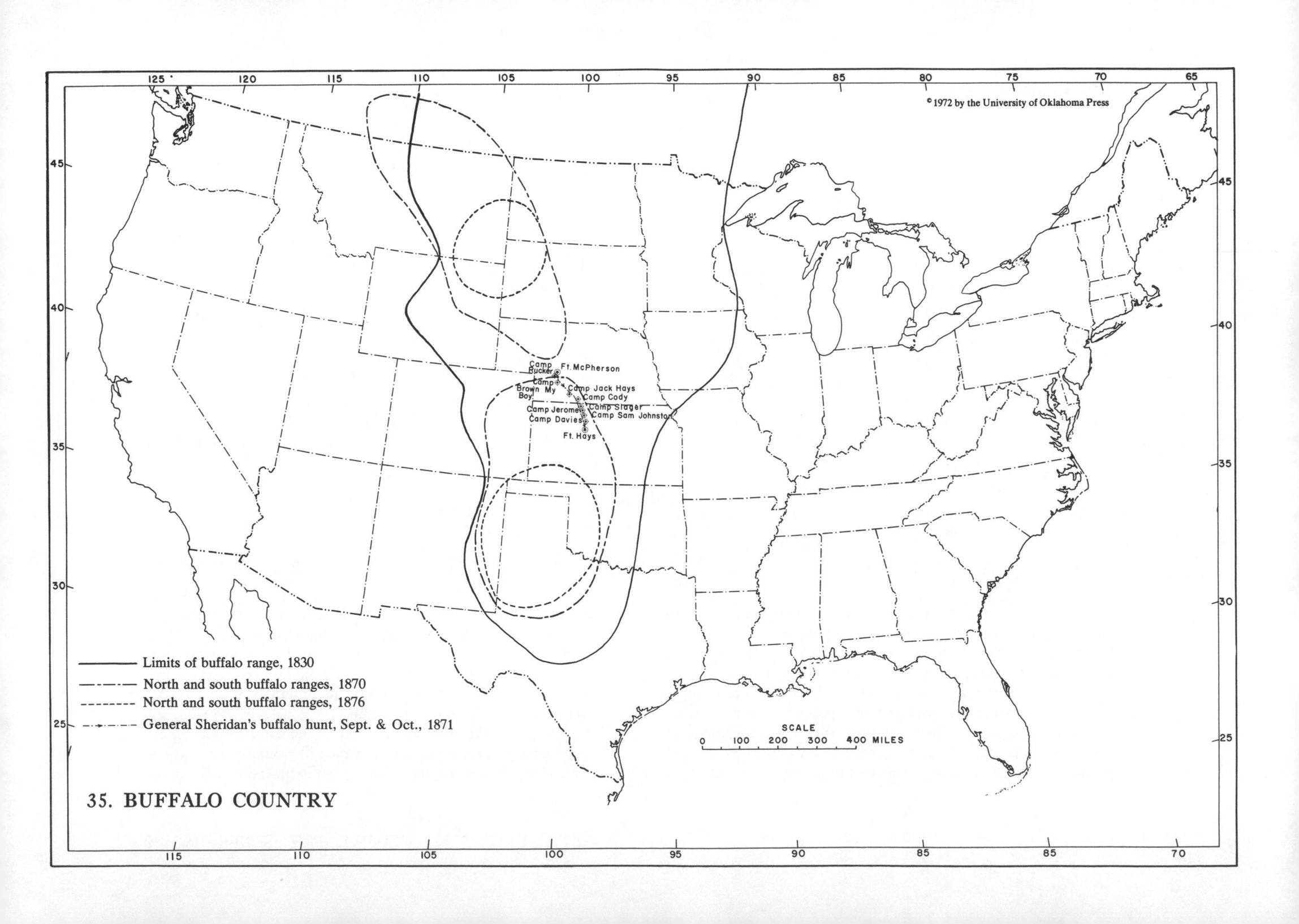

© 1972 by the University of Oklahoma Press

Camp Ft. McPherson
Bucker
Camp
Brown My
Boy! Camp Jack Hays
Camp Cody
Camp Jerome Camp Stager
Camp Davies Camp Sam Johnston
Ft. Hays

——— Limits of buffalo range, 1830

—·—·— North and south buffalo ranges, 1870

------- North and south buffalo ranges, 1876

—·►—·— General Sheridan's buffalo hunt, Sept. & Oct., 1871

SCALE
0 100 200 300 400 MILES

35. BUFFALO COUNTRY

35. BUFFALO COUNTRY

THE GRASSLAND OF THE GREAT PLAINS was a natural habitat for the buffalo, or American Bison, whose numbers in early historic times may have been as high as sixty million. By 1830 the limit of the buffalo range was on the fringe of settlement in Missouri, and in the next generation the eastern limit of the buffalo retreated with great speed.

The buffalo was the supermarket for the Indian of the Great Plains. Food, shelter, clothing, fuel, and some war materials could be fashioned from a buffalo carcass. The Plains Indian followed the buffalo for his livelihood.

With the completion of the Union Pacific railroad through Nebraska and Wyoming by the late 1860's the huge buffalo herd of the plains was split into a northern and a southern herd. Buffalo did cross the track, but the railroads brought the buffalo grounds into closer contact with the country, and hunting buffalo became a popular sport. By the early 1870's the procedure for making good leather from buffalo hide was developed, and professional hunters accepted the chance for easy money.

The decade of the 1870's was a time of the big buffalo hunt, first in the valleys penetrated by railroads, the Platte, the Smoky Hill, and the Arkansas. Then well-organized hunting parties sought buffalo at a greater distance from rail lines. So rapid was the extermination and so inefficient were some skinners that as few as two hides out of every twelve buffalo killed reached market. Still, the deliveries of millions of hides from Dodge City and other rail points was astounding. Relatively few buffalo remained by 1880, and four years later the entire buffalo population in the country was down to about one thousand.

Two interesting buffalo hunts, organized for sporting purposes, were under the direction of Lieutenant General Philip H. Sheridan. The first was in September and October, 1871, in which Sheridan combined the necessity of traveling from Fort McPherson, Nebraska, to Fort Hays, Kansas, with a chance to hunt buffalo. Each camp was named for a member of the party, and from reports a hilarious time was enjoyed by everyone. The second Sheridan-organized hunt, in January, 1872, was for the entertainment of the Russian Grand Duke Alexis. General George Armstrong Custer and other high officials met the Grand Duke's party at Omaha, escorted them to North Platte, Nebraska, and rode horseback to a camp fifty miles away. Buffalo were located nearby and Buffalo Bill Cody and Custer directed the Grand Duke in making his kill. After several days of hunting and visiting with the Brulé Sioux the party returned to the train, went west to Cheyenne, Wyoming, south to Denver, and east over the Kansas Pacific to Kit Carson, Colorado, where another hunt was staged. The royal hunting expedition then proceeded to Topeka, met with the Kansas legislature then in session, feasted on a seven-course dinner, and departed from Kansas.

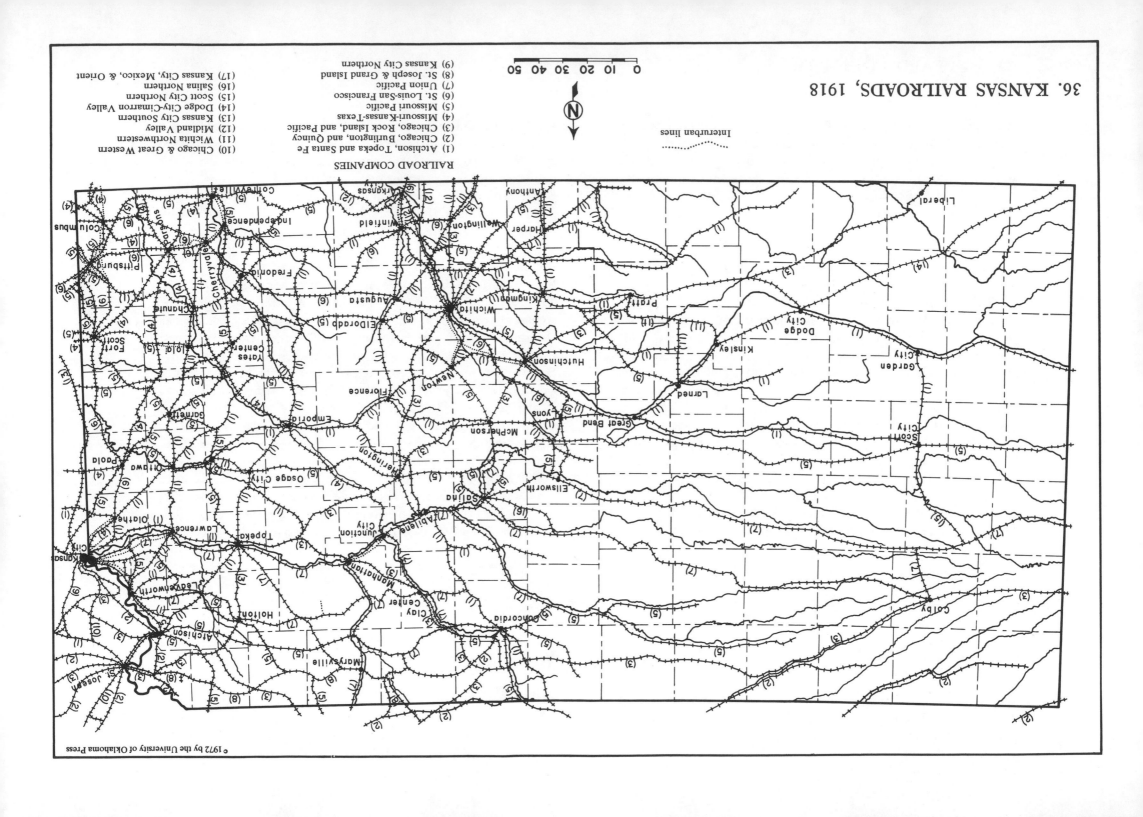

36. KANSAS RAILROADS, 1918

36. KANSAS RAILROADS, 1918

FOR YEARS AN EXCELLENT MEASURE of railroad development was the number of miles of track operated in a region. Railroads in Kansas operated 8,806.45 miles of track in 1890. The 1890's were economically unprofitable for railroad expansion, and many of those years saw the abandonment of track already laid. By 1904 the total mileage in the state was only five miles longer than in 1890. Thereafter for a decade railroads in the state show a steady expansion, and except for a half-mile decrease in 1914, total mileage increased regularly to the high point of December 31, 1916, when the figure was 9,408.99 miles.

These figures cover miles of operating line and do not include second and third tracks or yards and sidings. When these auxiliary tracks are added to the 1916 figure, a grand total in excess of 12,500 miles is recorded. In addition, the tracks of terminal railroads in the state and street and interurban lines could account for another 400 miles.

Naturally, the tracks, the bridges, the rolling stock, and the buildings housing the railroad operations in 1916 were much improved over 1878. The railroad in 1916 was still the primary mode of transportation for other than short distances. The car, truck, and bus had not yet appeared on the scene in a form reliable enough to effectively compete with the transportation service offered by railroads.

In some ways World War I wrought important changes on American railroads including those in Kansas. The federal government, as a war measure, took over the operation of railroads. Effort was made to reduce competing lines and to increase efficiency, thus some track was abandoned. The Kansas mileage for 1918, the year of this map, was 9,386.02. Major east-west railroads in the state were the Atchison, Topeka and Santa Fe; the Missouri Pacific; the Chicago, Rock Island and Pacific; and the Union Pacific. The longer lines with a north-south operation in Kansas were the Missouri, Kansas and Texas; and the St. Louis and San Francisco.

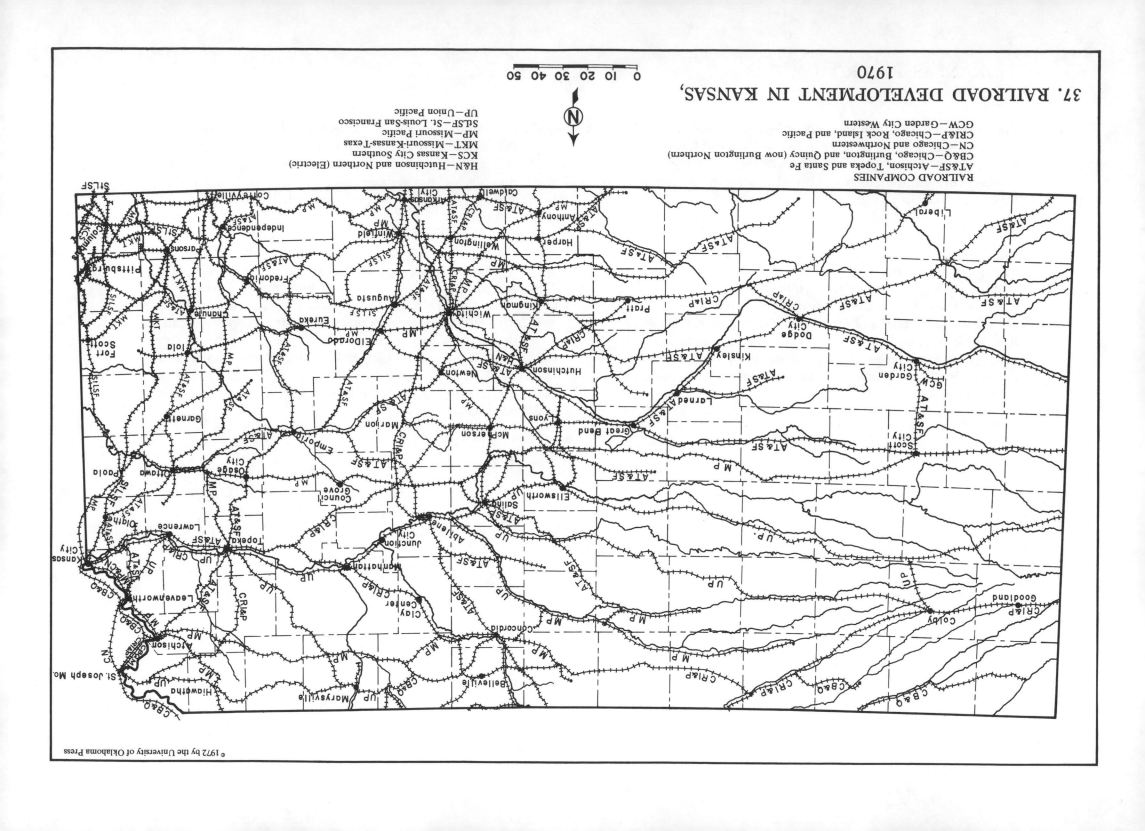

37. RAILROAD DEVELOPMENT IN KANSAS, 1970

RAILROAD COMPANIES

AT&SF—Atchison, Topeka and Santa Fe
CB&Q—Chicago, Burlington, and Quincy (now Burlington Northern)
CN—Chicago and Northwestern
CRI&P—Chicago, Rock Island, and Pacific
GCW—Garden City Western

H&N—Hutchinson and Northern (Electric)
KCS—Kansas City Southern
MKT—Missouri-Kansas-Texas
MP—Missouri Pacific
SLSF—St. Louis-San Francisco
UP—Union Pacific

37. RAILROAD DEVELOPMENT IN KANSAS, 1970

ONE HAS TO GO BACK to the mid-1880's to find Kansas rail track mileage as low as the 1970 figure, approximately 8,000 miles. But there is no comparison in the condition of the 1970 rail property and the skill of the 1970 rail worker to that of the earlier period. The poorly constructed track, bridges, and roadbed of the 1880's were vastly improved by the peak year of 1916, and the heavy steel rails, smooth roadbed, and new bridges of 1970 show a continual upgrading of rail equipment. Kansas rail track mileage generally ranks sixth in the nation, an indication of its central location and the prominence of railroad activity in the state. This position is further supported by the fact that a larger proportion of Kansans work in some part of the transportation field than is the case nationally.

Since 1916 more than 1,500 miles of Kansas track have been abandoned, rail companies have consolidated or gone out of business, and a vast new network of transportation involving private automobiles, buses, trucks, pipelines, river barges, and airlines, has come into existence. Where railroads once dominated the intercity passenger and freight hauling business, all other forms of transportation now successfully compete for a larger share of the business than is retained by railroads. Passengers in 1970 used almost every other means of travel and seemingly avoided passenger trains, and rail companies avoided the carrying of passengers. The federal AMTRAK corporation in 1971 contracted for several rail passenger lines through the state, to preserve a portion of a once significant transportation facility. Rail companies, in 1970, concentrated on hauling long-distance, heavy freight, the kind of thing they can do best. No longer in the late twentieth century do rail companies possess the dominant political influence in local and state politics which they demonstrated fifty and a hundred years earlier.

Railroad statistics for many years differentiated between steam railroads, street and interurban lines, and terminal railroads. Street and interurban lines in 1970 were non-existent in Kansas; terminal railroads remained in central terminals; and steam railroads have been entirely replaced by diesel-electric lines. Kansas rail companies, in keeping with the national trend, began the switch to diesel in the 1930's. Thus by 1970 powerful diesel-electric locomotives pulled far heavier freight trains, in excess of one hundred cars, at double the speed of earlier locomotives. The longer freight trains at increased speed, the vastly decreased passenger service, mechanical operations for track maintenance, and closing of many railroad offices also meant that less human labor was required, and employment opportunities with rail lines decreased.

About seven thousand of the eight thousand miles of track in Kansas are owned and operated by four railroad companies. In order of their size in the state they are Atchison, Topeka and Santa Fe; Missouri Pacific; Chicago, Rock Island and Pacific; and Union Pacific. Almost all of the remaining track in Kansas is operated by three railroads—St. Louis and San Francisco; Missouri, Kansas and Texas; and Burlington Northern, formerly the Chicago, Burlington, and Quincy.

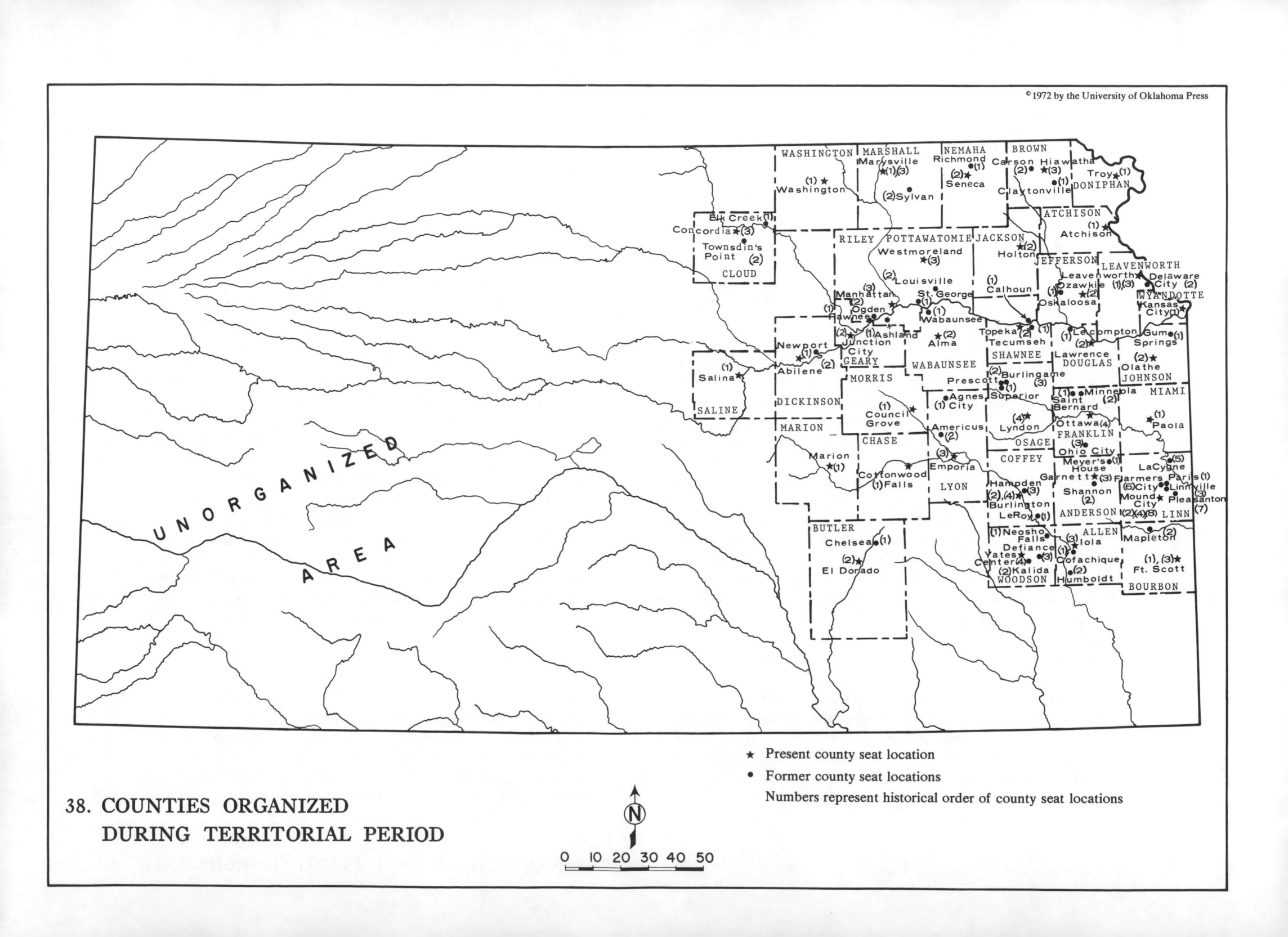

★ Present county seat location

● Former county seat locations

Numbers represent historical order of county seat locations

38. COUNTIES ORGANIZED
DURING TERRITORIAL PERIOD

0 10 20 30 40 50

38. COUNTIES ORGANIZED DURING TERRITORIAL PERIOD

COUNTY ORGANIZATION in Kansas responded to settlement, and this map and the three following illustrate the settlement process in action through a period of more than thirty years. Within the state of Kansas these thirty-four counties were the first organized, although in the territorial period a few counties were organized in the far western part that became a portion of the neighboring state of Colorado.

There were frequent changes in county boundaries and in many other activities associated with the territorial government of early day Kansas. The boundaries shown here are the more permanent borders of later years. The vast number of changes made in county boundaries are well-illustrated by Helen G. Gill in "The Establishment of Counties in Kansas," *Transactions of the Kansas State Historical Society (1903–4)* Vol. VIII, 449–72. By 1860 the population of these counties was approximately 100,000.

The pressure for change during the territorial period can be seen in the large number of county seats, most of them products of this very early time. Altogether there were eighty county seats in these thirty-four counties, with Leavenworth, Marysville, and Mound City each serving two or three times. The large number of changes in the location of county government was due, in part, to the older age of this portion of Kansas, which was settled when the phenomenon of changing a county seat location was a regular part of inter-community rivalry. Also, after some county seats had been designated by the pro slave legislature, Free Staters gained control and a county seat change was an expected result.

The county seat removal from Tecumseh to Topeka in Shawnee County, and from Lecompton to Lawrence in Douglas County illustrate this point.

These county seat conflicts, sometimes identified as "county seat wars," were prompted by the business advantages which could be gained for the community which was also the chief point of political interest in the county. The largest community in the county could not automatically expect to become the county seat. Usually, a location on a railroad line near the center of the county, with local community support for providing land or a public building for the county would help assure a county seat for a community. Where these factors were missing, as in Pottawatomie or Linn counties, or rival towns could offer all of these advantages as in Osage or Coffey counties, the location of a county seat was in doubt.

Eight counties in this group obtained new names during this period or later. They were Jackson, Morris, Osage, and Wabaunsee, whose names prior to 1859 were respectively Calhoun, Wise, Weller, and Richardson. Miami was the new name for Lykins in 1861. The following year Lyon replaced Breckinridge County. As a consequence of a legislative joke in 1867 Cloud County for a year was known as Shirley County. In 1889 the voters of Davis County, named after Jefferson Davis, secretary of war and later president of the Confederate States of America, changed the name to Geary County, after the third territorial governor.

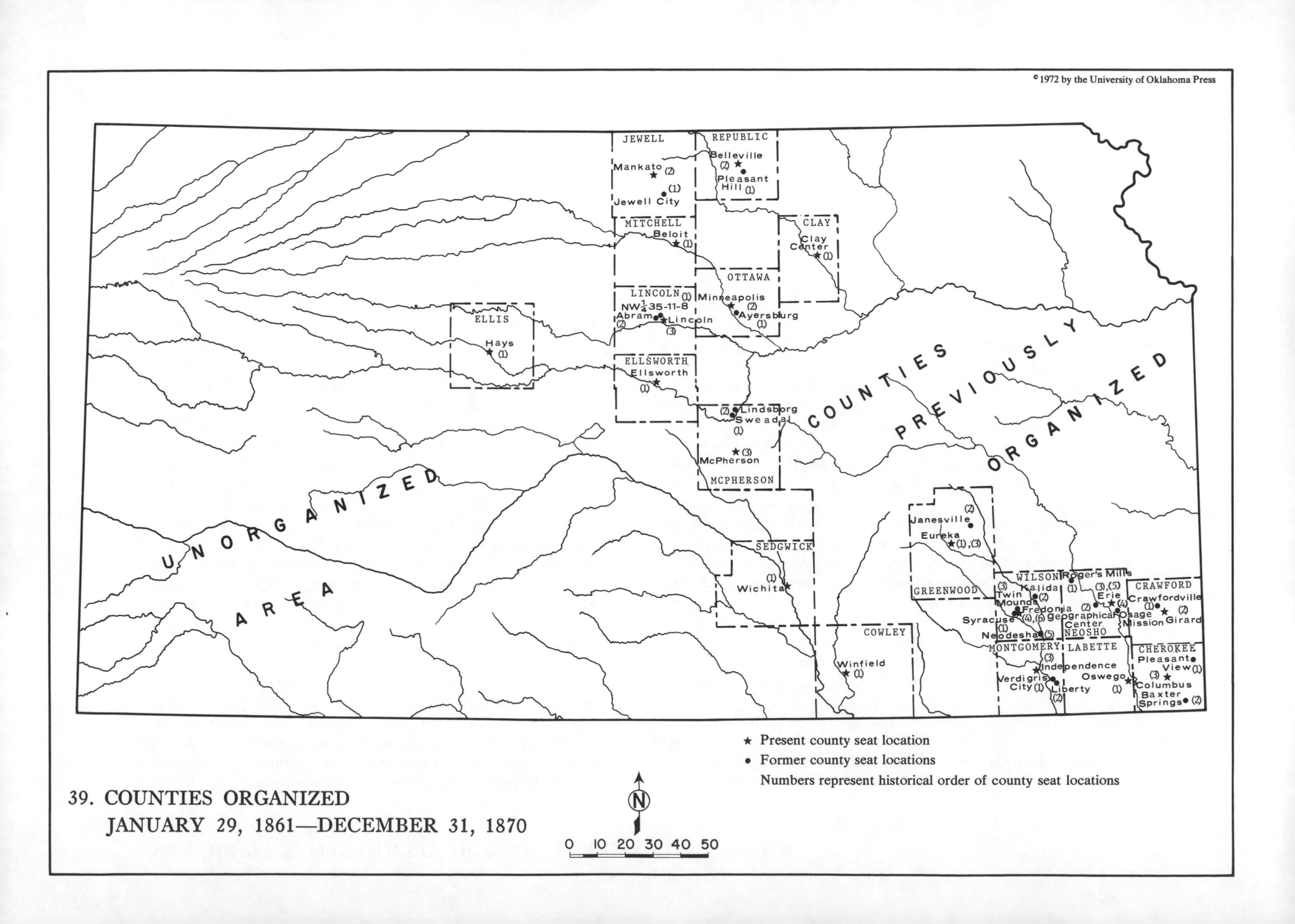

JEWELL

REPUBLIC

Mankato ★ (2)

Belleville (2) ★

(1)

Pleasant Hill (1)

Jewell City

MITCHELL
Beloit
★ (1)

CLAY

Clay Center (1)

OTTAWA

LINCOLN (1)
NW¼ 35-11-8
Abram (2) ★ Lincoln (3)

Minneapolis
★ ●
Ayersburg (1)

ELLIS

Hays ★ (1)

ELLSWORTH
Ellsworth
(1)

● Lindsborg
Sweadal (2)
(1)

McPherson ★ (3)

MCPHERSON

C O U N T I E S

P R E V I O U S L Y

O R G A N I Z E D

U N O R G A N I Z E D

A R E A

SEDGWICK

Wichita ● (1) ★

Janesville ●
Eureka ★ (2)
(1),(3)

GREENWOOD

WILSON Roger's Mills
(3) Kalida (1) (3),(5)
● (2) Erie
Twin ★ (4)
Mounds Fredonia
Syracuse (4),(6) (2) Osage
(1) Geographical Mission
Neodesha Center
(5) NEOSHO

CRAWFORD
Crawfordville
(1) ●
★ (2)
● Girard

COWLEY

MONTGOMERY LABETTE

CHEROKEE
Pleasant
● View (1)

Winfield ★ (1)

Verdigris (3)
City (1) ★ Independence
Liberty
(2)

Oswego
★
(1)

★ Columbus
Baxter
Springs ● (2)

★ Present county seat location
● Former county seat locations
Numbers represent historical order of county seat locations

39. COUNTIES ORGANIZED
JANUARY 29, 1861—DECEMBER 31, 1870

N

0 10 20 30 40 50

THE COUNTIES ORGANIZED in the first decade of Kansas statehood show the advance of settlement into regions adjacent to previous settlement or along lines of railroad construction. The impact of Civil War times retarded political and economic development in this decade. Settlement during the period was extended into the eastern fringe of the Great Plains region, attracted there by generous new land legislation and by other opportunities.

Even though the organizers of these eighteen counties had not been parties to the political strife of the territorial period they were emotionally tied up in the business of establishing their homes and local governments. "County seat wars" were also a feature of this period of county organization in Kansas. In histories of two southeastern Kansas counties local historians reported that corruption was rampant and bitter feelings had developed as a result of "county seat wars." One said that, "Persons who were considered good and honest citizens seemed to have no scruples in encouraging and assisting illegal and fraudulent voting, in tampering with ballot-boxes, and fixing up returns to suit the emergency, so as to give the place for which they were working a majority." Another reported that the county seat agitation was "a question that arose early and stayed up late, and permeated the whole county with its evil influence and demoralizing effect upon the sacredness and purity of the ballot."

In all, there were forty-one county seats for these eighteen counties, with Erie, Eureka, and Fredonia each serving twice. Kansas population tripled in this decade and these new counties contributed significantly to that increase. County names changed in this group were Dorn County, eventually divided between Neosho and Labette, and Cowley, which replaced Hunter. Seven of these counties had only a single county seat, and they were the real winners, for the other counties suffered through an average of three.

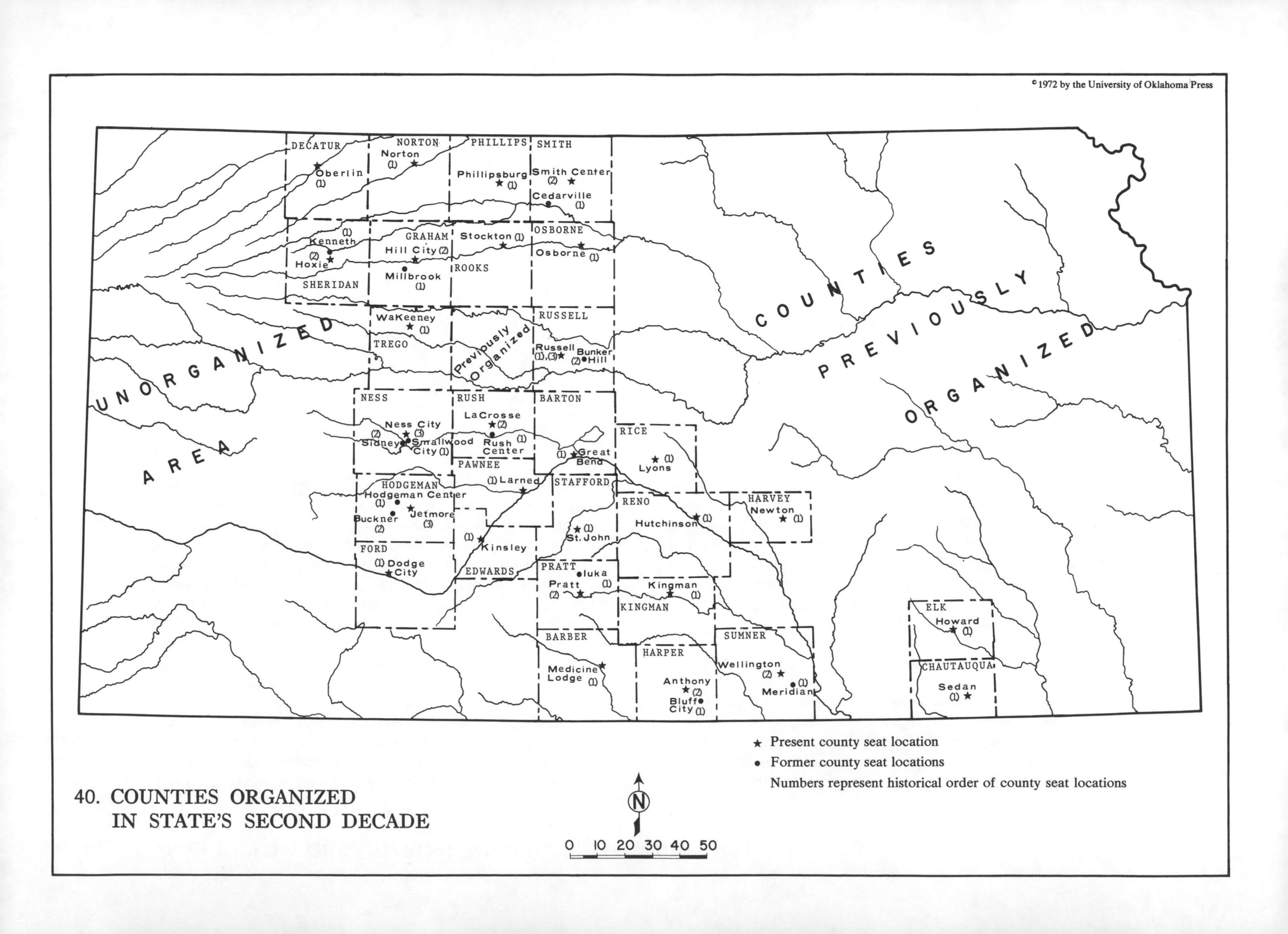

DECATUR
NORTON
PHILLIPS
SMITH
Norton (1)
Oberlin (1)
Phillipsburg (1)
Smith Center (2)
Cedarville (1)

Kenneth (1)
GRAHAM
Stockton (1)
OSBORNE
Hoxie (2)
Hill City (2)
Osborne (1)
Millbrook (1)
ROOKS
SHERIDAN

WaKeeney (1)
RUSSELL
TREGO
Previously Organized
Russell (1), (3)
Bunker Hill (2)

NESS
RUSH
BARTON
LaCrosse (2)
Ness City (3)
RICE
Sidney (2)
Smallwood City (1)
Rush Center (1)
Great Bend (1)
Lyons (1)
PAWNEE
Larned (1)
STAFFORD
HODGEMAN
Hodgeman Center (1)
RENO
HARVEY
Newton (1)
Buckner (2)
Jetmore (3)
Hutchinson (1)
St. John (1)
FORD
Kinsley (1)
Dodge City (1)
EDWARDS
PRATT
Iuka
Pratt (2)
Kingman (1)
ELK
Howard (1)
KINGMAN
BARBER
SUMNER
CHAUTAUQUA
HARPER
Wellington (2)
Sedan (1)
Medicine Lodge (1)
Anthony (2)
Meridian (1)
Bluff City (1)

UNORGANIZED AREA

COUNTIES PREVIOUSLY ORGANIZED

★ Present county seat location
● Former county seat locations
Numbers represent historical order of county seat locations

**40. COUNTIES ORGANIZED
IN STATE'S SECOND DECADE**

N

0 10 20 30 40 50

40. COUNTIES ORGANIZED IN STATE'S SECOND DECADE

WITH THE COMPLETION of two railroads across the state, county development proceeded rapidly, with twenty-eight counties organized in the second decade of statehood. In spite of the conditions brought on by the Panic of 1873, resulting in five or six years of low-level economic activity, the push to open the region to settlement continued, and homesteaders and railroad land purchasers rapidly took up land. Several of the counties in this group were initially organized fraudulently—notably Harper and Pratt—but on the whole the organization was accomplished without great difficulty.

Seventeen of these twenty-eight counties got a county seat on the first try. However, the counties of Elk and Chautauqua had previously made up Howard County, then the second largest county in the state. The reports of county seat conflict in Howard County sound exaggerated. One author reported, "So bitter did county-seat struggles become that they not only broke up neighborhoods but divided churches and plunged families into strife." As many as seven small Howard County communities actively sought the county seat, and after much confusion, balloting, stolen county records, and losses in taxes, the solution was a "county bustin'" one—a division of the area into two new counties. Because the towns earlier seeking the county seat were near the border of the new counties they lost out entirely to new contestants, and each county started with a sizable debt incurred in earlier county seat elections.

LaCrosse finally won the county seat race in Rush County after nearly a decade of argument. In a bitter rather than humorous vein the opposition press invariably identified their rival as the town of "LaX." Pratt County's decision on a county seat also took almost ten years. Iuka was the first county seat, and rivals Saratoga and Anderson sought the prize. With the arrival of the railroad the support for Iuka shifted to the new town of Pratt Center, with Saratoga as its principal rival. In this phase of the county seat war the courthouse was burned, amidst shooting which wounded several people. The state's adjutant general was sent to investigate, and order was soon restored, with the issue decided in favor of Pratt.

CHEYENNE RAWLINS

St. Francis
(2) ★ ● Bird (1)
City ★ (1)
★ Atwood

Eustis
(2) ★ ● (1)
Goodland ● Colby ★ (1)
SHERMAN

THOMAS

WALLACE Oakley ★ GOVE
(2) (1)
Pond City (1) Wallace (2) Russell ★ Gove
(3) ★ SPrings
Sharon Springs (1)
LOGAN

GREELEY WICHITA LANE
SCOTT
(1),(3) Farmer ★ (1) Dighton
● Leoti ★ City ★ Scott (1) ★
(1) ★ (2) City
Tribune

HAMILTON KEARNY FINNEY

Coolidge (1)
● (3) Kendall (1),(3) Garden
Syracuse ★ Lakin City
(2) (4) ★ (1)
Hartland GRAY
(2) Ingalls (2)
● ★
Cimarron
STANTON GRANT HASKELL (1),(3)

Ulysses KIOWA
★ (1) Santa Fe (1)
★ (1) ● (1) ★ Greensburg
Johnson
Sublette ★ (2) MEADE
MORTON STEVENS SEWARD CLARK COMANCHE
Springfield Meade Coldwater
Richfield (1) (1) ★ ★ (1)
Hugoton Ashland
★ (1) (1) ★
Elkhart Liberal
★ (2) ★ (2)

★ Present county seat location
● Former county seat locations
Numbers represent historical order of county seat locations

41. COUNTIES ORGANIZED
IN STATE'S THIRD DECADE

COUNTIES PREVIOUSLY ORGANIZED

N

0 10 20 30 40 50

THE LAST TWENTY-FIVE COUNTIES to be organized in Kansas were created in a period of intense optimism which wilted quickly after 1887 with the return of dry years to western Kansas. Perhaps for this reason the county seat wars, which resulted in killings in three counties, brought far more bloodshed than had occured in all previous county organization in Kansas.

Governor John A. Martin (1885–89) strongly endorsed the contagious enthusiasm for settlement in western Kansas. Early in his term he told an audience that, "To populate a county thirty miles square within six months, and round out the half-year with a fight over the county seat between six towns, or to build a fair-sized city within a twelvemonth–these achievements may seem like fiction, but they have been realities in Kansas." During his years as governor the conditions he described ceased to be a laughing matter, and on several occasions the state militia was called out to restore order.

Why these last county seat wars in Kansas were so bloody is difficult to explain. Stanley Vestal, in describing the character of the sod-busting farmers of the Great Plains explained that, "Sedentary people—all legend to the contrary—are more blood-thirsty and vindictive than nomads . . . . The cowboys and gamblers had killed personal enemies. But the plowmen who swarmed in to file on free land fought for their towns and their homesteads—grimly, ferociously, relentlessly. . . . The county-seat boosters and land-hungry boomers too often had no conscience and no remorse."

Vestal's interpretation may help explain what happened in Gray, Garfield, Wichita, and Stevens counties. Gray County's fight for the county seat was between Cimarron and Ingalls. Rival newspapers in the two communities whipped up emotions over the county seat issue. Bribery was reported and gunmen were imported from Dodge City. When Ingalls men went to Cimarron to forcibly remove the county records, an innocent bystander was killed.

Neighboring Garfield County, the ill-fated 106th county in Kansas, had as county seat rivals the communities of Ravanna and Eminence. The battle was largely fought in the press, and an embittered Ravanna lost to Eminence. In retaliation they ordered a resurvey of the county which disclosed that the area was slightly smaller than the 432 square miles then required for a new county in Kansas. There were no killings here, but Garfield County was disorganized and attached to Finney County.

Imported gunmen from Wallace and Dodge City were also featured in the county seat war between Leoti and Coronado in Wichita County. Some of Leoti's "tough hombres" visited Coronado one Sunday afternoon. After the Leoti invaders spent some time lording it over their rivals and ridiculing them, the Coronado citizens countered vocal insults with a volley of well-aimed shots, hitting seven Leoti men, four of whom were killed. Arrests were made, but the case was never prosecuted, and Leoti eventually won the county seat.

Stevens County, with a single county seat, had the most violence of any county in Kansas. Charles E. Cook, forceful leader of Hugoton and former postmaster of McPherson, and Samuel N. Wood, factional leader of Woodsdale and longtime champion of the political underdog in Kansas, were able to evoke in their backers a bitterness which aroused their two communities to a fever pitch. After four Woodsdale men were slaughtered by a Hugoton partisan in the Hay Meadow Massacre of July 25, 1888, in No Man's Land, just south of the Kansas border, the state

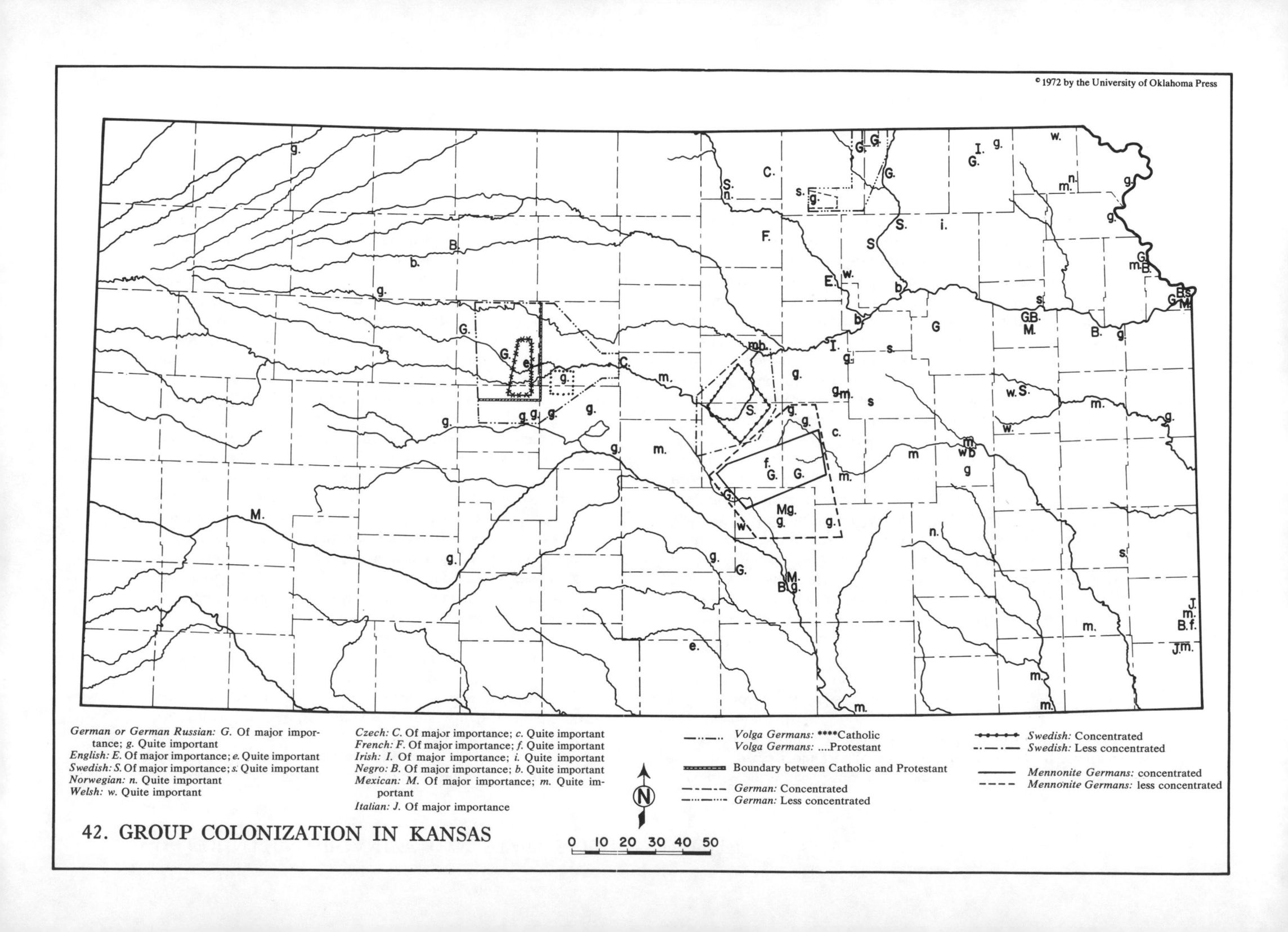

German or German Russian: *G.* Of major importance; *g.* Quite important
English: *E.* Of major importance; *e.* Quite important
Swedish: *S.* Of major importance; *s.* Quite important
Norwegian: *n.* Quite important
Welsh: *w.* Quite important

Czech: *C.* Of major importance; *c.* Quite important
French: *F.* Of major importance; *f.* Quite important
Irish: *I.* Of major importance; *i.* Quite important
Negro: *B.* Of major importance; *b.* Quite important
Mexican: *M.* Of major importance; *m.* Quite important
Italian: *J.* Of major importance

Volga Germans: ****Catholic
Volga Germans: ....Protestant
Boundary between Catholic and Protestant
German: Concentrated
German: Less concentrated

Swedish: Concentrated
Swedish: Less concentrated
Mennonite Germans: concentrated
Mennonite Germans: less concentrated

N

0 10 20 30 40 50

42. GROUP COLONIZATION IN KANSAS

militia was sent to the county for ten days. Wood sought to bring indictments against the murderers, and he finally found a federal court in Paris, Texas, which would accept jurisdiction in the case. Six Hugoton ringleaders were convicted and sentenced to be hanged. Their case was appealed on a writ of error, they were freed, and the case was finally dropped. A last gasp of this tragic county seat war was the daytime murder of Wood in front of witnesses in 1891. His killer escaped prosecution.

In 1873 all of the remaining area of the state was divided into named counties by the Kansas legislature. For the region of the twenty-five counties which came into existence between 1881 and 1888, this earlier legislature supplied names not necessarily used when the county was eventually settled and organized. County names that disappeared in this process were Arapahoe, Buffalo, Foote, Kansas, St. John, and Sequoyah. Counties in this far-western part of the state were small in area, like their counterparts in the east. Early boomers of the area expected far greater population than came to live there, but the primary reason for the small-sized counties—about six or seven hundred square miles in area—was the desire that every citizen should be able to travel by horseback from his home to the county seat and return in one day.

42. GROUP COLONIZATION IN KANSAS

THE POPULATION OF KANSAS has always been one that was largely native-born American. Slightly fewer than 14 per cent of the Kansans listed in the 1870 census were of foreign birth, the largest proportion of any census. Most people who migrated to Kansas did so alone or with their immediate families. At the same time, there were rural areas in settlement days where most of the residents were from Iowa or Illinois, or Pennsylvania or St. Louis, or some other specific area. Private communication would influence relatives or former neighbors to migrate to the new area, and it was natural for the newcomers to locate with friends or acquaintances.

Longer-lived settlements of special character, such as those established by religious congregations, or by foreign-born or other ethnic groups, have been the basis for much study in Kansas history. In early-day Kansas, the largest foreign-born group came from the British Isles. These people, accounting for half of all the foreign born in 1870, came from England, Scotland, Wales, and Ireland, and they scattered throughout the state because they encountered little language difficulty. The primary English settlement was at Wakefield, with interesting communities at Victoria and Runnymede. Welsh settlements were located at Emporia, Bala, and Arvonia. Irish, some from big cities in the United States, were located in large numbers near Chapman, near Seneca, and in Pottawatomie County. In 1895 there were still 4,500 people of Scottish birth in Kansas, with about a fourth of them concentrated in the coal-mining counties of Osage, Crawford, and Cherokee.

By 1890 the German-speaking foreign-born residents of Kansas, whether from Germany, Hungary, Russia, or neighboring areas, had grown to 43 per cent of the total foreign born and out-

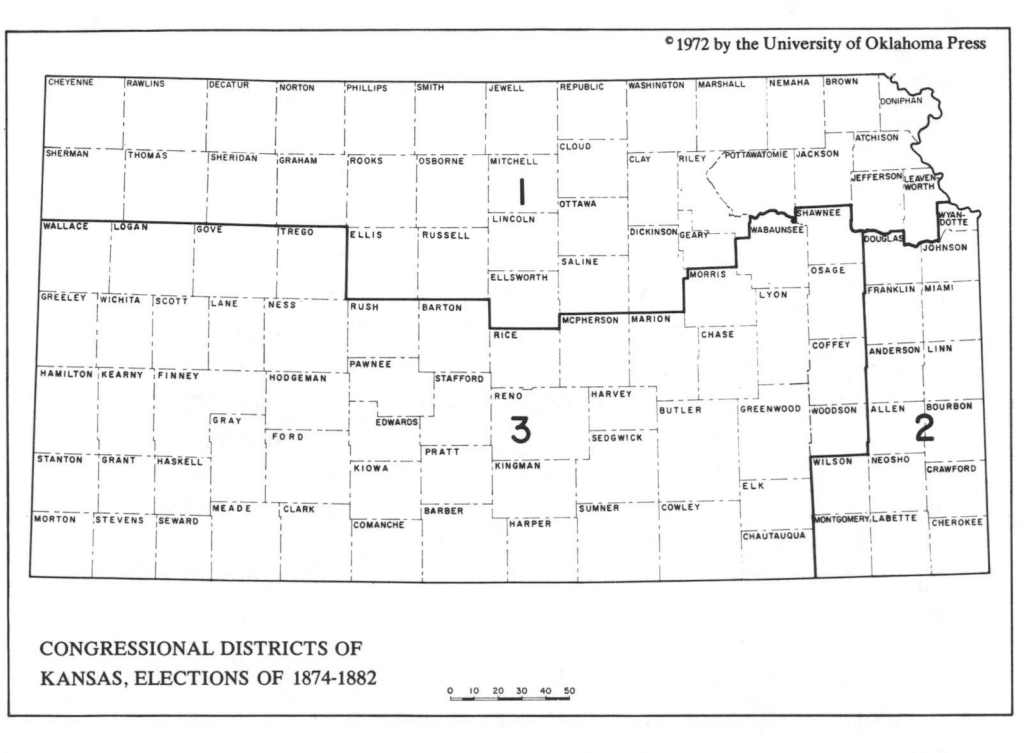

CONGRESSIONAL DISTRICTS OF
KANSAS, ELECTIONS OF 1874-1882

0 10 20 30 40 50

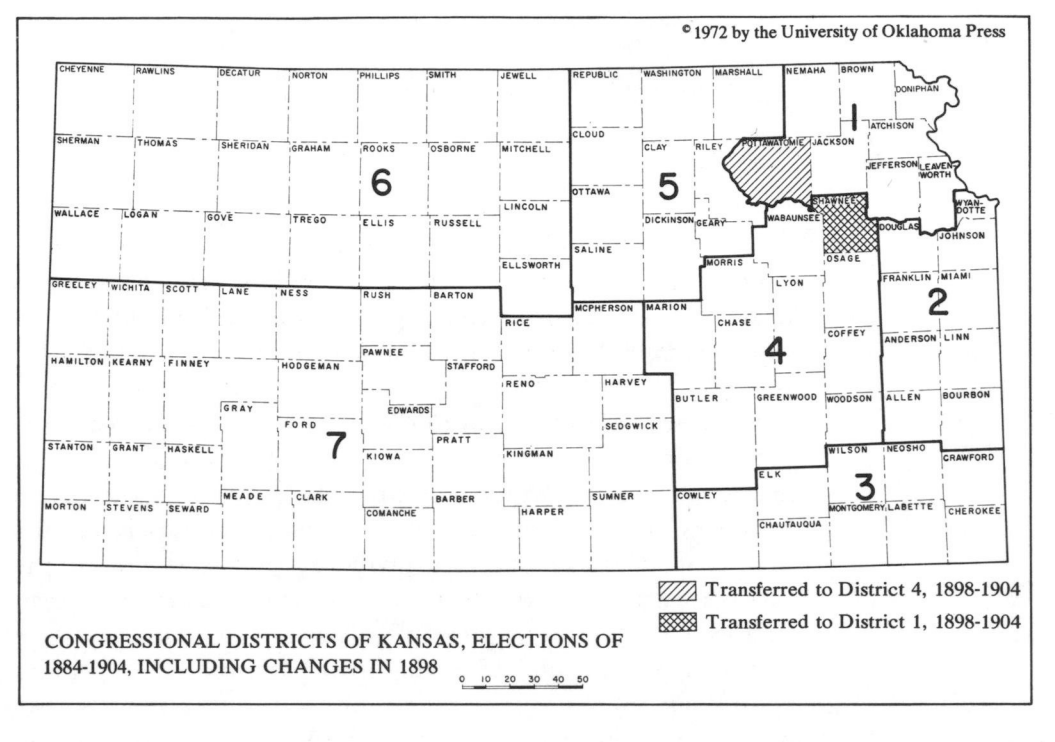

▨ Transferred to District 4, 1898-1904
▩ Transferred to District 1, 1898-1904

CONGRESSIONAL DISTRICTS OF KANSAS, ELECTIONS OF
1884-1904, INCLUDING CHANGES IN 1898

0 10 20 30 40 50

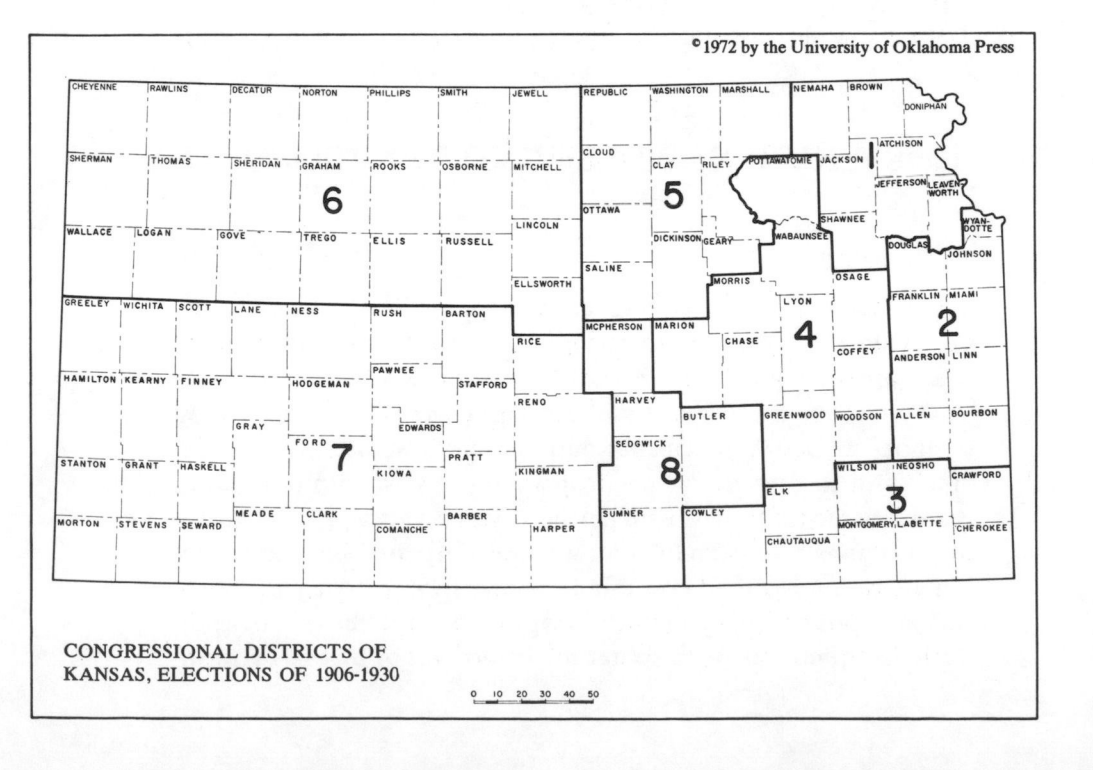

CONGRESSIONAL DISTRICTS OF
KANSAS, ELECTIONS OF 1906-1930

0 10 20 30 40 50

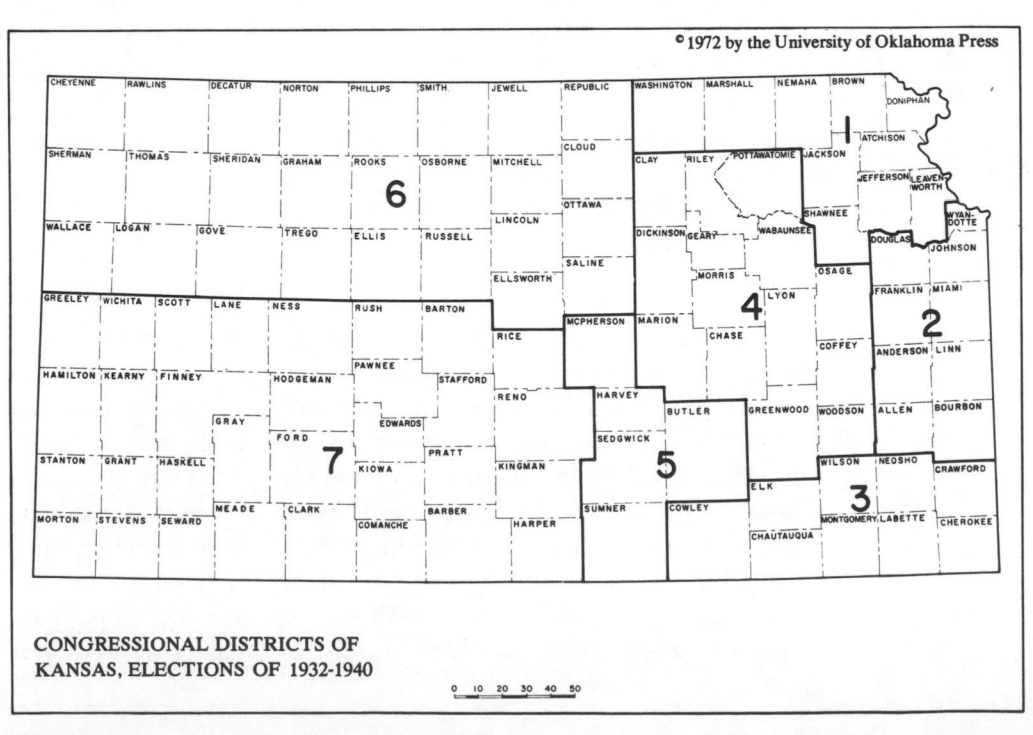

CONGRESSIONAL DISTRICTS OF
KANSAS, ELECTIONS OF 1932-1940

0 10 20 30 40 50

numbered all others. Germans were located in all counties and had large settlements in Kansas City, Leavenworth, Seneca, Alma, and Topeka. Southeast McPherson and adjoining Marion, Harvey, and Reno counties became the home of German-Russian Mennonites and other German-speaking people. Ellis County had a large number of German-Russian Catholics, and German Lutherans congregated in Marshall and Washington counties.

The third largest foreign-born group in nineteenth-century Kansas came from Sweden. Their primary colony was located at Lindsborg, with other areas of Swedish influence in Republic, Osage, and the Blue River parts of Riley and Pottawatomie counties. A few settlers also came from other Scandinavian countries.

Foreign-born Kansans who spoke French were either Canadian or Belgian in background or had departed France after the ill-fated 1848 revolution. Cloud County had the largest French settlements. Many Italians, also, entered Kansas after about 1900 and settled in the southeastern mining district. Another distinc-

tive foreign-born group in Kansas was the Bohemians or Czechs. Their largest settlements were at Wilson in Ellsworth County and in eastern Republic County, with smaller concentrations elsewhere.

Native-born American Negroes increased in Kansas like all other elements of the population. Their proportion of the population remained remarkably constant for a hundred years at 3½ to 4 per cent. Kansas population tripled between 1870 and 1880, and this was the period of the "Exodus" of blacks from the deep South to the promised land of Kansas, when their numbers in the state increased from 17,108 to 43,107. Many blacks arrived in Kansas impoverished, and they settled in the larger towns, where they could find employment. Their primary rural settlement was Nicodemus, the first community in Graham County.

The last ethnic group to enter Kansas in large numbers were Spanish-speaking Mexicans, brought to the state as laborers for various railroad companies. Numbering only 71 in 1900, their totals reached 13,570 in 1920 and 19,042 in 1930. Their primary population concentrations were in railroad centers.

43. KANSAS CONGRESSIONAL DISTRICTS THROUGH 1940

As a consequence of the Wyandotte Constitution, in 1859 Kansans elected their first congressman to the House of Representatives, and he took office soon after statehood. There was a single congressional district for the state until the results of the 1870 census raised the Kansas share of the House of Representatives to three, who ran as at-large candidates in the election of 1872, and thereafter ran from specified districts. The 1880 census showed that Kansas had grown so rapidly that the 1 per cent share of the nation's population in 1870 had almost doubled to 2 per cent, and seven seats were assigned to the state. Four seats were filled in 1882 by at-large candidates, and the seven districts

were determined by the legislature in time for the 1884 election. For the next twenty years the Kansas population increased at a slower pace than that of the nation, but the size of the House of Representatives was enlarged after 1890. Kansas received an eighth congressional seat which was served by an at-large candidate until 1906, when eight congressional districts were assigned by the legislature. These districts existed through the census of 1930, when it was determined that Kansas had 1.53 per cent of the national population. One seat in Congress was lost, necessitating redistricting. These congressional districts lasted through the election of 1940.

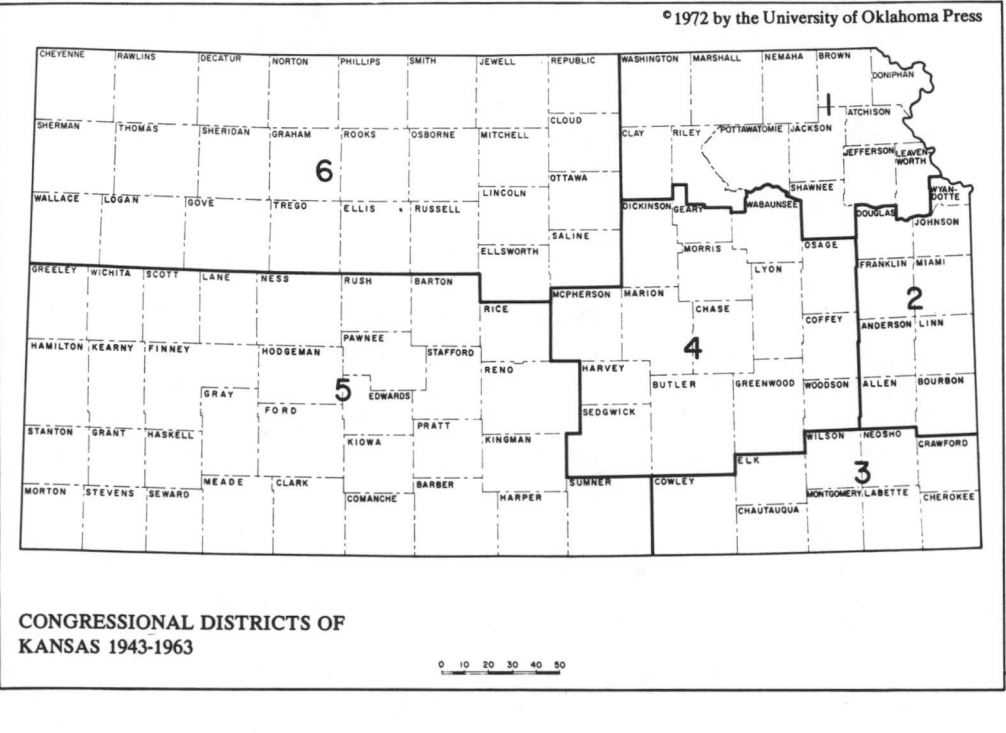

CONGRESSIONAL DISTRICTS OF
KANSAS 1943-1963

0 10 20 30 40 50

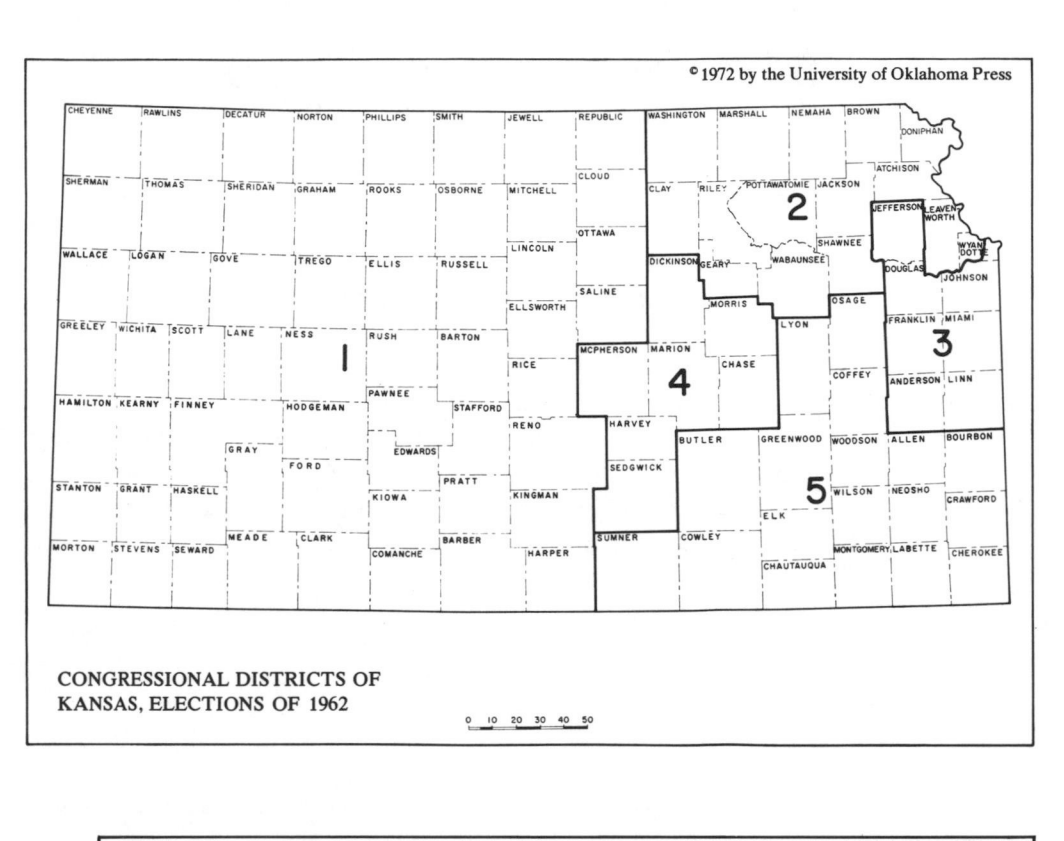

CONGRESSIONAL DISTRICTS OF
KANSAS, ELECTIONS OF 1962

0 10 20 30 40 50

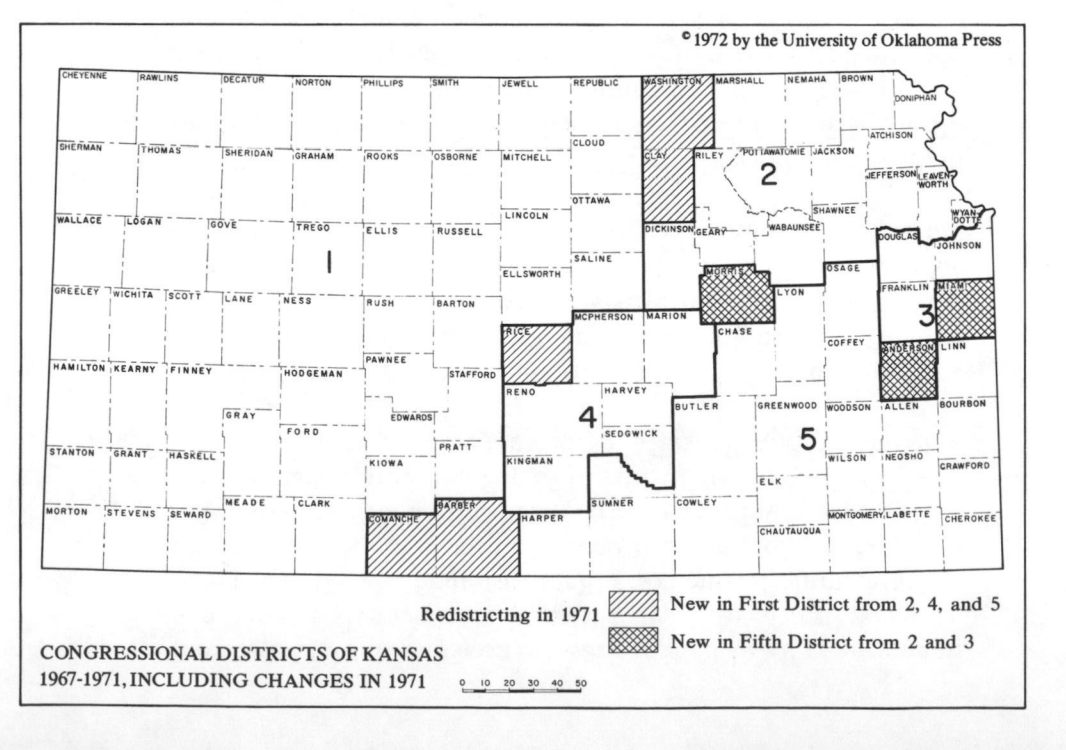

Redistricting in 1971   ▨ New in First District from 2, 4, and 5
                        ▨ New in Fifth District from 2 and 3

CONGRESSIONAL DISTRICTS OF KANSAS
1967-1971, INCLUDING CHANGES IN 1971

0 10 20 30 40 50

CONGRESSIONAL DISTRICTS OF KANSAS
AS DETERMINED BY FEDERAL COURT
ORDER, 1982

0 10 20 30 40 50
MILES

44. CONGRESSIONAL DISTRICTS IN KANSAS AFTER 1940

THE 1940 FEDERAL CENSUS was the only one to show a decline in Kansas population, and the number of congressmen in the state dropped from seven to six. The rural-dominated state legislature sought to diffuse the influence of the three largest cities, as they had done in previous redistricting. They placed Kansas City, Wichita, and Topeka in separate districts, a practice that continued in subsequent redistricting.

The proportion of the national population residing in Kansas in 1940 was 1.36 per cent. As a consequence of the rapid growth in the next twenty years, the proportion of Americans living in Kansas declined. Kansas population grew but at a slower rate than national population, and in 1960 Kansas had 1.21 per cent of the nation's population. Again Kansas lost a congressional seat. The one-man, one-vote ruling made it mandatory that new districts be established, each showing a population near the average for the state's districts. The state legislature responded by redistricting in 1965, effective for terms beginning in January, 1967. Additional redistricting involving eight counties took place in 1971 in time for the 1972 election.

In congressional districts of the 1960's and 1970's, Wyandotte County was divided between two districts, and in the 1970's, Sedgwick County was divided between two districts. The 1980 federal census showed that Kansas had 1.04 per cent of the national population, still enough for five representatives. Internal shifts in population, however, brought a federal court order in 1982 mandating slight changes in congressional districts. An effort was made this time to avoid dividing a county between more than one district. An indication of the differences in population for Kansas counties is shown by the number of counties in each district: 1—58 counties; 2—13; 3—4; 4—5; and 5—25.

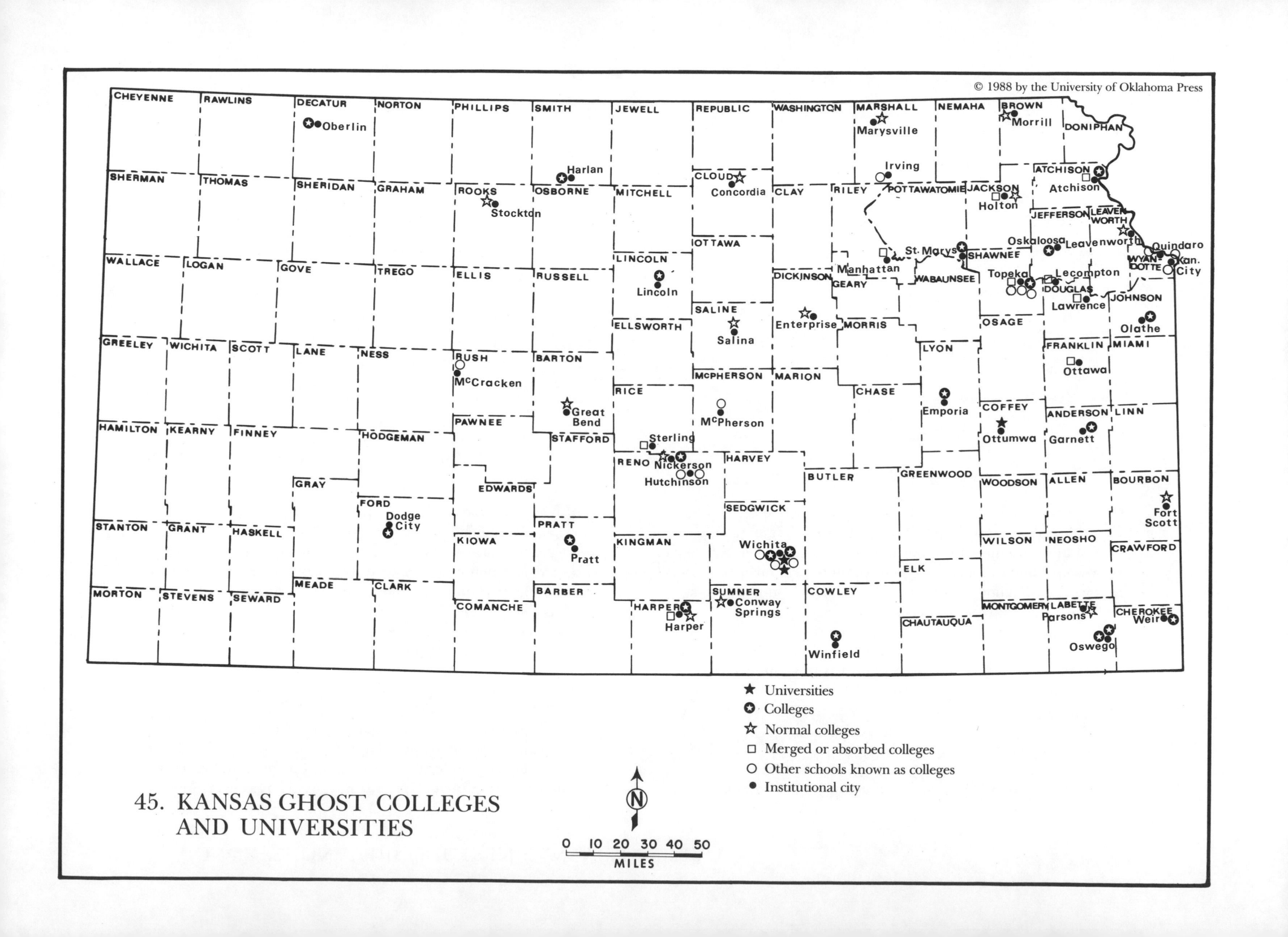

45. KANSAS GHOST COLLEGES
AND UNIVERSITIES

★ Universities
✪ Colleges
☆ Normal colleges
□ Merged or absorbed colleges
○ Other schools known as colleges
● Institutional city

N

0 10 20 30 40 50
MILES

45. KANSAS GHOST COLLEGES AND UNIVERSITIES

THE STORY OF KANSAS GHOST COLLEGES and universities is an account of high educational objectives frequently flawed by changing patterns of education, hard times, impractical promoters, and half-hearted support. The name university or college for these institutions was often a misnomer. Some communities tried a number of times to develop collegiate institutions and eventually succeeded. Many other communities had elaborate plans which got little further than the talking stage, although more than 140 corporation charters were obtained for such organizations. The communities with institutions of higher education, the names, and years of operation are as follows:

ATCHISON — Atchison (or Monroe) Institute (1870–84)

CONCORDIA — State Normal School—Concordia (1874–76)

CONWAY SPRINGS — Conway Normal College (1890–94)

DODGE CITY — Soule College (1893–97, 1902–1907)

EMPORIA — College of Emporia (1887–1974)

ENTERPRISE — Central College (1891–96)

FORT SCOTT — Kansas Normal College (1880–1902)

GARNETT — Mount Carmel (or Scipio) College (1871–84)

GREAT BEND — Central Normal College (1887–1901)

HARLAN — Gould College (1882–88)

HARPER — Harper Normal College (1886–96); Kansas Christian College (1899–1901); Harper College (1915–24)

HOLTON — Campbell Normal University (1882–1902); Campbell College (1902–13)

HUTCHINSON — Arkansas Valley Collegiate Institute (ca. 1874); Western Business College and Normal School (1886–89)

IRVING — Wetmore Institute (1864–80)

KANSAS CITY — Western Eclectic College of Medicine and Surgery (1888–1909); Kansas City Academy of Medicine and Surgery (1893–94); Kansas City Medical College (ca. 1896–1905); College of Physicians and Surgeons (1894–1905); Kansas City University (1894–1931)

LAWRENCE — Lawrence University (1861–64)

LEAVENWORTH — State Normal School—Leavenworth (1870–75)

LECOMPTON — Lane University (1882–1903)

LINCOLN — Kansas Christian College (1884–ca. 1912)

MANHATTAN — Bluemont Central College (1859–63)

MARYSVILLE — Modern Normal College (1892–1903)

McCRACKEN — Entre Nous College (1906–12)

McPHERSON — Walden College (1901–1905)

MORRILL — Morrill Normal College (1882–88)

NICKERSON — Nickerson Normal and Nickerson Business College (1898–1903); Nickerson College (1903–19)

OBERLIN — National G.A.R. Memorial College (1890–ca. 1893)

OLATHE — Olathe Normal University (ca. 1888)

OSKALOOSA — Enoch Marvin College (1878–80)

OSWEGO — Oswego College (1870–82); Oswego College for Young Ladies (1886–89, 1904–21)

OTTAWA — Roger Williams University (1860–65)

OTTUMWA — Western Christian University (1863–74)

PARSONS — Hobson Normal Institute (1882–90's)

PRATT — Baptist College (1891–93)

QUINDARO — Western University (formerly Freedman University, 1865–?) (1890–1943)

SALINA — Salina Normal University (1884–1904)

ST. MARYS — St. Mary's College (1869–1931; then part of St. Louis University until 1967)

STERLING — Cooper Memorial College (1887–1909); Cooper College (1909–19)

STOCKTON — Stockton Normal School (ca. 1898)

TOPEKA — Lincoln College (1865–68); College of Physicians and Surgeons, North Topeka (ca. 1872); College of the Sisters of Charity (ca. 1875); Kansas Medical College (1890–1902); Topeka Dental College (1909–11); College of the Sisters of Bethany (1873–1926)

WEIR — Kansas School of Mines (1912–17)

WICHITA — Southwest Kansas Institute (ca. 1877–79); Southwest Kansas College (ca. 1884); Garfield University (1887–90) [Central Memorial University (1892–94)]; Wichita University (1887–95); Albertus Magnus College (ca. 1901); Western School of Elocution and Oratory (1891–1902); American Socialist College (ca. 1903); Fairmont College (1896–1926); University of Wichita (1926–64)

WINFIELD — St. John's College (1893–1986)

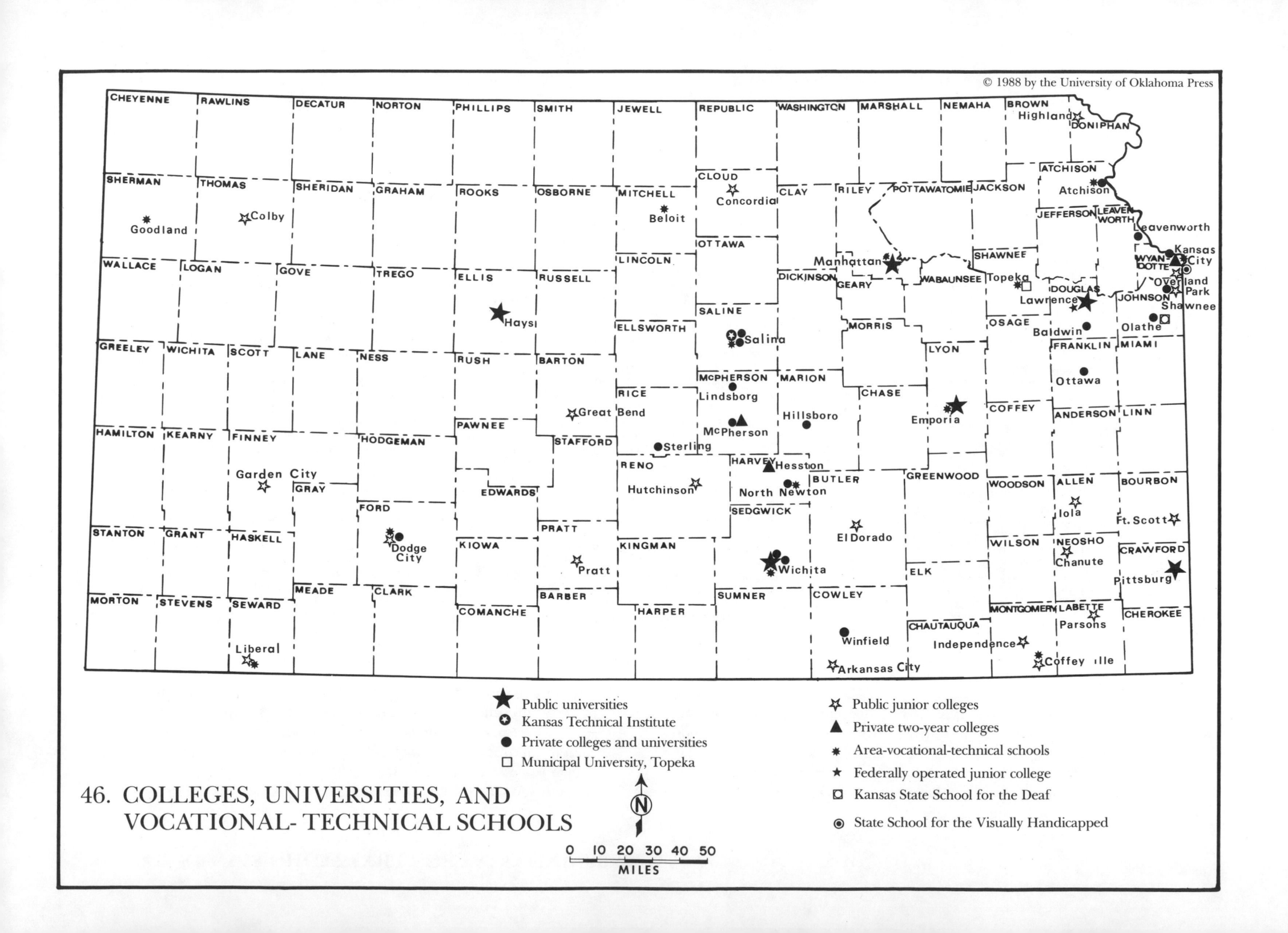

Public universities
⊛ Kansas Technical Institute
● Private colleges and universities
▢ Municipal University, Topeka

✪ Public junior colleges
▲ Private two-year colleges
✳ Area-vocational-technical schools
★ Federally operated junior college
⬚ Kansas State School for the Deaf
◉ State School for the Visually Handicapped

46. COLLEGES, UNIVERSITIES, AND VOCATIONAL- TECHNICAL SCHOOLS

N

0 10 20 30 40 50
MILES

46. COLLEGES, UNIVERSITIES, AND VOCATIONAL-TECHNICAL SCHOOLS

ACADEMIC AND VOCATIONAL EDUCATION is available in Kansas in diverse forms and places. They are as follows:

STATE INSTITUTIONS OF HIGHER LEARNING

EMPORIA	Emporia State University
HAYS	Fort Hays State University
LAWRENCE	University of Kansas
MANHATTAN	Kansas State University
PITTSBURG	Pittsburg State University
WICHITA	Wichita State University

MUNICIPAL UNIVERSITY

Washburn University	TOPEKA

PRIVATE FOUR-YEAR COLLEGES

ATCHISON	Benedictine College
BALDWIN CITY	Baker University
DODGE CITY	St. Mary of the Plains College
HILLSBORO	Tabor College
LEAVENWORTH	Saint Mary College
LINDSBORG	Bethany College
MCPHERSON	McPherson College
NORTH NEWTON	Bethel College
OLATHE	Mid-America Nazarene College
OTTAWA	Ottawa University
SALINA	Kansas Wesleyan College
	Marymount College
STERLING	Sterling College
WICHITA	Friends University
	Kansas Newman College
WINFIELD	Southwestern College

PUBLIC COMMUNITY TWO-YEAR JUNIOR COLLEGES

ARKANSAS CITY	Cowley County Community College
CHANUTE	Neosho County Community College
COFFEYVILLE	Coffeyville Community College
COLBY	Colby Community College
CONCORDIA	Cloud County Community College
DODGE CITY	Dodge City Community College
EL DORADO	Butler County Community College
FORT SCOTT	Fort Scott Community College
GARDEN CITY	Garden City Community College
GREAT BEND	Barton County Community College
HIGHLAND	Highland Community College
HUTCHINSON	Hutchinson Community College
INDEPENDENCE	Independence Community College
IOLA	Allen County Community College
KANSAS CITY	Kansas City Kansas Community College
LIBERAL	Seward County Community College
PARSONS	Labette County Community College
PRATT	Pratt County Community College
SHAWNEE MISSION	Johnson County Community College

PRIVATE TWO-YEAR COLLEGES

HESSTON	Hesston College
KANSAS CITY	Donnelly College
MCPHERSON	Central College

FEDERALLY OPERATED TWO-YEAR COLLEGE

LAWRENCE	Haskell Indian Junior College

AREA VOCATIONAL-TECHNICAL SCHOOLS

ATCHISON	Northeast Kansas Area Vocational-Technical School
BELOIT	North Central Area Vocational-Technical School
COFFEYVILLE	Southeast Kansas Area Vocational-Technical School
DODGE CITY	Southwest Kansas Area Vocational-Technical School
EMPORIA	Flint Hills Area Vocational-Technical School
GOODLAND	Northwest Kansas Area Vocational-Technical School
KANSAS CITY	Kansas City Area Vocational-Technical School
LIBERAL	Liberal Area Vocational-Technical School
MANHATTAN	Manhattan Area Vocational-Technical School
NEWTON	Central Kansas Area Vocational-Technical School
SALINA	Salina Area Vocational-Technical School
TOPEKA	Kaw Area Vocational-Technical School
WICHITA	Wichita Area Vocational-Technical School

KANSAS TECHNICAL INSTITUTE

SALINA	Schilling Institute

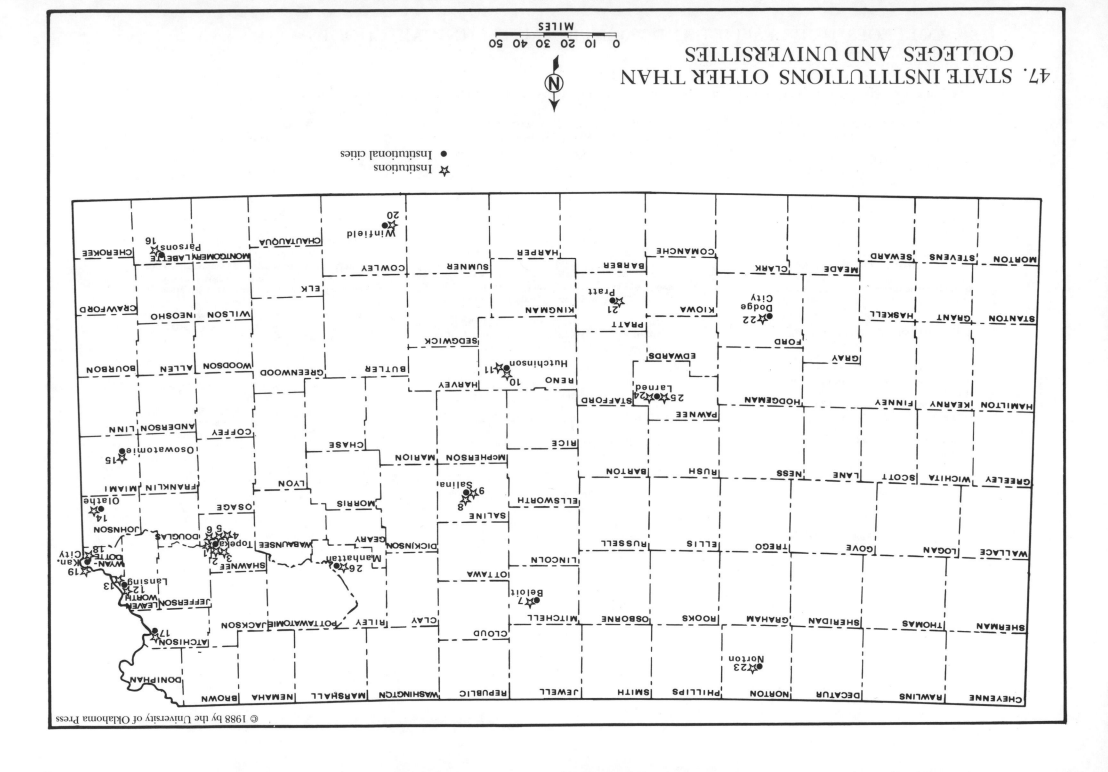

☆ Institutions
● Institutional cities

N

MILES
0 10 20 30 40 50

47. STATE INSTITUTIONS OTHER THAN COLLEGES AND UNIVERSITIES

A LARGE NUMBER of state institutions other than the colleges and universities have been developed throughout the state. Topeka, with the state capitol and other major state offices included in the Capitol Area Complex, might be expected to have other state institutions, and it does. Their names and the names and locations of other state institutions are as follows:

1. State Industrial School for Boys, Topeka
2. Topeka State Hospital, Topeka
3. Kansas Neurological Institute, Topeka
4. Kansas State Reception and Diagnostic Center, Topeka
5. Kansas Correctional-Vocational Training Center, Topeka
6. Youth Center at Topeka, Topeka
7. Youth Center at Beloit, Beloit
8. Kansas Technical Institute, Salina
9. Kansas Vocational Rehabilitation Center, Salina
10. Kansas State Industrial Reformatory, Hutchinson
11. Kansas State Fair, Hutchinson
12. Kansas State Penitentiary, Lansing
13. Kansas State Industrial Farm for Women, Lansing
14. Kansas School for the Deaf, Olathe
15. Osawatomie State Hospital, Osawatomie
16. Parsons State Hospital and Training Center, Parsons
17. Youth Center at Atchison, Atchison
18. Kansas State School for the Visually Handicapped, Kansas City
19. Rainbow Mental Health Facility, Kansas City
20. Winfield State Hospital and Training Center, Winfield
21. Kansas Fish and Game Commission, Pratt
22. Kansas Soldiers' Home, Fort Dodge
23. Norton State Hospital, Norton
24. Larned State Hospital, Larned
25. Youth Center at Larned, Larned
26. Kansas Wheat Commission, Manhattan

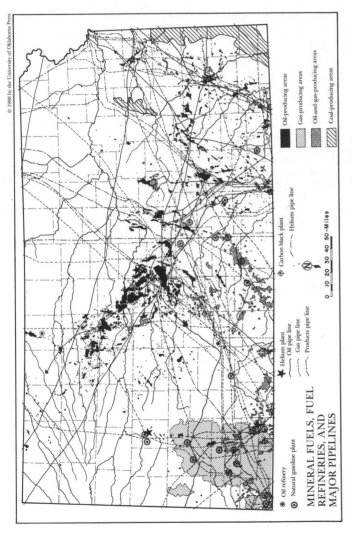

Oil-producing areas

Gas-producing areas

Oil-and-gas-producing areas

Coal-producing areas

● Oil refinery

◉ Natural gasoline plant

★ Helium plant

◈ Carbon black plant

—·— Oil pipe line

——— Gas pipe line

— — — Helium pipe line

——— Products pipe line

N

0 10 20 30 40 50 Miles

MINERAL FUELS, FUEL REFINERIES, AND MAJOR PIPELINES

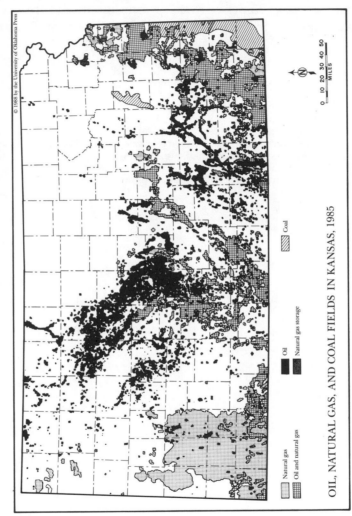

N

0 10 20 30 40 50
MILES

Natural gas

Oil and natural gas

Oil

Natural gas storage

Coal

OIL, NATURAL GAS, AND COAL FIELDS IN KANSAS, 1985

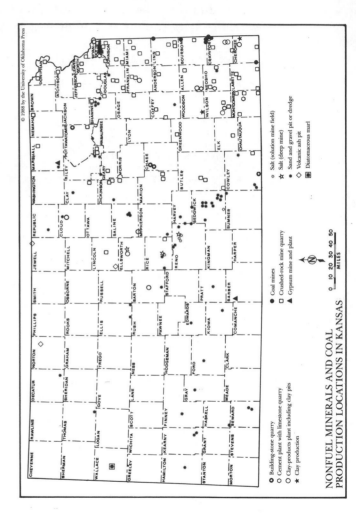

◇ Building-stone quarry

○ Cement plant with limestone quarry

◎ Clay-products plant including clay pits

★ Clay production

● Coal mines

□ Crushed-rock mine quarry

▲ Gypsum mine and plant

◇ Salt (solution mine field)

✩ Salt (deep mine)

△ Volcanic ash pit

◇ Sand and gravel pit or dredge

▨ Diatomaceous marl

N

0 10 20 30 40 50
MILES

NONFUEL MINERALS AND COAL PRODUCTION LOCATIONS IN KANSAS

Mineral Fuels, Fuel Refineries, and Major Pipelines

THE VALUE of mineral production in Kansas exceeded half a billion dollars in 1956 and in every year since 1962. In most of the years since 1918 Kansas has consistently been in the top dozen states in value of mineral production. As is true in most other states possessing a high value in minerals, the largest contributor to this underground Kansas wealth is petroleum, which, along with natural gas and derivatives of natural gas, accounts for four-fifths or more of the value of mineral production in the state.

Indians made use of "tar springs" in the eastern Kansas area in preterritorial times. Less than a year after Drake's discovery of the first oil well in Pennsylvania, the first shallow oil well in Kansas was dug near Olathe in June, 1860. Similar low-producing wells were found in other eastern counties, and in the 1890's a new, larger, deeper oil field was brought in near Neodesha. Big expansion for Kansas petroleum production began after 1915, with the discovery of the outstandingly productive El Dorado Oil Pool. By 1925 oil production began in Russell County, and important discoveries were made in central Kansas. Since then, discoveries in the huge Mid-Continent field of either oil or natural gas have expanded production in the El Dorado and Russell areas and beyond.

Natural gas production in Kansas has paralleled petroleum output, since gas was found in most oil wells, and most Kansas counties have one or both minerals. Early large gas fields near Iola led to heavy withdrawals to provide fuel for zinc smelters there. Production of natural gas in Kansas, second in value among minerals, has come, for the most part, from the huge Hugoton field of southwestern Kansas. The Hugoton field also includes the neighboring parts of the Oklahoma and Texas panhandles. Natural gasoline and LPG products, derived from natural gas, have been third-highest in value among Kansas minerals. Helium, another natural gas by-product, showed phenomenal growth in production after 1961 because of demands coming from the National Aeronautics and Space Administration.

Coal, the other mineral fuel produced in Kansas, was discovered in the area prior to the formation of the territory. For many years it played a prominent part in the economy of the state when more than ten thousand coal miners worked the mines in southeast Kansas and in Osage County. Coal production in the 1980's is a small fraction of total mineral output in Kansas and comes largely from a few open-pit mines in five counties. Production of lead and zinc, formerly mined in Cherokee County as a part of the tri-state lead and zinc mining area, is no longer reported.

More than 40,000 miles of Kansas pipelines augment the other transportation facilities of the state. These lines carry huge tonnages of natural gas, crude petroleum, and refined gas and petroleum products to major markets throughout the nation.

Oil, Natural Gas, and Coal Fields in Kansas, 1985

IN THE MID-1980's oil, natural gas, and coal production in Kansas is carried on in all but ten of the state's counties. Coal deposits in Kansas are quite restricted, whereas petroleum or natural gas is found in 80 of the 105 counties. Public policy related to severance taxes has a large and interested constituency. World price levels for fossil fuels have a local impact, felt both in good times and bad.

Nonfuel Minerals and Coal Production Locations in Kansas

SOME KIND of mineral production may be found in virtually every county in the state. Portland cement, accounting for the largest nonfuel mineral value in Kansas, is produced in five counties. Gypsum mines and plants exist in two counties, diatomaceous marl in one county, volcanic ash pits in three counties, some form of salt production in four counties, clay products plant and production in ten counties, and there is widespread production of sand, gravel, and crushed rock.

Mining in the 1980's accounts for almost 1 percent of all Kansas jobs, down more than half from 1955. Income for Kansas miners, especially those in the gas and oil fields, and the value added to refining of Kansas minerals is a significant part of the Kansas economy.

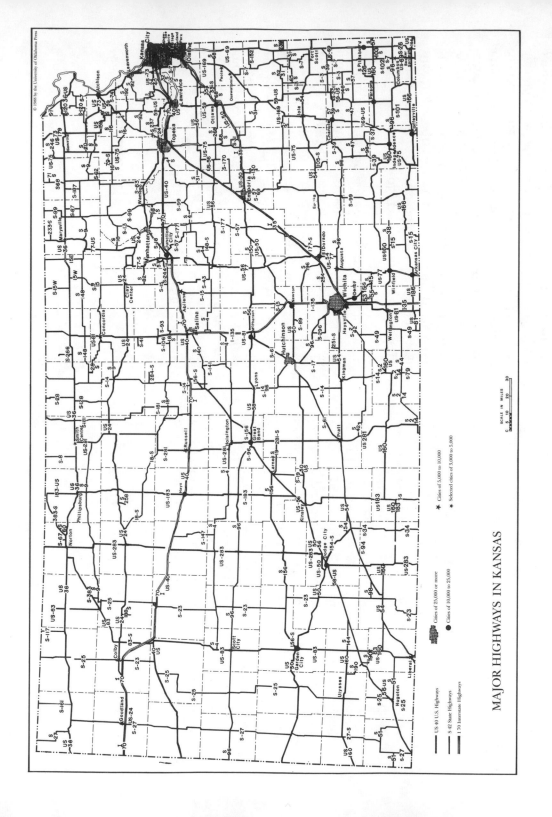

MAJOR HIGHWAYS IN KANSAS

US 40 U.S. Highways
S 42 State Highways
I 70 Interstate Highways

Cities of 25,000 or more
Cities of 10,000 to 25,000
Cities of 5,000 to 10,000
Selected cities of 3,000 to 5,000

SCALE IN MILES
0 5 10 20 30

© 1988 by the University of Oklahoma Press

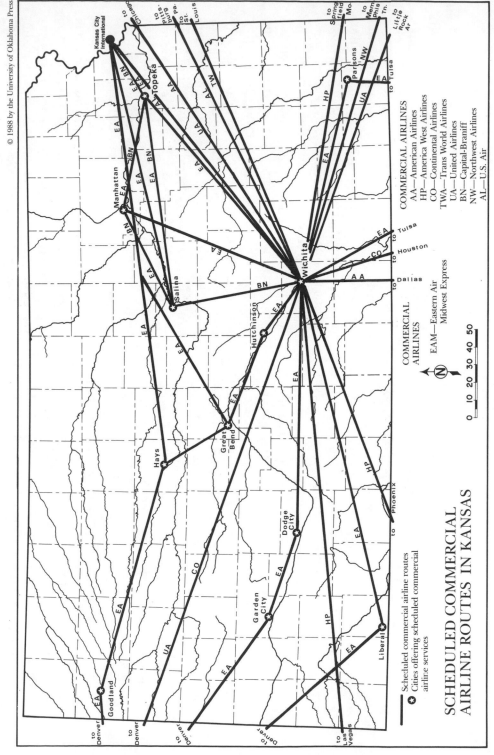

SCHEDULED COMMERCIAL AIRLINE ROUTES IN KANSAS

Scheduled commercial airline routes
Cities offering scheduled commercial airline services

COMMERCIAL AIRLINES
EAM—Eastern Air Midwest Express

COMMERCIAL AIRLINES
AA—American Airlines
HP—America West Airlines
CO—Continental Airlines
TWA—Trans World Airlines
UA—United Airlines
BN—Capital-Braniff
NW—Northwest Airlines
AL—U.S. Air

N

0 10 20 30 40 50

© 1988 by the University of Oklahoma Press

Major Highways in Kansas

THE TOTAL RURAL road mileage in Kansas is greater than 110,000 miles, somewhat smaller than authorized by the territorial legislature, which permitted the opening of a public road on every section line. Before World War I these roads were almost entirely under local governmental control. With the passage in 1916 of a federal rural roads act that provided fifty per cent of the funds to build major roads, Kansas began a transition to state control of major roadways, climaxed in 1929 with the establishment of the State Highway Commission, later known as the State Department of Transportation.

Efforts to upgrade all Kansas state and federal highways in the 1930's were delayed by depression and stopped by war. A long-range highway building program initiated in 1946 was substantially completed in the late 1960's, but by then most travelers desired better roads than those planned twenty years earlier. Because of the success of the Pennsylvania Turnpike toll-road operations, the Kansas legislature created the Kansas Turnpike Authority in 1953, which built the 236-mile, $160,000,000 Kansas Turnpike between Kansas City, Topeka, Wichita, and on south to the Oklahoma border.

Later major improvements in roadways in Kansas came with enactment of the federal Interstate Highway Act of 1956. Improvements were made with 90 per cent federal and 10 per cent state funds. Interstate 70, completed in 1970, crosses Kansas from Kansas City to the Colorado border west of Goodland and makes use of the Kansas Turnpike from Kansas City to Topeka. North-south interstate highways, Interstate 35 and Interstate 135 were almost complete at the same time. I-35 parallels part of the Kansas Turnpike from Kansas City to Emporia and makes use of the turnpike from there south. I-135 starts as I-70 at Salina and joins I-35 at Wichita and continues south. Urban links in the Kansas City area to these important highways were completed in the 1980's.

Scheduled Commercial Airline Routes in Kansas

AIR PASSENGERS who travel on scheduled commercial planes from points in Kansas generally depart by air from either the Kansas City International Airport, north of the Kansas City metropolitan area and just east of Leavenworth, or from the Wichita Mid-Continent Airport. Following deregulation of the airlines by the Civil Aeronautics Board in 1978, commercial airline service in Kansas changed greatly and was still in a state of flux in the 1980's. With the exception of Wichita most internal airports are served by a combination of commuter airlines, flying on a scheduled basis, and the major commercial airlines flying planes of much larger size.

Wheat

Other field crops

Cattle and calves

Other livestock and livestock products

Government payments to farmers

State distribution

50. AVERAGE ANNUAL VALUE OF FARM CROPS, LIVESTOCK, LIVESTOCK PRODUCTS, AND GOVERNMENT PAYMENTS TO FARMERS, 1980–1984

$170,000,000
110,000,000
90,000,000
70,000,000
50,000,000
30,000,000
15,000,000

N

0 10 20 30 40 50
MILES

50. AVERAGE ANNUAL VALUE OF FARM CROPS, LIVESTOCK, LIVESTOCK PRODUCTS, AND GOVERNMENT PAYMENTS TO FARMERS, 1980–1984

KANSAS REMAINS ONE of the leading agricultural states in the nation, as shown by its standing second in cropland, third in land in farms, and usually sixth or seventh in cash receipts from farming. According to an agency of the U.S.D.A., Kansas is first among the states in acreage of prime farmland—land that is best suited for producing food, feed, forage, fiber, and oilseed crops. A considerable portion of Kansas's agricultural production must find a market overseas. The proportion of farmers in the Kansas population has declined significantly, but it remains about double the national average. Total annual receipts and payments received by Kansas farmers between 1980 and 1984 ranged from $5,397,867,000 to $6,389,300,000. When production expenses were counted, net farm income from this total (the amount that farmers really earned) was 8.3 to 15.6 per cent. Sizable increases in production costs have severely reduced the ability of Kansas farmers to prosper.

Kansas is also the nation's number one wheat producer, harvesting about one-fifth of each year's national total. About ten million acres of Kansas farmland are generally devoted to wheat production. Kansas flour mills rely on this dependable source of supply and produce heavily for national and international consumption. But Kansas farmers gained a larger portion of their income during this period from beef cattle products than from wheat. The categories of (1) other livestock and livestock products and (2) other crops individually have a value almost equal to wheat. Because of the large number of cattle and calves on Kansas farms (nearly six million in a typical year) and the large number of cattle in adjacent states, Kansas has become the first or second state in numbers of cattle slaughtered each year.

Government payments are about 3 per cent of the total in an average year. While still important to the success of the individual farmer, they are a smaller part of the total annual income for farmers than they were in the 1960's or earlier.

Between 1950 and 1983 crop yields in Kansas showed a tremendous increase because of a number of technological and scientific factors including increased use of fertilizer, higher yielding seeds, improved implements for planting and harvesting, use of herbicides and pesticides, and heavier use of irrigation. The statewide average for five crops in 1950 and 1983 was as follows:

	1950	1983
WHEAT	14.5 bu. per acre	41.5 bu. per acre
CORN	35.5 bu. per acre	95.0 bu. per acre
GRAIN SORGHUM	25.0 bu. per acre	43.0 bu. per acre
SORGHUM SILAGE	8.5 tons per acre	9.5 tons per acre
SORGHUM FORAGE	2.1 tons per acre	2.5 tons per acre

Similar increases have come in animal production in Kansas.

The map shows the annual relative value of five different sources of farm income for each county. Also illustrated is the amount of each county's farm income, from the premier agricultural county, Finney, to the largely urbanized small county of Wyandotte. Between 1980 and 1984 the dominance of irrigation agriculture in southwestern and west-central Kansas is shown not only by the leadership of Finney but also by four other counties. Ford, Haskell, Gray, and Scott had greater average value in agricultural products than Reno, the leader from 1959 to 1968. Closely following Reno, which was number six between 1980 and 1984, were Sumner, Sedgwick, and Barton, with Seward, another western Kansas county, as number ten.

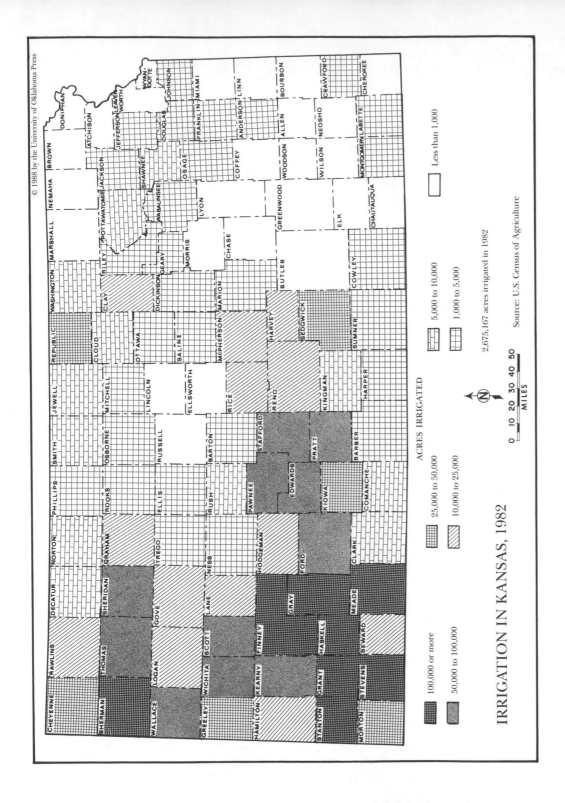

ACRES IRRIGATED

- 100,000 or more
- 50,000 to 100,000
- 25,000 to 50,000
- 10,000 to 25,000
- 5,000 to 10,000
- 1,000 to 5,000
- Less than 1,000

2,675,167 acres irrigated in 1982

Source: U.S. Census of Agriculture

N

0 10 20 30 40 50
MILES

IRRIGATION IN KANSAS, 1982

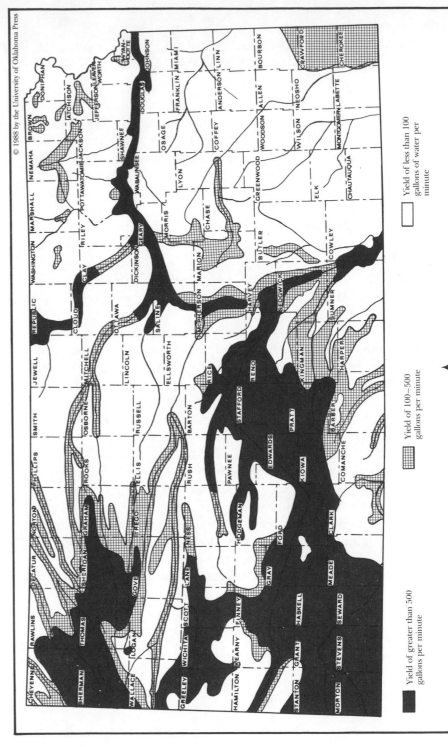

- Yield of greater than 500 gallons per minute
- Yield of 100–500 gallons per minute
- Yield of less than 100 gallons of water per minute

N

0 10 20 30 40 50
MILES

GENERAL AVAILABILITY OF GROUNDWATER IN KANSAS, 1985

51. IRRIGATION AND GENERAL AVAILABILITY OF GROUNDWATER IN KANSAS

Irrigation in Kansas, 1982

WATER HAS ALWAYS BEEN a significant resource in Kansas. Aside from small tracts irrigated by Indians in preterritorial western Kansas, the use of irrigation in a limited way began with settlement along the Arkansas River in the 1880's. These initial operations, even with the construction of hundreds of miles of irrigation canals supplied by the Arkansas River, were generally unsuccessful. Heavy upstream use in Colorado left little water in the river when it reached Kansas. Except for gardens irrigated by water from nearby windmills, some fifty thousand acres near Garden City and about the same amount elsewhere was the extent of Kansas irrigation as late as 1940.

By late 1982 acres under irrigation had grown to 2,675,167. Using the slightly different criteria of "total acres that could be irrigated if conditions warrant," the Kansas State Board of Agriculture reported 3,354,000 acres available in 1981. These irrigation figures are almost double those of 1968. Kansas has 30,019,593 acres of cropland by a recent estimate, so acres irrigated represent 8.9 per cent of the cropland, and acres available is slightly more than 11 per cent. Groundwater resources account for almost all of the irrigation on Kansas farms. Large reservoirs, generally those constructed by the federal government, have also been used to supply irrigation water to Kansas farmland.

The needs of irrigation are greatest in the low-rainfall areas of western Kansas. Three multicounty groundwater-management districts have been developed there. The fourteen counties of southwest Kansas have more than half of the acres available for irrigation. Seven leading irrigated counties in the state—Finney, Haskell, Gray, Stanton, Grant, Stevens, and Meade—are in that district. Sherman

County, in northwest Kansas, and Wichita County, in west-central Kansas, are also heavily irrigated. The groundwater taken primarily from the Ogallala aquifer has been utilized on more than one hundred thousand acres in eight western Kansas counties. Ten other counties in western and central Kansas have more than fifty thousand acres under irrigation. These groundwater resources are drawn to the surface with centrifugal, high-speed pumps powered by natural gas, diesel fuel, gasoline, or electricity. The depth of the well, the cost of fuel, and the value of an irrigated crop enter into calculations to use high-cost irrigation for crop production. Crops under irrigation in Kansas, in order of acreage, are corn, grain sorghum, and wheat.

General Availability of Groundwater in Kansas, 1985

GROUNDWATER AVAILABILITY in Kansas is determined largely by the underground geologic structure from the surface for a few hundred feet downward. Rocks in eastern Kansas are less porous than those in the west, with a lessened capacity to retain groundwater. The Ogallala aquifer in western Kansas is a saturated, water-bearing rock formation more than a hundred feet deep that has accumulated water slowly over the past several thousand years, mostly from surface water filtering downward. Extensive irrigation in the area has in some years depleted ten feet of water from this resource, while recharge is usually only a few inches. The valleys of most of the state's large rivers contain water-saturated sands and gravels called alluvial aquifers. Except in times of severe drouth, these aquifers are dependable sources of water and serve as an important resource for irrigation, industry, and municipal water supplies.

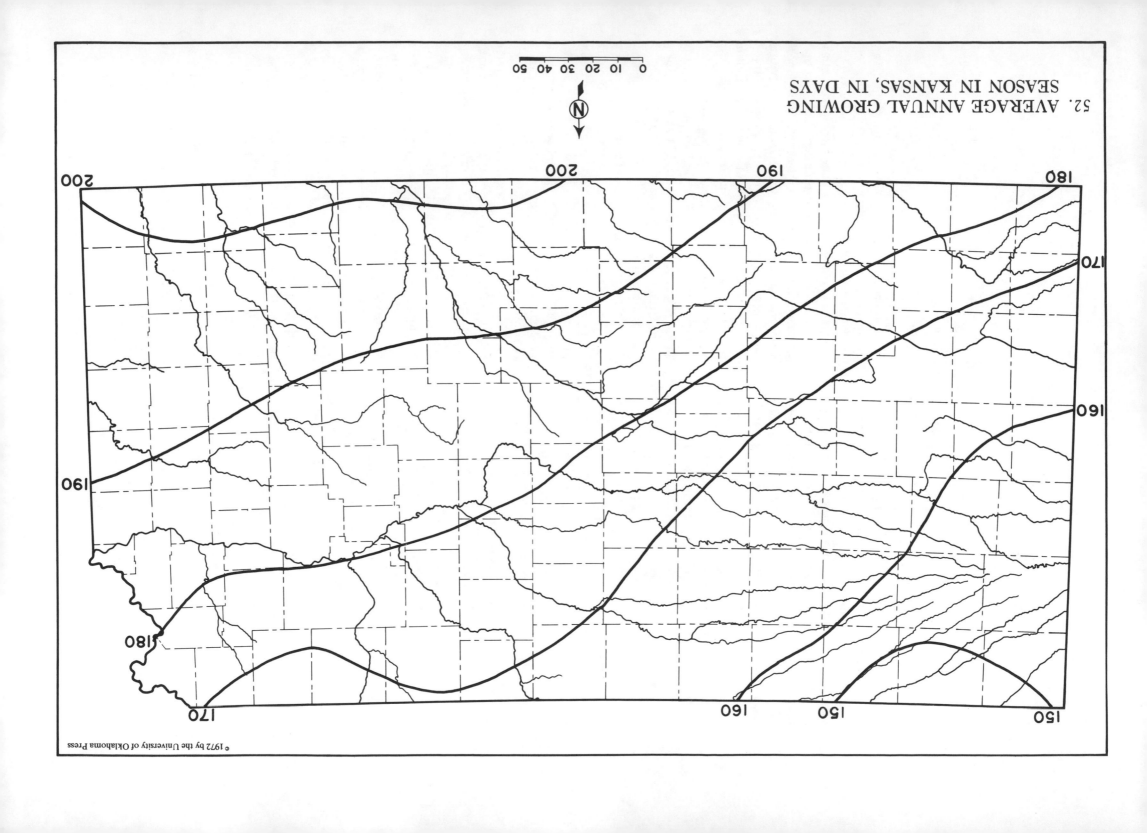

52. AVERAGE ANNUAL GROWING SEASON IN KANSAS

THE AVERAGE ANNUAL growing season is the number of days between the last killing frost in the spring and the first killing frost in the fall. It becomes a decisive factor in the choice of kinds of crops to plant and the time to plant them. Most types of corn require 140 frost-free days to mature, so corn will grow in all parts of Kansas, but cotton takes more time to mature than is normally available. The number of frost-free days is influenced to some extent by elevation. At this latitude the annual average temperature decreases about 3.3° F for each additional 1,000 feet of elevation.

The annual average temperature for Kansas is 55° F. July is the hottest month, with an average of 79.2° F, and January's average is below freezing at 30° F. The many days of bright sun in Kansas and the generally low humidity allow its residents to feel comfortable at temperatures which would be decidedly unpleasant with higher humidity.

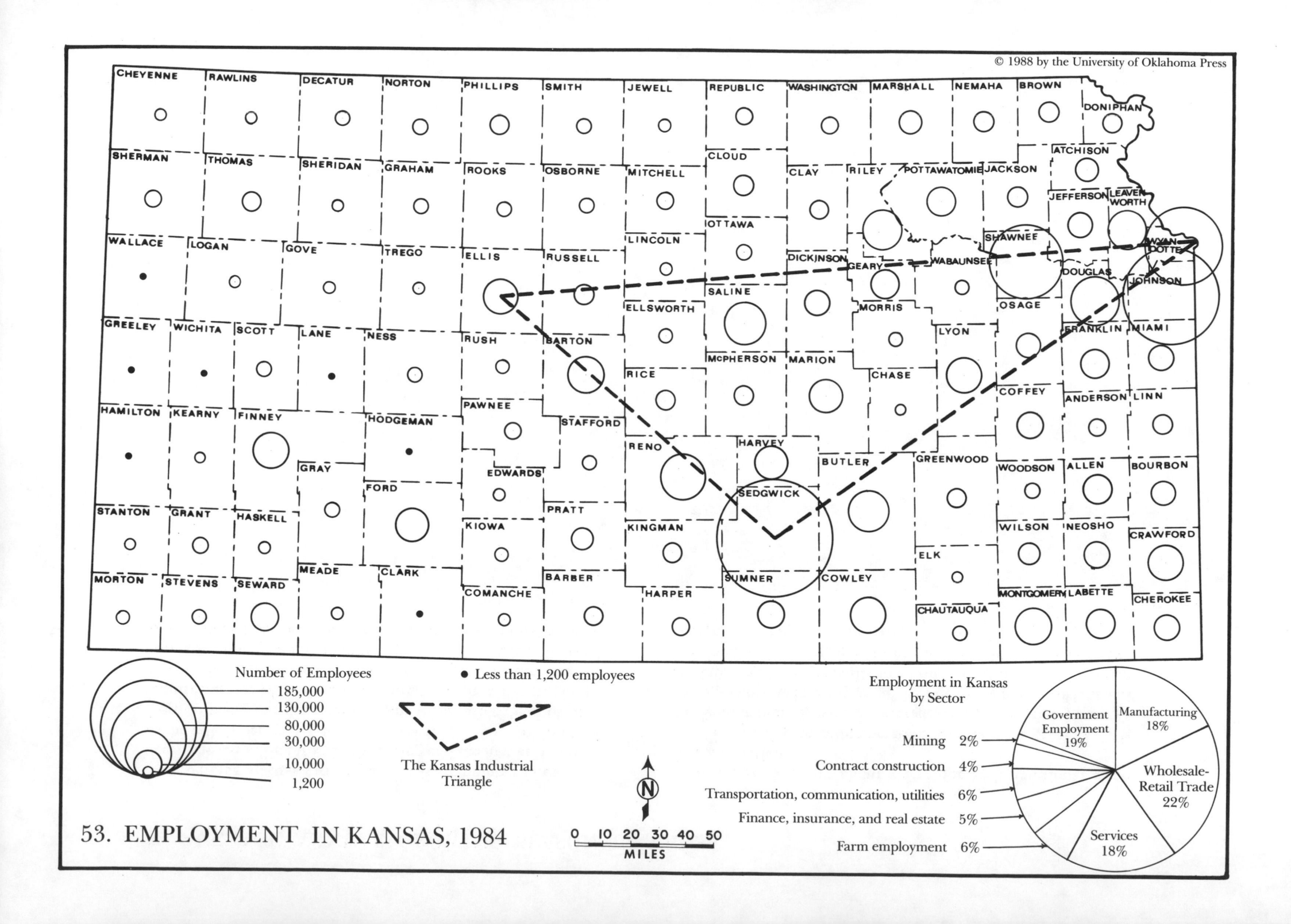

© 1988 by the University of Oklahoma Press

Number of Employees

• Less than 1,200 employees

— 185,000
— 130,000
— 80,000
— 30,000
— 10,000
— 1,200

The Kansas Industrial
Triangle

N

0 10 20 30 40 50
MILES

53. EMPLOYMENT IN KANSAS, 1984

Employment in Kansas
by Sector

Government
Employment
19%

Manufacturing
18%

Mining   2%

Contract construction   4%

Transportation, communication, utilities   6%

Finance, insurance, and real estate   5%

Farm employment   6%

Wholesale-
Retail Trade
22%

Services
18%

53. EMPLOYMENT IN KANSAS, 1984

MOST KANSAS INDUSTRY is based on changing agricultural products and available mineral resources into finished goods. Typically, industry in nineteenth-century Kansas was small, with 7,830 industrial establishments in 1900 employing 35,193 wage earners. In 6,400 of these places the business was carried on by five or fewer workers. The leading industries at that time were slaughtering and meat packing, flour and grist mill production, construction and maintenance of railroad cars, smelting and refining of zinc, dairy processing, and printing and publishing.

In 1984 there were about 3,200 manufacturing firms, with 174,500 employees, up five times over 1900. A revolution in Kansas industry came with wartime demands, particularly those of World War II and afterward. Except for property income the largest single source of personal income in the state came from manufacturing. The total number in the civilian labor force in Kansas in 1984 was 1,197,000. The proportion of that total who were in manufacturing has declined since 1970 with sizable increases recorded in wholesale-retail, government, and services. But leading industries continue to be food and kindred products, chemicals and allied products, transportation equipment, petroleum and coal products, machinery, and printing and pub-

lishing. For instance, two of the nation's largest meat slaughtering plants are located in Kansas, at Emporia and at Holcomb, and flour mills are located throughout the state. Mineral resources, particularly gas, oil, and salt, provide the basis for the chemical industry. With an automobile assembly plant in Kansas City, railroad car shops in Topeka and elsewhere, and a sizable aircraft industry in Wichita, the building of transportation equipment looms large in the Kansas economy.

The map shows the total industrial-business employment in many different sectors of the economy. The Kansas industrial triangle indicates the area of concentration of industry and business within the state. Most of the top Kansas firms or those transacting more than half of their business within the state are located in this twenty-nine county region. This triangle cuts or encloses the ten largest counties based on the 1980 census and counties with about one-fourth of the total land area of the state. Containing slightly less than 70 per cent of the population, the industrial-business triangle has 80 per cent of the manufacturing employees and a greater proportion of the total number of jobs in Kansas than their share of the population.

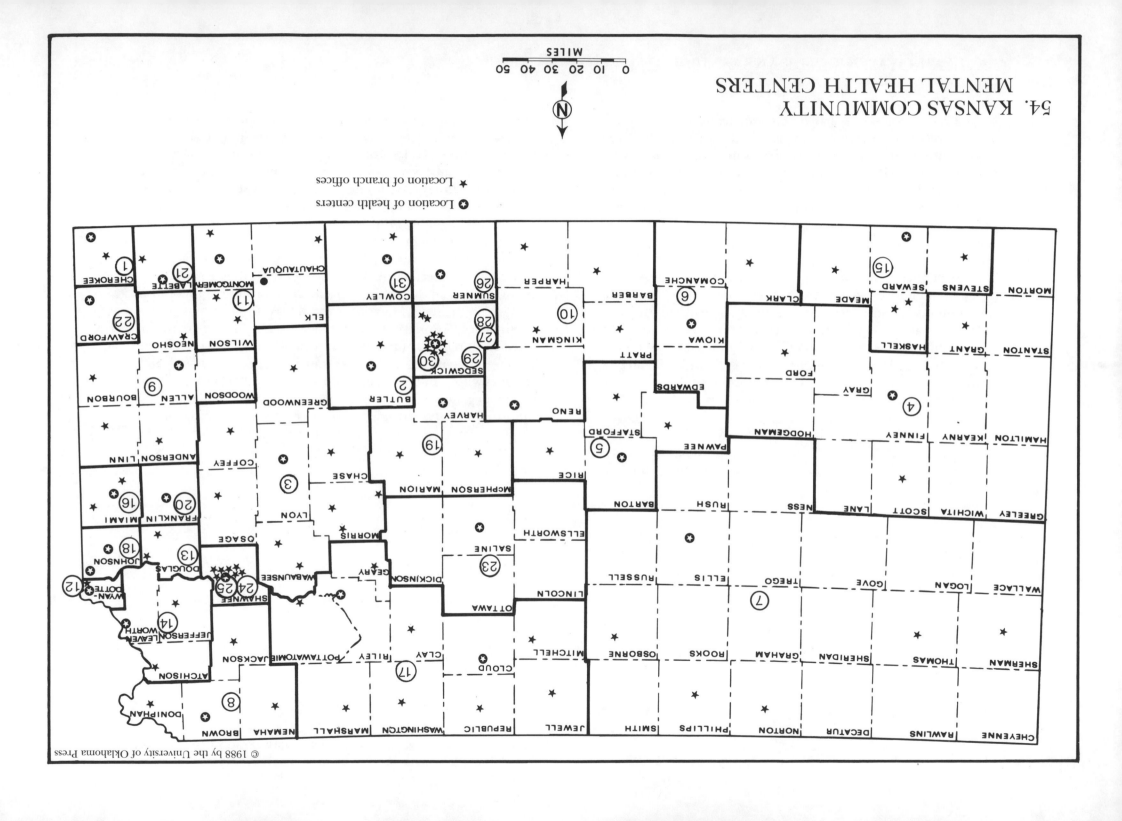

⊛ Location of health centers

★ Location of branch offices

54. KANSAS COMMUNITY MENTAL HEALTH CENTERS

THROUGH CO-OPERATION WITH THE Menninger School of Psychiatry and the Veterans Administration, the State of Kansas in the late 1940's and 1950's expended large resources on upgrading the treatment for mental illnesses. The hospitals for treatment of mental illness were transformed into viable institutions that successfully cured most patients. An important part of the Kansas mental health program, which augments the state hospitals at Larned, Osawatomie, and Topeka, are the Kansas Community Mental Health Centers, with well-established outpatient clinics. During the past decade clinics have been extended to everyone in the state. Earlier they served 85 counties containing 92 per cent of the population. These support centers are:

1. BAXTER SPRINGS — Cherokee County Mental Health Center, Inc.
2. EL DORADO — South Central Mental Health Counseling Center, Inc.
3. EMPORIA — Mental Health Center of East Central Kansas
4. GARDEN CITY — Area Mental Health Center
5. GREAT BEND — The Center for Counseling and Consultation
6. GREENSBURG — The Iroquois Center for Human Development, Inc.
7. HAYS — High Plains Comprehensive Community Mental Health Center
8. HIAWATHA — Kanza Mental Health and Guidance Center
9. HUMBOLDT — Southeast Kansas Mental Health Center
10. HUTCHINSON — Horizons Mental Health Center
11. INDEPENDENCE — Four County Mental Health Center
12. KANSAS CITY — Wyandotte Mental Health Center, Inc.
13. LAWRENCE — Bert Nash Community Mental Health Center, Inc.
14. LEAVENWORTH — Northeast Kansas Mental Health and Guidance Center
15. LIBERAL — Southwest Guidance Center
16. PAOLA — Miami County Mental Health Center
17. MANHATTAN — Pawnee Mental Health Services
18. MISSION — Johnson County Mental Health Center
19. NEWTON — Prairie View Mental Health Center
20. OTTAWA — Franklin County Mental Health Clinic
21. PARSONS — Labette Center for Mental Health Services, Inc.
22. PITTSBURG — Crawford County Mental Health Center
23. SALINA — Central Kansas Mental Health Center
24. TOPEKA — Family Service and Guidance Center of Topeka, Inc.
25. TOPEKA — Shawnee Community Mental Health Center, Inc.
26. WELLINGTON — Sumner County Mental Health Center
27. WICHITA — Family Consultation Service
28. WICHITA — Holy Family Center
29. WICHITA — Sedgwick County Department of Mental Health
30. WICHITA — Wichita Guidance Center
31. WINFIELD — Cowley County Mental Health Center

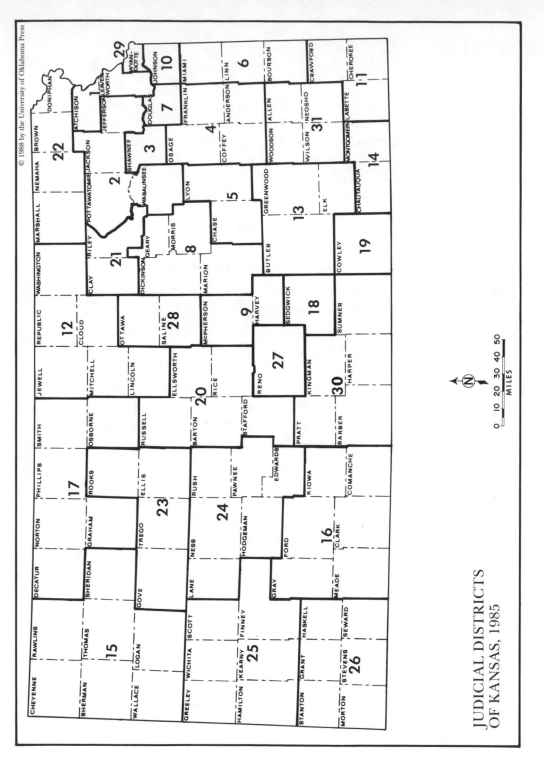

JUDICIAL DISTRICTS
OF KANSAS, 1985

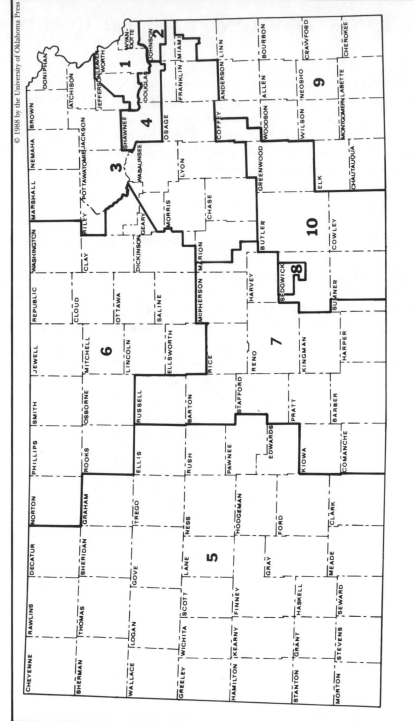

STATE BOARD OF
EDUCATION DISTRICTS, 1985

55. JUDICIAL AND STATE BOARD OF EDUCATION DISTRICTS OF KANSAS

Judicial Districts of Kansas, 1985

IN AN EFFORT to equalize the case load of district judges, the 1968 state legislature abolished forty-one judicial districts and authorized twenty-nine districts with sixty-one judges. A major overhaul of the state's judicial system came in the 1970's with the formation of a Unified Judicial Department. A Court of Appeals was created in 1977 to ease the heavy work load of the Supreme Court. By 1985 there were 31 judicial districts presided over by 70 district judges. The state pays the entire cost of the personnel in the judicial system.

State Board of Education Districts, 1985

With the reorganization of the Kansas State Department of Education, the state legislature in 1968 created an elective State Board of Education to help formulate policy. Initially, the ten districts were based on previous state senatorial districts, with each member of the Board of Education representing four senatorial districts. That plan has continued in the districts of 1985.

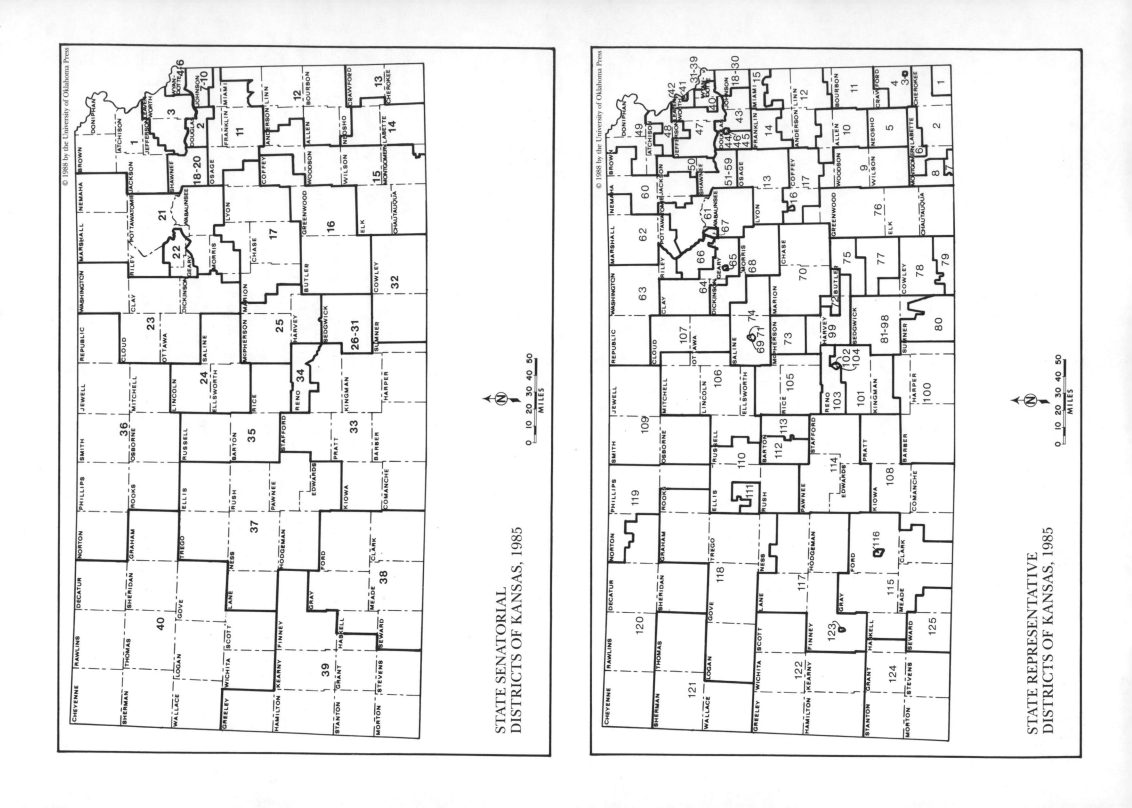

STATE SENATORIAL
DISTRICTS OF KANSAS, 1985

STATE REPRESENTATIVE
DISTRICTS OF KANSAS, 1985

State Senatorial Districts of Kansas, 1985

FOR MANY YEARS the forty state senators allowed by the Kansas constitution were elected from districts more equal in population than the districts from which the state representatives were elected. In a sense, Kansas state senators represented population, while the representatives represented area. Under the impact of the one-man, one-vote ruling, the Kansas legislature reorganized all legislative districts. In a decree handed down by the federal district court for the District of Kansas, filed March 28, 1968, twenty-eight senatorial districts were imposed on Kansas, with additional senators serving from certain districts. All other districts elected a single senator.

In responding to population changes shown by the 1970 census, the 1972 legislature redistricted the state into forty state senatorial districts, which was vetoed by the governor. A panel of three judges from the Federal District Court of Kansas provided a new plan on March 31, 1972. In the new required districts major and minor shifts or alterations were made in thirty-one voting areas. No changes were developed for nine districts in the western half of the state or along the southern border. The forty senatorial districts of 1985, shown on the map, are

an effort to comply with the requirement that each legislative district be of about equal size, which in the 1980's is a population of 59,106.

State Representative Districts of Kansas, 1985

THE KANSAS CONSTITUTION provided that each county in the state have at least one representative in the state's House of Representatives. Eventually, the number of counties increased to 105, and each county had a representative. Twenty additional representatives were distributed among the most populous counties. This pattern produced a tendency for the lower house of the Kansas legislature to represent territory, just as the United States Senators represent states.

As a consequence of the one-man, one-vote issue the Kansas legislature met in special session in 1966 and enacted a new law for organizing representative districts. The character of the House of Representatives, long dominated by representatives from rural areas, was greatly altered. In 1985, for instance, many of the representative districts were multicounty, while others were only a few square miles in the city. A typical representative in the 1980's represents 19,702 people.

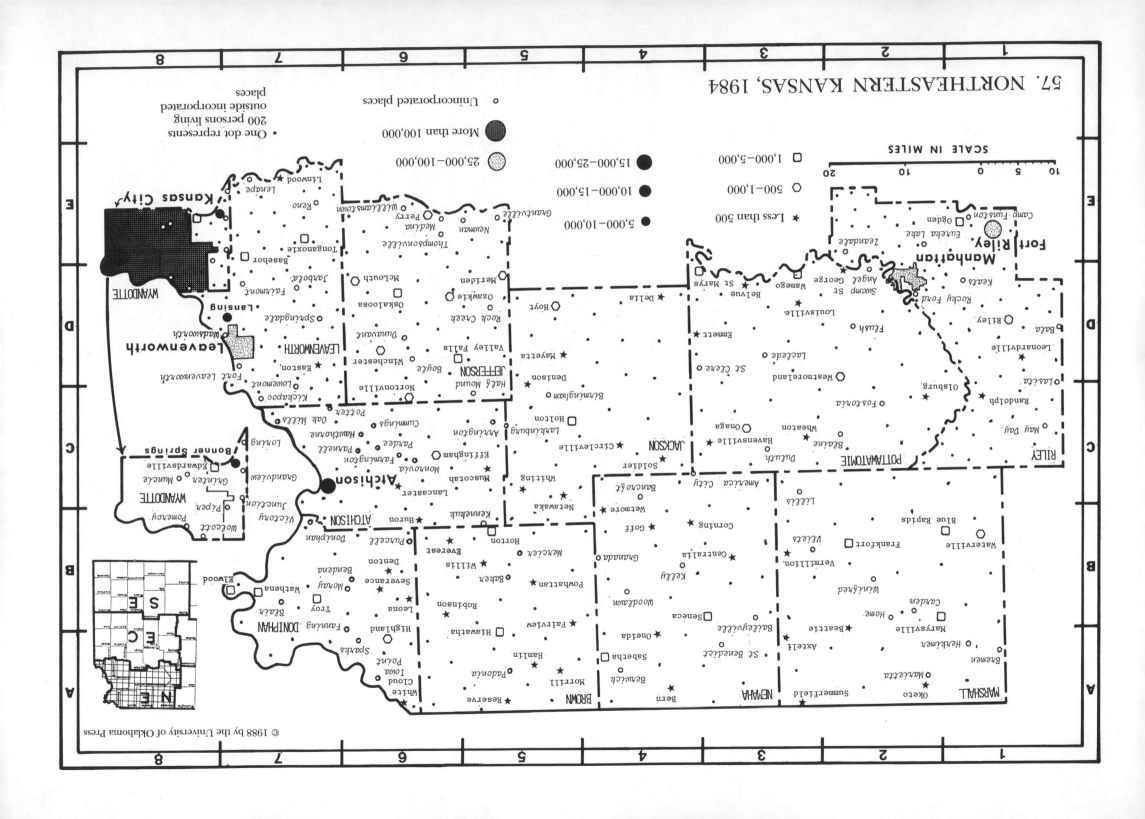

57. NORTHEASTERN KANSAS, 1984

57. NORTHEASTERN KANSAS, 1984

THE ELEVEN COUNTIES of northeastern Kansas were created by the territorial legislature. Their location, along the Missouri River and near the other early access routes to Kansas, gave them a longer history than most Kansas areas. Fort Leavenworth is the oldest spot of continuous human occupancy in Kansas, and much of the preterritorial history of the area revolved around the fort. The area was also occupied by many emigrant tribes in the preterritorial period, and it is the only part of Kansas that retains Indian reservations—the Pottawatomie Reservation west of Mayetta; the Kickapoo Reservation west of Horton; and the Iowa, Sauk and Fox Reservation near Reserve.

The rolling, grass-covered countryside of this region of Kansas was produced by the action of a prehistoric glacier that pushed south about as far as the Kansas River, followed by long years of erosion. These counties, in the tall bluestem area, are among the leading Kansas producers of corn and livestock, particularly swine and cattle. The ten thousand farms in this region average slightly more than one-half section in size. Agricultural production here is about one-eighth of the state's total.

Kansas City has long served as an important wholesale center for this part of Kansas. Its factories and other businesses employ many thousands of workers. Its city boundaries in the 1960's were greatly enlarged in order to produce a substantial increase in population for Kansas City and thus preserve its position as the second largest community in Kansas with a total population in 1984 of 160,468. Leavenworth was the early metropolis of Kansas, and in the twentieth century it maintains an important position next to historic Fort Leavenworth. Atchison's location on the Missouri River has been basic to its economic development. Manhattan is the home of Kansas State University.

The population of these eleven counties in 1880 reached 167,-812. By 1984 the figure had more than doubled, to 400,063 up 4,127 from the 1970 figure. Two counties in this group, Jefferson and Nemaha, lack population centers big enough to fit the census definition of urban—2,500 or more. Four counties, Atchison, Leavenworth, Riley, and Wyandotte, have urban totals of two-thirds or more of their population. These four counties are primarily responsible for the increases in population in this area.

58. EAST CENTRAL KANSAS, 1984

Legend:

- One dot represents 200 persons living outside incorporated places

incorporated places:

- ★ Less than 500
- ○ 500–1,000
- ◌ 1,000–5,000
- ● 5,000–10,000
- ◗ 10,000–15,000
- ● 15,000–25,000
- ◉ 25,000–100,000
- ⬤ More than 100,000

○ Unincorporated places

SCALE IN MILES
10 5 0 10 20

Counties and places:

LINN — Prescott, Blue Mound, Mound City, Pleasanton, Centerville, Parker, Goodrich, Farlinville, Trading Post, Boicourt, LaCygne, Cadmus, Greeley, Harris, Scipio, Lane, Beagle, Fontana, Jingo, New Lancaster

ANDERSON — Kincaid, Colony, Lone Elm, Welda, Selma, Bush City, Mount Ida, Westphalia, Garnett, Scipio, Richmond, Williamsburg

COFFEY — LeRoy, Gridley, Aliceville, Burlington, Sharpe, New Strawn, Olpe, Hartford, Neosho Rapids, Waverly, Agricola, Aliceville, Lebo

FRANKLIN — Princeton, Rantoul, Homewood, Pomona, Ottawa, Richter, Peoria, Le Loup, Centropolis, Wellsville, Lane, Quenemo

MIAMI — Somerset, Paola, Louisburg, Wagstaff, Hillsdale, Chiles, Bucyrus, Antioch

DOUGLAS — Baldwin City, Worden, Pleasant Grove, Lone Star, Clinton, Vinland, Lawrence, Eudora, Stull

JOHNSON — Gardner, Edgerton, Spring Hill, Stilwell, Bonita, Olathe, Monse, Clare, Stanley, Lackmans, De Soto, Cedar Junction, Overland Park, Lenexa, Shawnee, Merriam, Leawood, Prairie Village, Fairway, Mission, Roeland Park, Mission Woods, Westwood Hills, Westwood, Mission Hills, Countryside, Lake Quivira, Wilder, Ocheltree, Aubry, Craig, Gum Springs, McCamish, Leipmont, Lackland

OSAGE — Overbrook, Scranton, Carbondale, Burlingame, Osage City, Michigan Valley, Vassar, Lyndon, Barclay, Reading, Miller, Admire, Allen, Bushong, Olivet, Melvern, Arvonia, Lang

LYON — Americus, Emporia, Plymouth, Hartford, Dunlap, Neosho Rapids, Reading

WABAUNSEE — Harveyville, Eskridge, Bradford, Hessdale, Keene, Maple Hill, Paxico, McFarland, Alma, Alta Vista, Allendorph, Volland, Newbury, Wabaunsee, Dover

SHAWNEE — Topeka, Silver Lake, Rossville, Willard, Tecumseh, Pauline, Wakarusa, Auburn, Valencia, Vera, Maple Hill, Berryton, Grove, Elmont

MORRIS — White City, Dwight, Parkerville, Latimer, Wilsey, Council Grove, Helmick, Delavan, Skiddy, Dunlap, Diamond Springs, Burdick

CHASE — Strong City, Cottonwood Falls, Elmdale, Elinor, Saffordville, Neva, Clements, Bazaar, Gladstone, Rockland, Hymer, Matfield Green, Cedar Point, Homestead, Bazaar, Burdick, Clements

GEARY — Junction City, Grandview Plaza, Fort Riley, Milford, Wreford, Olson

Cities: Emporia, Topeka, Junction City, Ottawa, Olathe, Lenexa, Shawnee, Merriam, Leawood, Prairie Village, Overland Park, Lawrence

58. EAST CENTRAL KANSAS, 1984

ALL FOURTEEN OF THE COUNTIES in east central Kansas were organized by the territorial legislature, and they shared in the earliest history of settlement of the region. The violent actions of "Bleeding Kansas" were peculiarly a part of this region, including the sack of Lawrence in Douglas County, John Brown's Pottawatomie Massacre in southeastern Franklin County, and the Marais des Cygnes Massacre in eastern Linn County. During the Civil War Lawrence also lost heavily in lives and property to Quantrill and his guerrilla forces. The Battle of Mine Creek in Linn County, near Pleasanton, was the biggest battle ever fought in Kansas. The counties of this region have possessed much influence in state politics, and Topeka has served as capital throughout statehood.

Bounded along its western edge by the Flint Hills, this region is generally within the Osage Plain. Farms along the eastern edge of the area average less than half a section in size. Chase County, entirely within the Flint Hills, has farms and ranches averaging 1,125 acres, almost triple the average for east central Kansas.

Agricultural output in the diversified farms of this region amount to a seventh of the total in Kansas. The population of the east central region almost tripled from 206,097 in 1880 to 696,600 in 1984, 28 per cent of the state's total. Latest census reports show no urban population residing in Chase, Linn, Morris, and Wabaunsee counties, but more than four-fifths of the population of Douglas, Johnson, and Shawnee counties is urban. Franklin, Geary, and Lyon counties are more than half urban.

Junction City, next to Fort Riley, has maintained steady growth. Topeka, the third largest Kansas city, has developed as an important business and governmental leader. Lawrence is the home of the University of Kansas and Emporia State University is located at Emporia. The communities of Johnson County, within the Kansas City metropolitan area, have grown more rapidly than any other part of Kansas since World War II. Johnson County's population in 1984 was 296,435, up more than four and one-half times over that of 1950, and nine times larger than in 1940.

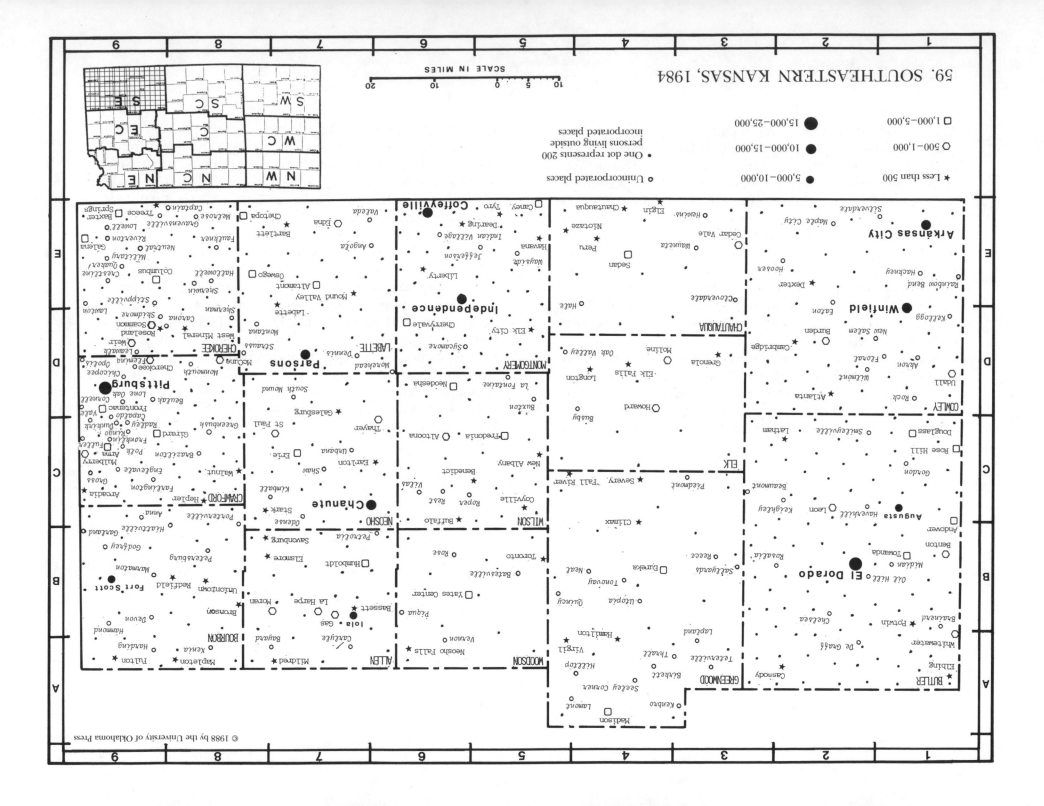

59. SOUTHEASTERN KANSAS, 1984

59. SOUTHEASTERN KANSAS, 1984

THE FOURTEEN COUNTIES of southeastern Kansas were settled, for the most part, in the years after the Civil War. Settlers came rapidly into this area of farming opportunity after the relocation of Indian tribes into Indian territory. The southeast corner of this region is known as the Cherokee Lowland and is on the edge of the Ozark Plateau. The Flint Hills encompasses the five western counties, and the rest of the area is in the Osage Plain. Farmers in the highest-rainfall area of Kansas raise diversified crops and livestock and in 1980 concentrated on forage crops for large herds of cattle and calves. The area is a leader in soybean production in the state. Farm size in the 1980's averages almost three-fourths of a section.

Most of the largest cities of this area were incorporated about 1870 or later. With fertile, well-watered farmland and abundant mineral resources, supported by numerous railroads, the area grew rapidly. In 1880 it boasted a population of nearly 220,000, almost a quarter of the state's total. Some writers have referred to the eastern portion of this region as the Kansas Balkans, presumably because of its relative geographical position in the state and the diversity of its population. The mineral resources of southeastern Kansas, especially coal, petroleum, zinc, and lead, were exploited in the late nineteenth and early twentieth centuries, and industry was developed that attracted many other people into the area. But the petroleum industry, coal mining, a changing transportation network, and small farms failed to hold people, and by 1920 six counties were already declining when the population for this fourteen-county area was 395,293. Since 1930 all of these counties have decreased in population, with the exception of Butler included in the Wichita metropolitan area. Their 1984 total was 298,061 or about one in eight Kansans.

Pittsburg, founded as a mining camp in 1876, was named for Pittsburgh, Pennsylvania. Now the home of Pittsburg State University, it has become the eighteenth largest city in the state and the largest in this group of counties. Coffeyville, the next largest city, is followed by Arkansas City, Parsons, Winfield, El Dorado, Independence and Chanute, all over ten thousand in population.

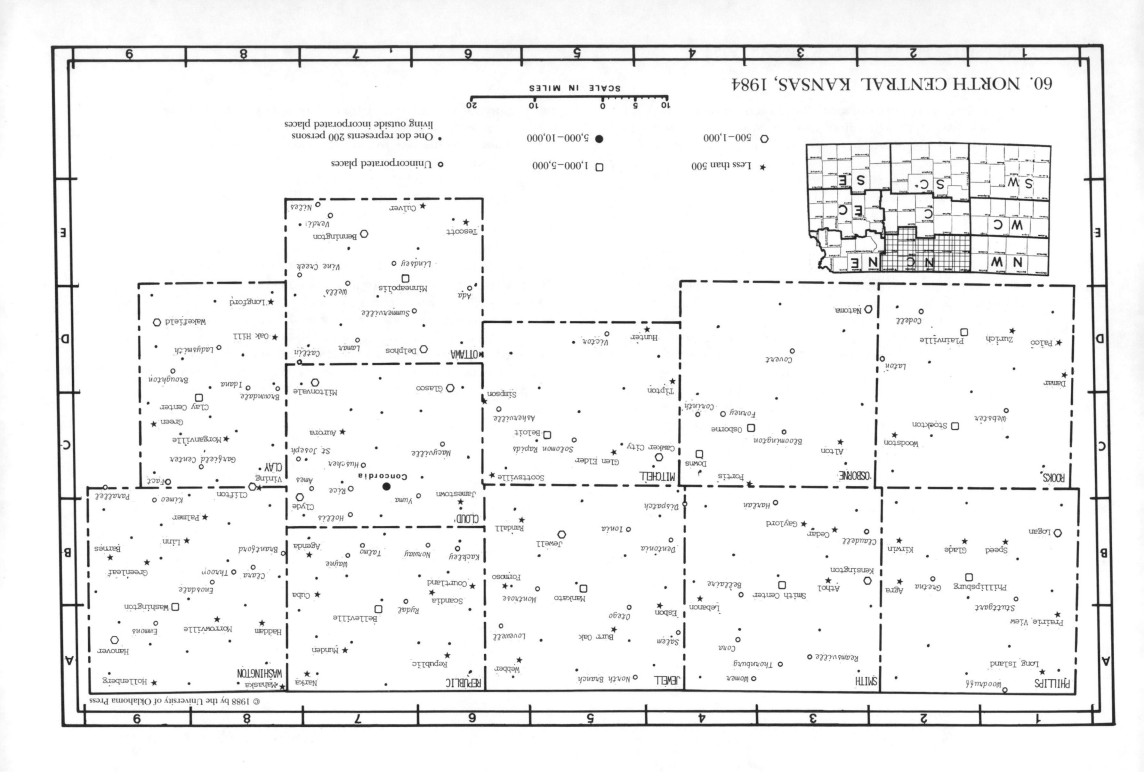

60. NORTH CENTRAL KANSAS, 1984

SCALE IN MILES

○ 500–1,000
● 5,000–10,000
□ 1,000–5,000
★ Less than 500
○ Unincorporated places
• One dot represents 200 persons living outside incorporated places

© 1988 by the University of Oklahoma Press

THE ELEVEN COUNTIES of north central Kansas are probably more representative of the homesteading frontier than any other area in the state. Relatively untouched by railroad land grants, this area was attractive to the quarter-section homesteader, whose eagerness to take up land under the Homestead Act of 1862 was described by Receiver Jeff Jenkins at the Concordia office on the first day of land office business, January 16, 1871. "The door was opened—a shout—a rush—a scramble over each other—a confused shouting of the number of the range and township, as half-dozen or more simultaneously presented their papers to the officers, who, in the tumult, could as well have told which animal was the first taken into the ark, as to have designated which one of the settlers was prior in time with presentation of his papers to the proper officer."

In many parts of the area there was a settler family on each quarter-section. Clay, Cloud, Mitchell, Ottawa, and Republic counties all reached their maximum population in 1890, a short generation after settlement began. Four other counties had their highest population in 1900, and the population in Osborne and Rooks counties peaked in 1910, when the total for the entire area had declined somewhat to 169,017. No large population centers developed in the region. Because of the dependence on the small family farm, where 160 acres was not enough land, the population had fallen to 81,429 in 1984, less than 50 per cent of the figure for either 1900 or 1910. Agricultural production in the region is diversified, with some of Kansas's top corn, sorghum, and swine counties located here. By the 1980's farm size averaged almost one section.

County seat towns in this region, with one exception, have the largest population and are the most active points for business and trade. Only in Rooks County, where Plainville has a source of jobs in neighboring oil fields, does the county seat, Stockton, fail to have the largest population. Relatively few industries are located in this eleven-county area.

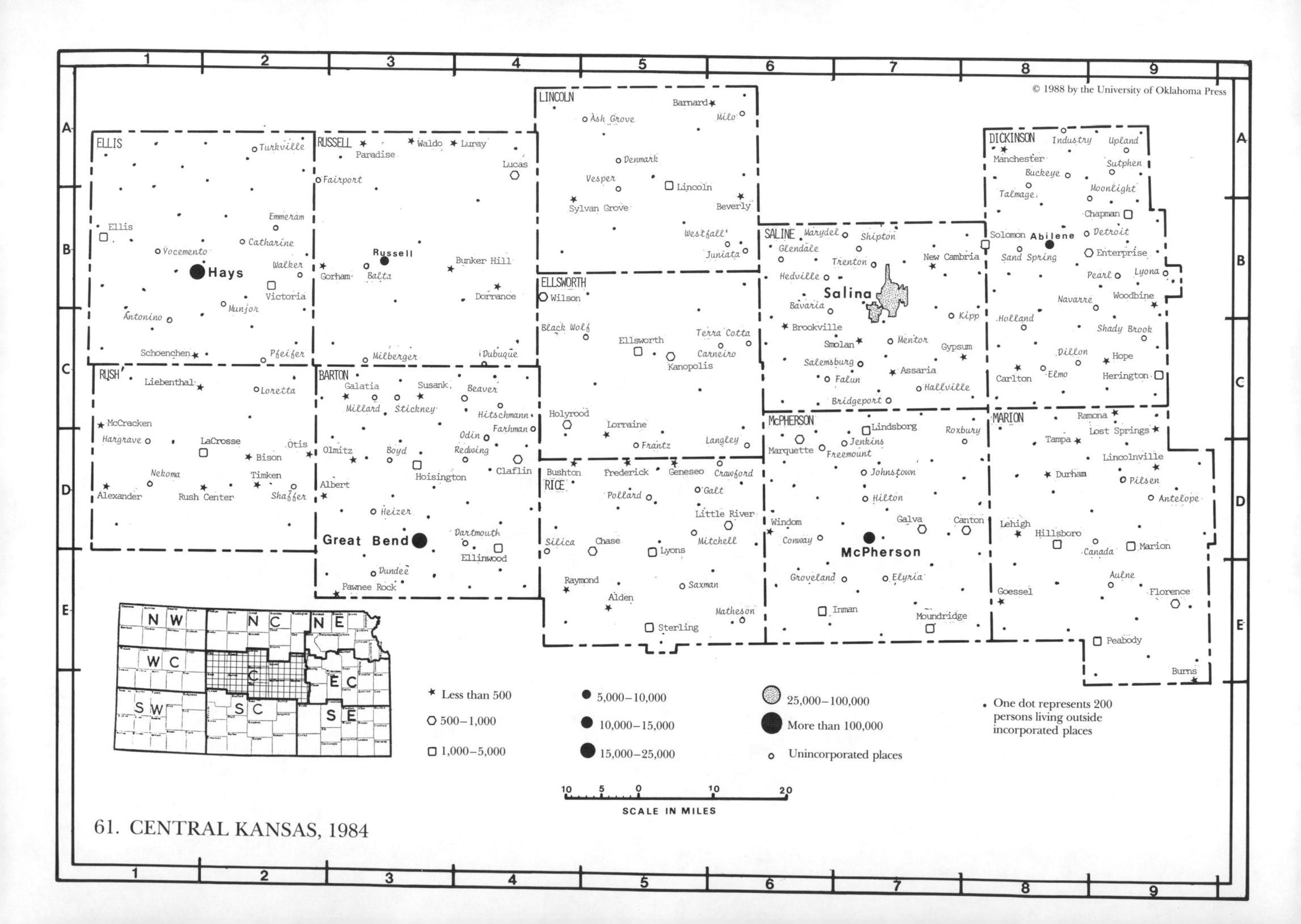

© 1988 by the University of Oklahoma Press

61. CENTRAL KANSAS, 1984

SCALE IN MILES

★ Less than 500

○ 500–1,000

◻ 1,000–5,000

● 5,000–10,000

● 10,000–15,000

● 15,000–25,000

◉ 25,000–100,000

● More than 100,000

○ Unincorporated places

• One dot represents 200 persons living outside incorporated places

61. CENTRAL KANSAS, 1984

THE ELEVEN COUNTIES in central Kansas were in the path of major transportation routes such as the Santa Fe Trail, the Kansas Pacific, and the Atchison, Topeka and Santa Fe railroads, and their development came in the 1860's and early 1870's. By 1880 the region claimed 114,361 population. Since then it has continued to grow, largely because of the expansion of Hays, Great Bend, McPherson, and Salina, to a 1984 population of 208,513. These four county seat towns cause their counties to be more than 50 per cent urban, with a peak population for most of them reflected in the 1984 estimated census, whereas the other counties in this region had their largest population from forty to seventy years earlier. Russell County is 61 per cent urban, and urban areas in Dickinson County account for 47 per cent of the county's total. Ellsworth, Lincoln, and Rush counties lack urban areas according to the census definition.

Widespread agricultural opportunities in central Kansas have resulted in bringing large areas under cultivation. Rainfall in this area approximates the state's average, and farm size, at seven-eighths of a section, is slightly smaller than the statewide average. This region is the heart of the winter wheat belt, and three or four counties here are among the top ten wheat producing counties each year. Other small grains and forage crops and large numbers of cattle are produced on farms in central Kansas.

Most of the counties in central Kansas have petroleum and gas production, and some salt is mined in the area. Blessed with an abundance of transportation facilities and a skilled labor force, this region has an expanded industry, which is often related to the agricultural and mineral resources near at hand. About a third of the denominational colleges in the state are located here, and Fort Hays State University is at Hays.

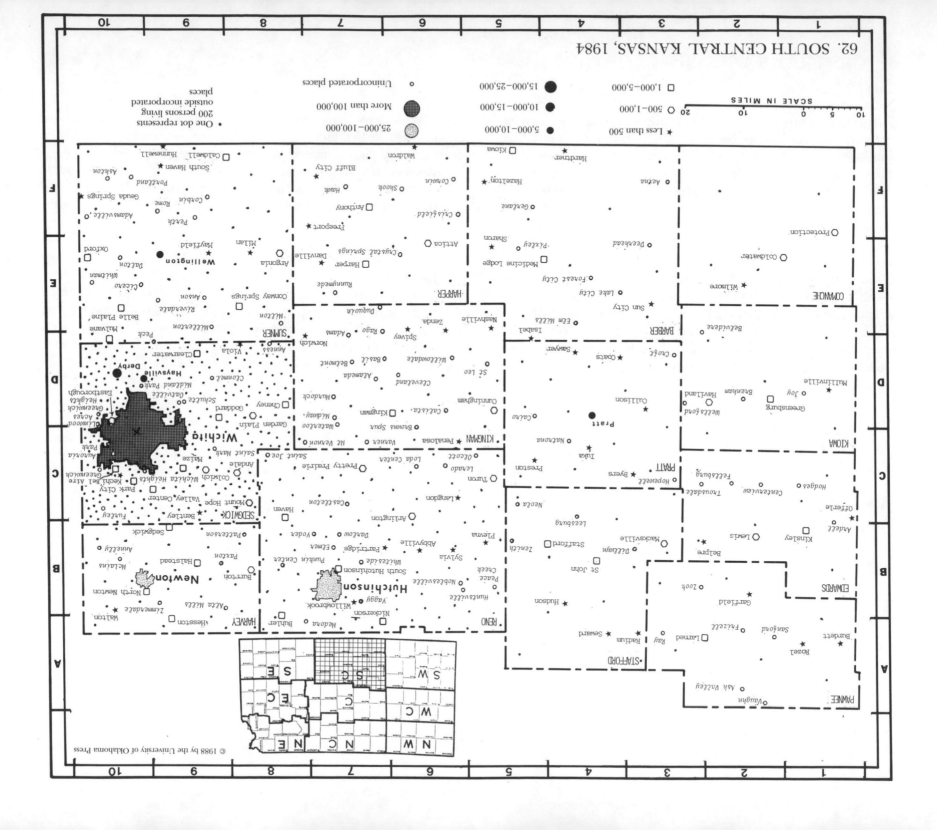

SCALE IN MILES

10   5   0   10   20

□ 1,000–5,000   ● 5,000–10,000   ◉ 25,000–100,000
○ 500–1,000   ● 10,000–15,000
★ Less than 500   ● 15,000–25,000   ▨ More than 100,000
                                                    ○ Unincorporated places

• One dot represents
200 persons living
outside incorporated
places

62. SOUTH CENTRAL KANSAS, 1984

THE FANTASTIC GROWTH of south central Kansas can be viewed largely as an extension of the growth of Wichita, which advanced from a population of 24,671 in 1900 to 283,496 in 1984, when Sedgwick County's 381,534 people made it the most populous county in the state. Almost one in six Kansans live in Sedgwick County, and more than one in five reside in these thirteen south central Kansas counties. Hutchinson and Newton, ranking eighth and twenty-first in population of Kansas cities, have also contributed to over-all growth of the region. Barber, Comanche, Edwards, Kiowa, and Stafford counties lack census-defined urban areas, while more than 50 per cent of the residents of Harvey, Pawnee, Pratt, Reno, and Sedgwick counties are counted as urban. County seats are the largest towns in each of these thirteen counties.

Reno County, the second largest Kansas county in area, has been a long-time state agricultural leader in terms of over-all production. As many as half of the top ten wheat producing counties in Kansas may come from this region in an average year. Sorghum and livestock production are also important to farmers here. Farm size in this group of counties is almost one section.

The industrial production coming from Wichita is a significant part of the state's total. Important in the aerospace industry, Wichita also contributes heavily in agricultural processing and in many manufacturing specialties. Other industries, making use of local agricultural and mineral resources, or of skilled workers, are located in the region. Sedgwick County's dominance in manufacturing by the late 1960's was illustrated by the location there of one-fifth of all manufacturing establishments in the state, with 39 per cent of all manufacturing employees, who received 42 per cent of all wages. These proportions changed little in later years.

Wichita, also, has gained importance in business and finance and has exhibited political strength in the state. News media from Wichita covers southern Kansas, far beyond this thirteen-county area. Wichita State University, which was formerly the municipally-operated University of Wichita, came into the state system in the 1960's.

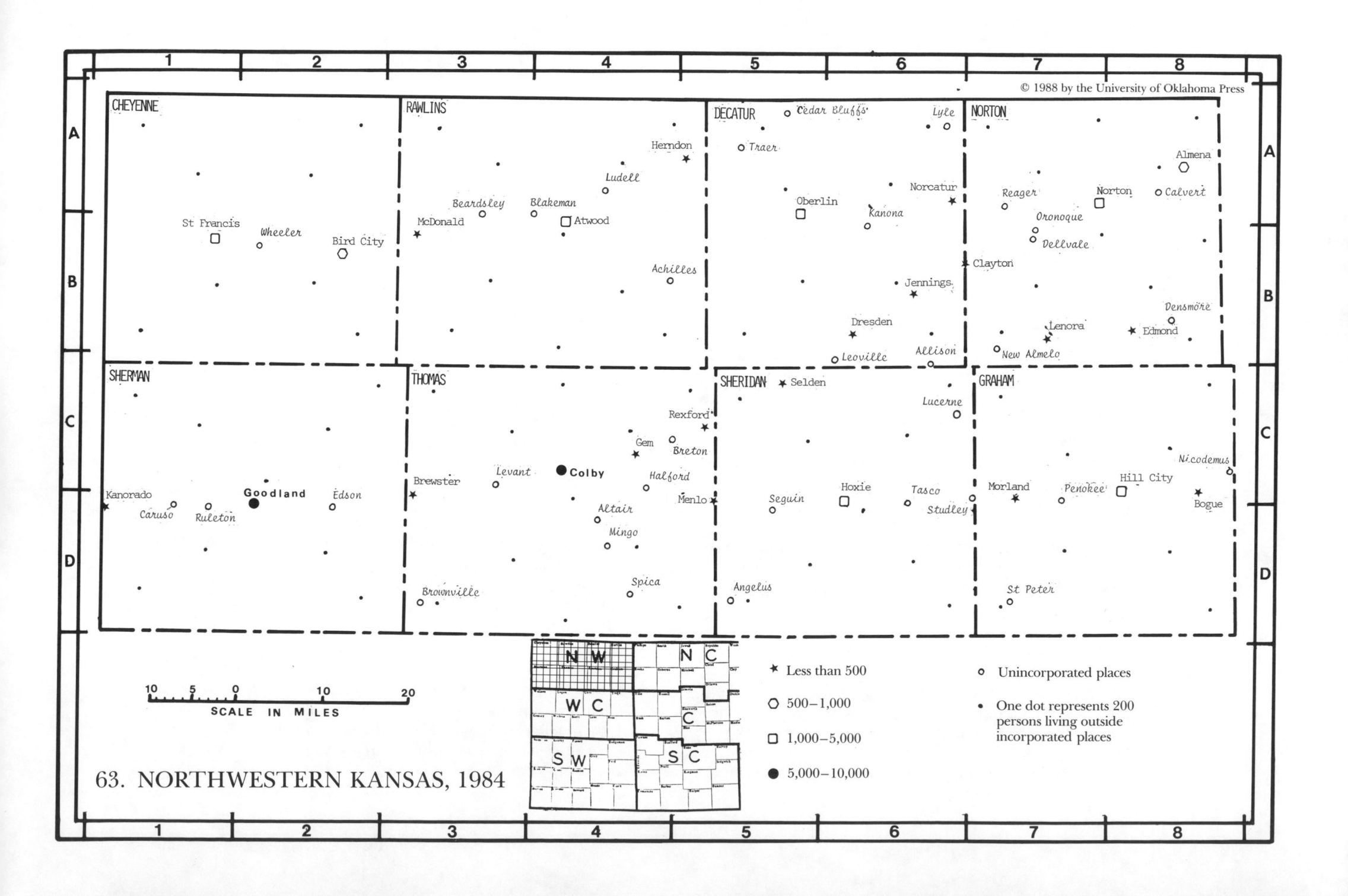

CHEYENNE

St Francis Wheeler Bird City

RAWLINS

Herndon
Ludell
Beardsley Blakeman
McDonald Atwood
Achilles

DECATUR

Cedar Bluffs Lyle
Traer
Norcatur
Oberlin Kanona
Jennings
Dresden
Leoville Allison

NORTON

Almena
Reager Norton Calvert
Oronoque
Dellvale
Clayton
Lenora Densmore
New Almelo Edmond

SHERMAN

Kanorado
Caruso Ruleton Goodland Edson

THOMAS

Selden
Lucerne
Rexford
Gem Breton
Brewster Levant Colby Halford
Menlo
Altair
Mingo
Brownville Spica

SHERIDAN

Seguin Hoxie Tasco
Studley
Angelus

GRAHAM

Nicodemus
Morland Penokee Hill City
Bogue
St Peter

SCALE IN MILES

10 5 0 10 20

NW NC
WC C
SW SC

★ Less than 500
○ 500–1,000
□ 1,000–5,000
● 5,000–10,000

○ Unincorporated places
• One dot represents 200 persons living outside incorporated places

63. NORTHWESTERN KANSAS, 1984

63. NORTHWESTERN KANSAS, 1984

EACH OF THE MAPS for the western third of Kansas shows only villages, towns, and cities, but they present by their arrangement the major arteries of transportation and the major rivers. For the most part, towns were established after the arrival of railroads, and the locations of these communities are like beads on a thread, with the railroad lines, highways, and rivers as the missing links in these map views of the area.

The eight counties of northwestern Kansas are all located in the High Plains country at elevations higher than 2,000 feet above sea level. Farms are large, averaging one and one half to two sections in size, and people in 1984 are fewer than the inhabitants of these counties in 1890. The precipitation for this region averages seventeen to twenty-one inches a year, generally inadequate for normal cropland agriculture. In addition, the variation of rainfall from one year to the next handicaps the farmer in his crop plans. In the flush of enthusiasm of the 1880's, when higher than average rainfall made many people believe that the climate was changing, many homesteaders entered this area to settle. Some enlarged their land holdings by first pre-empting land, at the same time establishing a tree claim on another quarter section under the Timber Culture Act of 1873, and then they homesteaded another quarter section. Use of a combination of the Pre-emption Act, the Homestead Act, and the Timber Culture Act permitted a settler to obtain a maximum of 480 acres of government land for a minimum cash outlay.

The years of high rainfall ended abruptly in 1887, and settlers began to leave the area. Population figures of 50,849 in 1890 decreased to 44,885 by 1900. Improvement in dry-farming techniques enabled later growth to more than 63,000 by 1930. In 1984 the population was 43,130. Goodland and Colby are the only towns exceeding 5,000 people. Norton was the only other urban center, based on the census definition.

Farming is the key activity in northwestern Kansas. Extended farming operations in this region, where the average farm is more than 1,000 acres, result in sizable crops, and in some years counties in this region are leaders in wheat production. Corn is raised under irrigation, and sorghum is the usual alternate to wheat production. Livestock production in this region is the smallest of any region in Kansas.

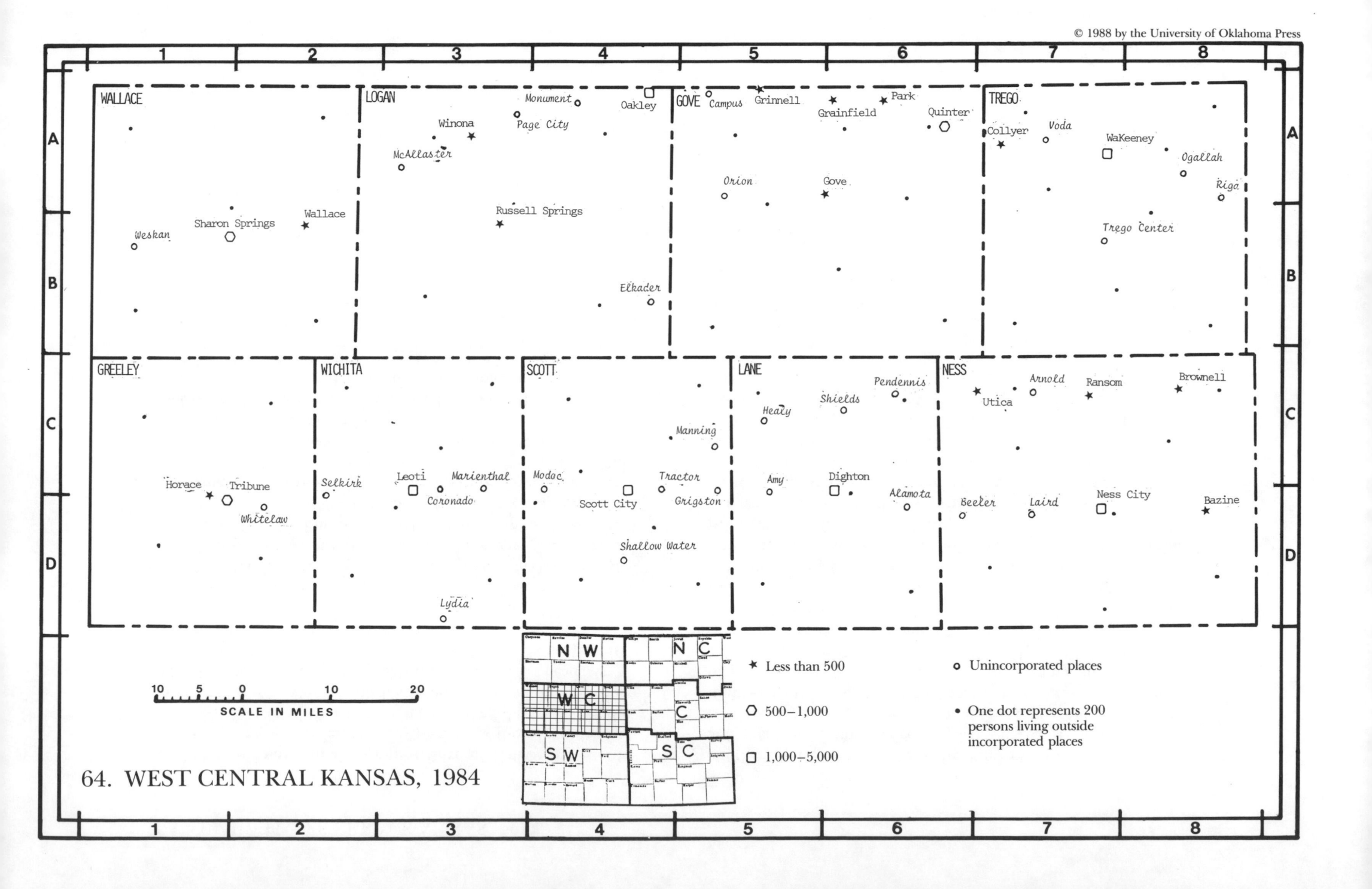

© 1988 by the University of Oklahoma Press

WALLACE

LOGAN

Monument

Oakley

GOVE Campus Grinnell Park Quinter **TREGO**

Winona Grainfield Collyer Voda

McAllaster Page City WaKeeney

Ogallah

Orion Gove Riga

Weskan Wallace

Sharon Springs Russell Springs Trego Center

Elkader

GREELEY **WICHITA** **SCOTT** **LANE** **NESS**

Arnold Ransom Brownell

Pendennis

Shields Utica

Healy

Manning

Horace Tribune Selkirk Leoti Marienthal Modoc Tractor Amy Dighton Ness City Bazine

Coronado Scott City Grigston Alamota Beeler Laird

Whitelaw

Shallow Water

Lydia

SCALE IN MILES

10 5 0 10 20

64. WEST CENTRAL KANSAS, 1984

NW NC

WC C

SW SC

★ Less than 500   ○ Unincorporated places

○ 500–1,000   • One dot represents 200
persons living outside
incorporated places

□ 1,000–5,000

64. WEST CENTRAL KANSAS, 1984

THE NINE COUNTIES of the west central region were among the last counties settled in Kansas, but the modern population was preceded by earlier inhabitants. El Cuartelejo ruins in northern Scott County is the remains of a pueblo-like structure presumably occupied by Indians from the Río Grande in the late seventeenth and early eighteenth centuries. In this short-grass High Plains country these early natives raised some crops with the aid of irrigation.

In 1880 the whole west central region was occupied by 8,800 people, and many others came in the next decade to increase the population to 22,738. As in neighboring areas in western Kansas, the 1890's saw a declining population here, with a slow growth later that leveled off near 32,000, about 8 percent of the state's total. Two counties, Wichita and Scott, posted their highest population in 1970, and Scott maintained growth in 1984. Scott City, with 71 per cent of the county's total and WaKeeney are considered the region's only urban areas according to the census definition.

To a visitor west central Kansas seems to be a new area, and comparatively it is. With a settlement history that goes back only a century, many of the residents of the area remember people who were among the earliest settlers.

Farm size in this region is large, averaging two sections per farm. The largest irrigated areas are located in Wichita and Scott counties, perhaps contributing to a higher recent population. In this region, where normal rainfall averages below twenty inches a year, corn is raised under irrigation for both grain and fodder. Wheat is a major crop, and sorghum production is large. Specialized truck farm crops are raised under irrigation. Livestock production is slightly higher than in the comparable area to the north.

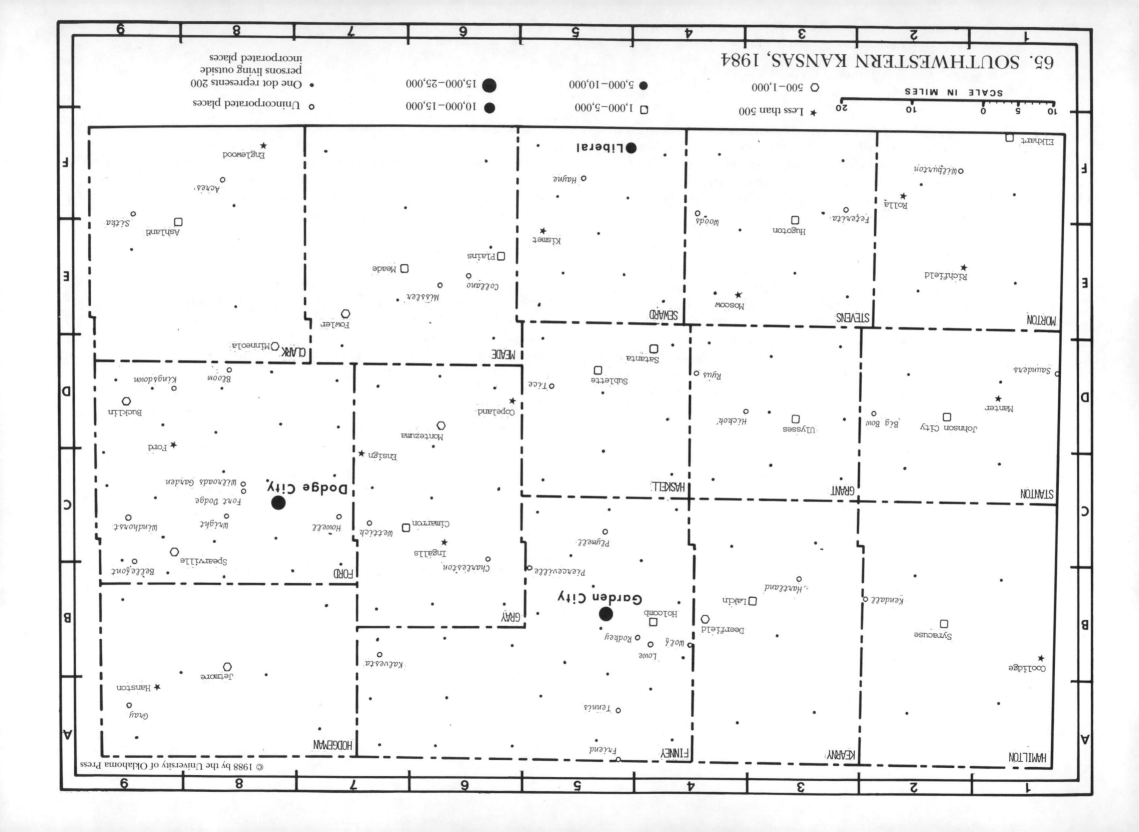

SCALE IN MILES

● 15,000–25,000	● 5,000–10,000	○ 500–1,000
● 10,000–15,000	□ 1,000–5,000	★ Less than 500

One dot represents 200 persons living outside incorporated places

○ Unincorporated places

65. SOUTHWESTERN KANSAS, 1984

THE ESTIMATED CENSUS OF 1984 shows the highest population ever for the fourteen counties of southwest Kansas, 115,937. This area was entered by many settlers in the boom times of the 1880's. Although people left the area with the collapse of the boom before the 1890 census, still almost 30,000 people were counted. In 1900 the figure was down to 21,029.

Weather cycles have influenced the ups-and-downs in population of this area. Average rainfall is marginal for normal cropland agriculture. The above-average rainfall years of the 1920's and 1940's were separated by deep drouth and the dust bowl days of the 1930's. Many people were forced out of the region because of those dry years. Farmers in the 1930's had the added handicap of entering the dry weather cycle after a severe economic depression for agriculture. When dry years returned to this region in the 1950's and later, most farmers had more capital working for them, and they could make use of the improved technology for dealing with the years of little rain.

Because of experience with drouth conditions and the availability of underground water supplies, this region of Kansas has become the most heavily irrigated part of the state. Early irrigation experiments near Garden City, using water from the Arkansas River, have been largely augmented for farmlands away from the river by irrigation water supplied from deep wells. In spite of higher costs of production, most farmers in the region believe that irrigation more than pays its way, and a certain insecurity in a farming operation is eliminated with the use of reliable sources of water. Farming is the leading economic activity of the region. Some of the state's top sorghum counties are located here. Other counties are leading producers of corn for silage or grain, of alfalfa hay and seed, and of cattle on farms. The average farm in this region is two sections in size. Heavy crop production supports an extensive cattle-feeding operation and a mammoth packinghouse in this area.

Five southwestern Kansas counties, Ford, Finney, Grant, Seward, and Stevens, show urbanized totals of 67 to 87 per cent of their population. Other counties have no cities over 2,500 and lack urban identification in the census. Mineral resources, particularly natural gas and its by-products, account for much economic activity. The cities showing the most growth are Dodge City, Garden City, and Liberal. In all counties the county seat is the largest community.

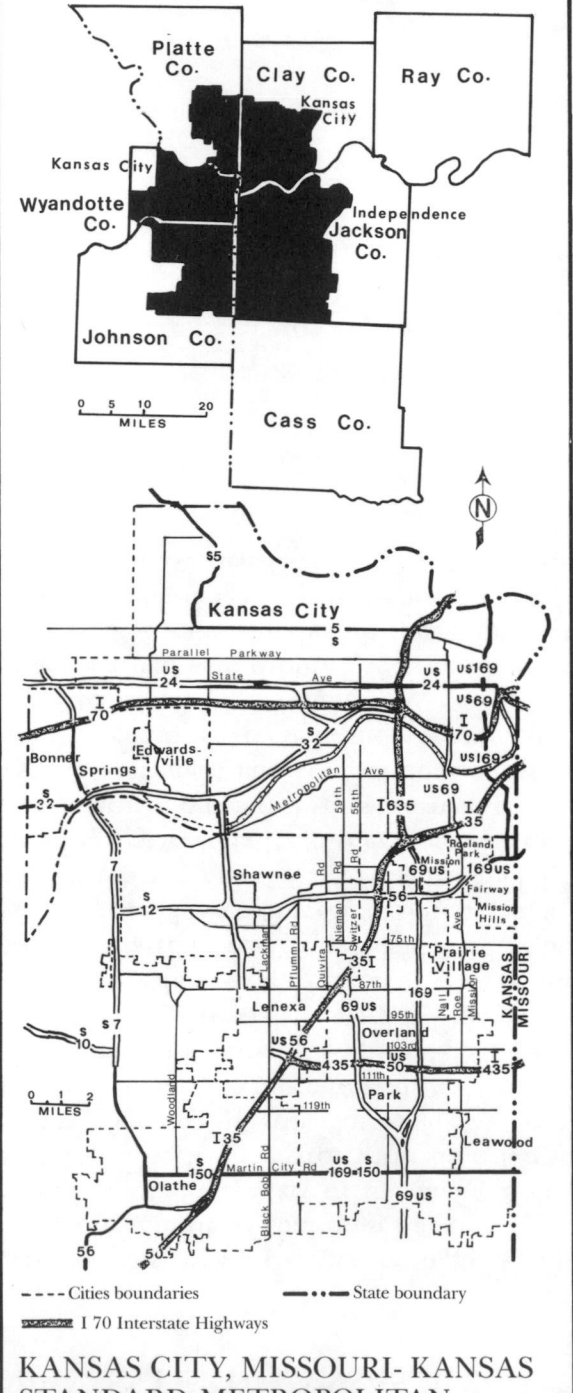

KANSAS CITY, MISSOURI- KANSAS
STANDARD METROPOLITAN
STATISTICAL AREA

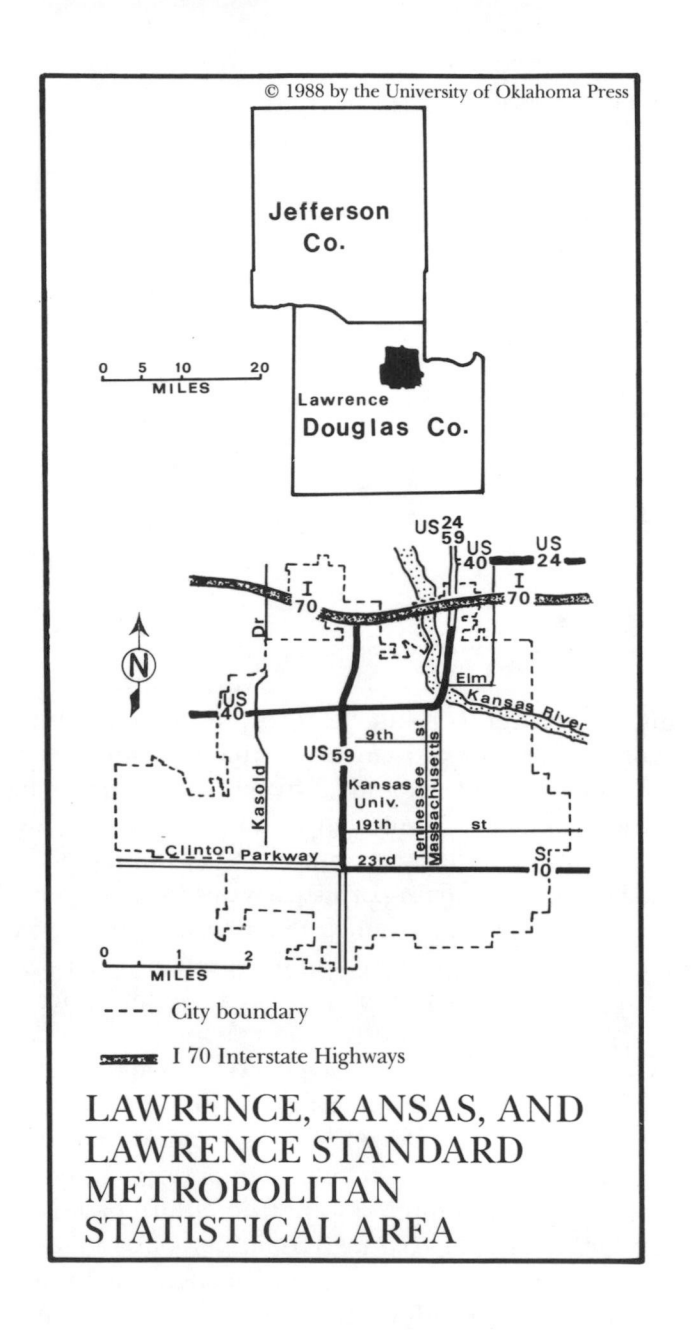

LAWRENCE, KANSAS, AND
LAWRENCE STANDARD
METROPOLITAN
STATISTICAL AREA

66. THE KANSAS CITY AND THE LAWRENCE STANDARD METROPOLITAN STATISTICAL AREAS

Kansas City, Missouri-Kansas SMSA

THE KANSAS CITY, Missouri-Kansas Standard Metropolitan Statistical Area covers six counties: Cass, Clay, Jackson, and Platte in Missouri; and Johnson and Wyandotte in Kansas. About half of the six-county population of 1,450,000 reside in Jackson County, Missouri. The population in 1980 in Johnson and Wyandotte counties, the second and third most populous counties in Kansas, was 442,604, about 30 per cent of the SMSA and 18.7 per cent of the Kansas population. Between 1940 and 1980 the Kansas population grew by 560,000, while 260,000 of that increase came from these two counties, 90 per cent of it from Johnson County alone.

Kansas City has long been the second largest city in Kansas. In Johnson County the communities of Overland Park, Olathe, Shawnee, Prairie Village, Lenexa, Leawood, and Merriam grew so rapidly after World War II that they were listed in the 1980 census as the fourth, eighth, eleventh, thirteenth, twenty-third, twenty-fourth, and twenty-ninth largest cities in Kansas. The concentration of population in the Kansas City SMSA has greatly expanded many economic opportunities available there.

The Lawrence SMSA

THE GROWTH OF population in Douglas County and adjacent Jefferson County has brought designation of this area as a Standard Metropolitan Statistical Area. The two-county population total in 1980 was 82,847, which was 3.5 per cent of the state's total. Lawrence is now the fifth most populous city in the state.

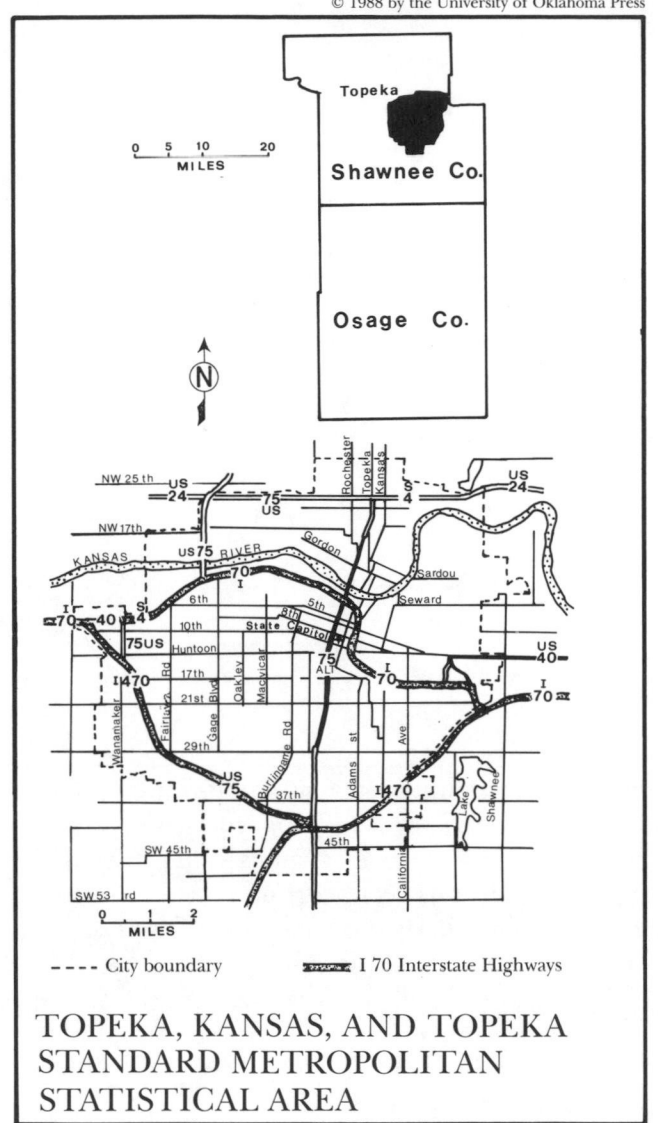

---- City boundary   ▬▬▬ I 70 Interstate Highways

TOPEKA, KANSAS, AND TOPEKA STANDARD METROPOLITAN STATISTICAL AREA

----- City boundary   ▬▬▬ I 35 Interstate Highways

WICHITA, KANSAS, AND WICHITA STANDARD METROPOLITAN STATISTICAL AREA

67. THE TOPEKA AND THE WICHITA STANDARD METROPOLITAN STATISTICAL AREAS

The Topeka SMSA

THE CAPITAL CITY of Kansas was laid out in 1854 on land claimed by the Topeka Association on the south bank of the Kansas River. Whether there was a faulty survey or whether it was intentional, the course of the streets varied 18.4° from the cardinal directions, a feature still evident on present-day maps of the downtown part of Topeka. Elsewhere, an effort to distinguish street names has brought additions such as Southwest 45th Street. After gaining the state capital Topeka continued to grow at a steady rate, and it has always been one of the ten largest cities in the state.

In the twentieth century Topeka has been either second or third in size, its 118,690 population in 1980 placing it third behind Wichita and Kansas City. Shawnee and Osage counties, counted in the Topeka SMSA, in 1980 had a combined population of 170,235 or 7.2 per cent of the state's population.

The Wichita SMSA

THE WICHITA STANDARD Metropolitan Statistical Area includes all of Sedgwick and Butler counties. Wichita has been the largest city in Kansas in every federal census year since 1950. It was third in 1900 and second from 1910 through 1940. Nine-tenths of the 411,870 population of the Wichita SMSA live in Sedgwick county, and 68 per cent live in the city of Wichita. Kansas grew by 560,000 people between 1940 and 1980, and these two counties accounted for 236,000 of that increase.

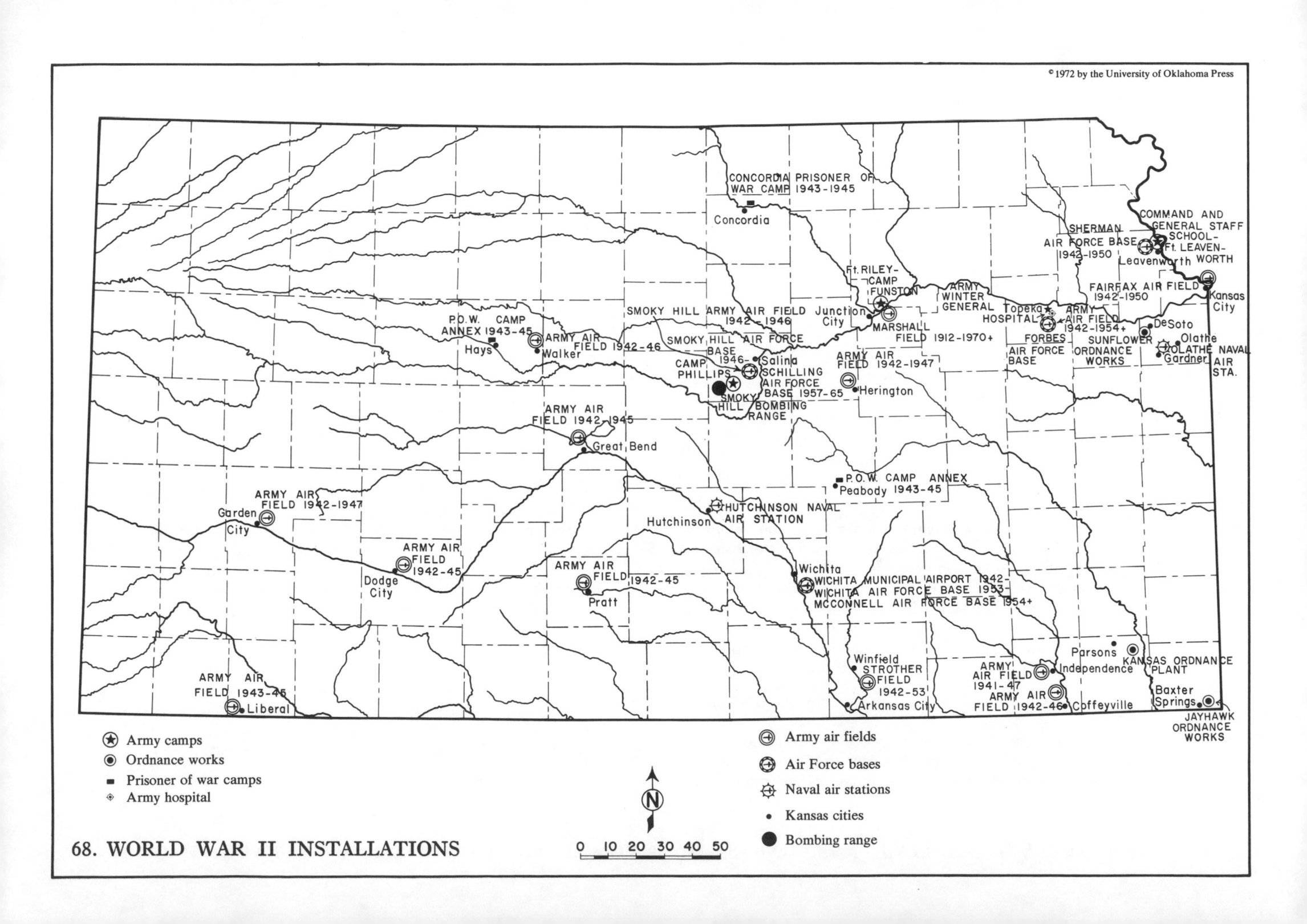

CONCORDIA PRISONER OF
WAR CAMP 1943-1945
Concordia

COMMAND AND
GENERAL STAFF
SCHOOL-
Ft. LEAVEN-
WORTH

SHERMAN
AIR FORCE BASE
1942-1950
Leavenworth

FAIRFAX AIR FIELD
1942-1950
Kansas
City

Ft. RILEY-
CAMP
FUNSTON

ARMY
WINTER
GENERAL
HOSPITAL

Topeka

ARMY
AIR FIELD
1942-1954+

DeSoto

P.O.W. CAMP
ANNEX 1943-45
Hays

ARMY AIR
FIELD 1942-46
Walker

SMOKY HILL ARMY AIR FIELD
1942-1946   Junction
City

MARSHALL
FIELD 1912-1970+

FORBES
AIR FORCE
BASE

SUNFLOWER
ORDNANCE
WORKS

Olathe
OLATHE NAVAL
AIR
Gardner   STA.

SMOKY HILL AIR FORCE
BASE
1946-   Salina
CAMP
PHILLIPS   SCHILLING
AIR FORCE
BASE 1957-65
SMOKY HILL BOMBING
RANGE

ARMY AIR
FIELD 1942-1947
Herington

ARMY AIR
FIELD 1942-1945
Great Bend

P.O.W. CAMP ANNEX
Peabody 1943-45

ARMY AIR
FIELD 1942-1947
Garden
City

HUTCHINSON NAVAL
AIR STATION
Hutchinson

ARMY AIR
FIELD
1942-45
Dodge
City

ARMY AIR
FIELD 1942-45
Pratt

Wichita
WICHITA MUNICIPAL AIRPORT 1942-
WICHITA AIR FORCE BASE 1953-
McCONNELL AIR FORCE BASE 1954+

ARMY AIR
FIELD 1943-45
Liberal

Winfield
STROTHER
FIELD
1942-53
Arkansas City

ARMY
AIR FIELD
1941-47
ARMY AIR
FIELD 1942-46

Parsons
Independence   KANSAS ORDNANCE
PLANT

Baxter
Springs
Coffeyville   JAYHAWK
ORDNANCE
WORKS

★ Army camps

◉ Ordnance works

■ Prisoner of war camps

✛ Army hospital

⊕ Army air fields

⊕ Air Force bases

✿ Naval air stations

• Kansas cities

⬤ Bombing range

N

0 10 20 30 40 50

68. WORLD WAR II INSTALLATIONS

68. WORLD WAR II INSTALLATIONS

DURING WORLD WAR II, the two permanent forts, Leavenworth and Riley, were vastly expanded, and many other military and naval installations were newly located in Kansas. The major growth of military operations came in the form of army air fields, placed in Kansas partly because of good flying conditions available there. These fields, dates for their period of active service, and the cities nearest their locations are as follows: Coffeyville (1942–46); Dodge City (1942–45); Garden City (1942–47); Great Bend (1942–45); Herington (1942–47); Independence (1941–47); Kansas City [Fairfax Field] (1942–50); Liberal (1943–45); Pratt (1942–45); Salina (1942–58+); Topeka (1942–54+); Walker (1942–46); Wichita (1942–57+); and Winfield [Strother Field] (1942–53). In addition, Marshall Field at Fort Riley and Sherman Field at Fort Leavenworth were used by the Army Air Corps. In later years Smoky Hill Army Air Field, at Salina, became an Air Force Base and was renamed Schilling Field. The air field at Wichita gained the name McConnell Air Force Base, and the one at Topeka was named Forbes Air Force Base.

Naval Air Stations were maintained near Olathe and near Hutchinson. The Jayhawk Ordnance Plant at Baxter Springs, the Kansas Ordnance Works at Parsons, and the Sunflower Ordnance Works near DeSoto were large-scale war industries. Expansion of war-related industry took place all over the state, and agricultural production also boomed.

In 1943 a prisoner-of-war camp was built near Concordia and for two years housed Italian and German captives. There were two side camps in Kansas, one at Peabody and the other at Hays, for holding prisoners who were willing to work at agricultural labor.

During World War II more than fifty sea-going vessels were named for Kansans, or for Kansas cities, counties, or rivers. Wichita and Topeka were used for cruisers, and Emporia, Hutchinson, and Abilene were the names of smaller ships. Clay, Haskell, Kingman, Logan, Ottawa, Rawlins, Sheridan, and Trego counties were recognized in names for a variety of naval vessels. Other naval and maritime ships had names of Kansans or rivers. Four of the Victory cargo vessels operated by the U.S. Maritime Commission were named the *Atchison Victory*, the *Chanute Victory*, the *Coffeyville Victory*, and the *Salina Victory*.

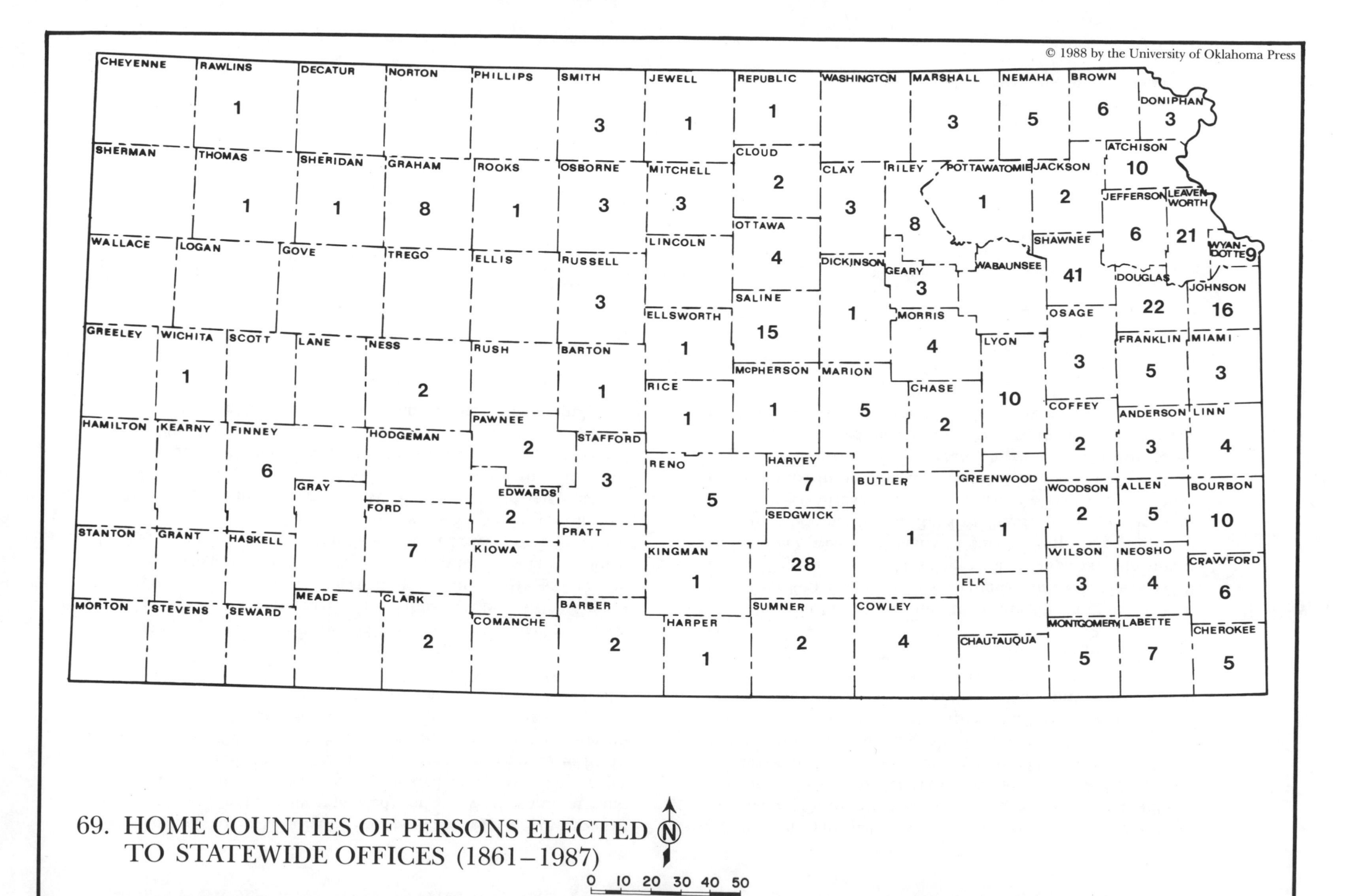

69. HOME COUNTIES OF PERSONS ELECTED TO STATEWIDE OFFICES (1861–1987)

N

0 10 20 30 40 50
MILES

THE OLDER AND MORE populous counties have a greater chance to help elect a home-county favorite to a statewide office. The western half of the state has gained only about 17 per cent of all statewide offices during more than a century. Only three of the forty-one governors came from that region. U.S. Highway 81 is often thought of as the dividing line between western and eastern Kansas. By extending western Kansas east to include another eight counties, all located west of that highway, another governor and a few other statewide officers would increase the total elected from western Kansas to 22 per cent. More than 70 per cent of those elected to statewide office, including 62 per cent of all governors, gave their residences as being in a location no more than three counties from the Missouri border.

Only four of the thirty United States senators from Kansas had their residences in the western half of the state. However, the only black ever elected to statewide office in Kansas came from that area: Edward P. McCabe, of Milbrook, was auditor of state from 1883 to 1887, a period when efforts to balance the ticket extended to various groups as well as geographical areas. United States Senator Nancy Landon Kassebaum, of Wichita, is one of four women represented by the numbers on this map. The others served as state superintendent of public instruction, secretary of state, and state treasurer.

On the whole, the distribution of the state's first forty-one governors among twenty-five counties indicates a tendency of Kansans to elect an attractive candidate no matter where he comes from. Shawnee County, for instance, has had only one governor among the forty-one persons from that county who have been elected to statewide office, and no governor has been elected from populous Wyandotte County.

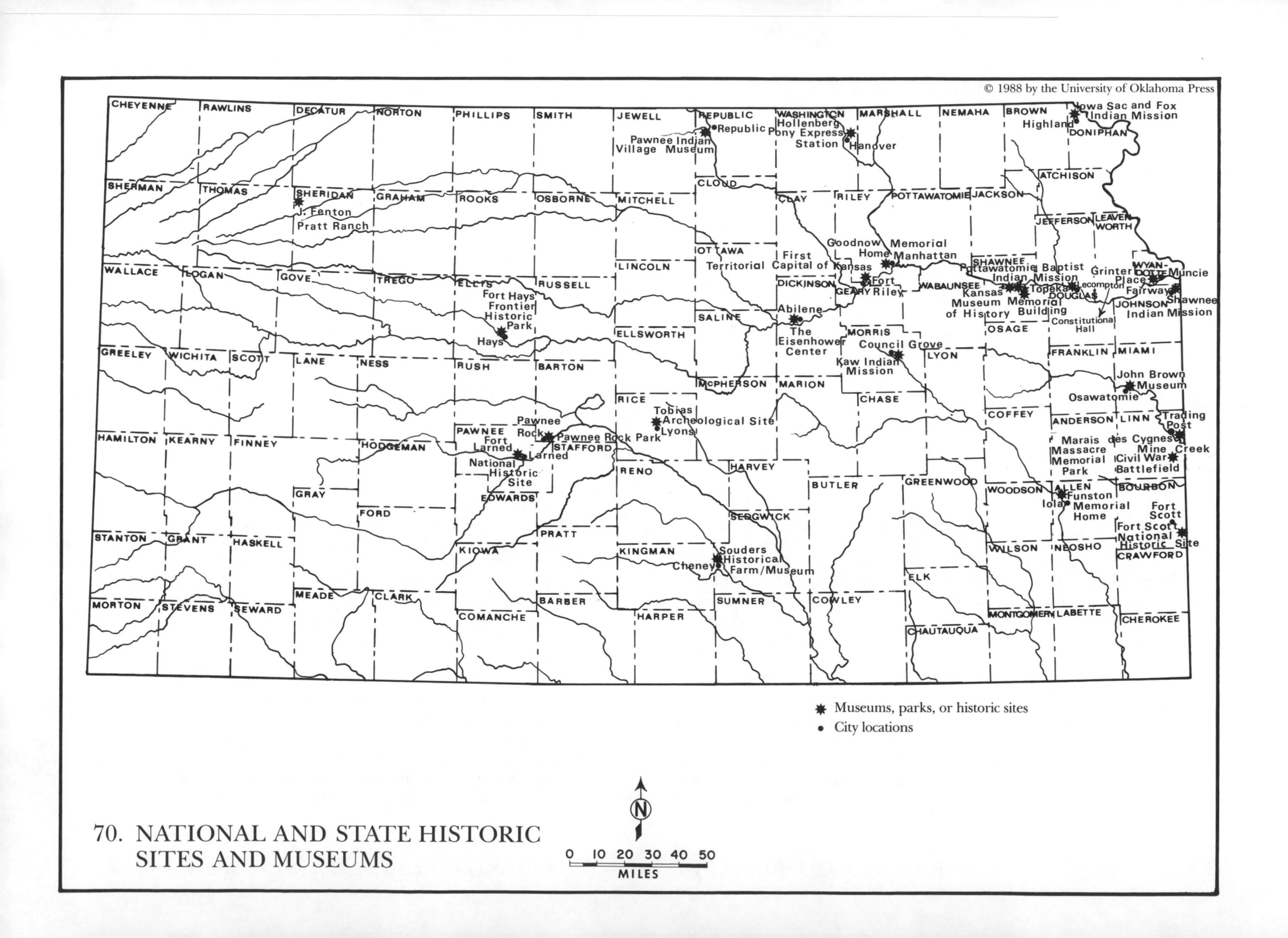

© 1988 by the University of Oklahoma Press

| CHEYENNE | RAWLINS | DECATUR | NORTON | PHILLIPS | SMITH | JEWELL | REPUBLIC | WASHINGTON | MARSHALL | NEMAHA | BROWN | | Iowa Sac and Fox Indian Mission |

Iowa Sac and Fox Indian Mission
Hollenberg
Pony Express
Station
Republic
Pawnee Indian
Village Museum
Handover
Highland
DONIPHAN
ATCHISON

J. Fenton
Pratt Ranch

Goodnow Memorial
Home Manhattan
First
Territorial Capital of Kansas
Pottawatomie Baptist
Indian Mission
Grinter
Place
Muncie
Fairways
Shawnee
Indian Mission
Fort Hays
Frontier
Historic
Park
Fort
Riley
Kansas
Museum
of History
Memorial
Building
Topeka
DOUGLAS
Constitutional
Hall
Hays
Abilene
The
Eisenhower
Center
Council Grove
Kaw Indian
Mission
John Brown
Museum
Osawatomie
Tobias
Archeological Site
Lyons
Trading
Post
Pawnee
Rock
Fort
Larned
Pawnee Rock Park
Larned
Marais des Cygnes
Massacre
Memorial
Park
Mine
Creek
Civil War
Battlefield
National
Historic
Site
Funston
Memorial
Home
Fort
Scott
Souders
Historical
Farm/Museum
Cheney
Fort Scott
National
Historic Site

✳ Museums, parks, or historic sites

● City locations

70. NATIONAL AND STATE HISTORIC SITES AND MUSEUMS

N

0 10 20 30 40 50
MILES

70. NATIONAL AND STATE HISTORIC SITES AND MUSEUMS

THREE HISTORIC SITES operated by the federal government in Kansas include the Eisenhower Center, in Abilene, under the guidance of the National Archives; the Fort Larned National Historic Site, near Larned; and the Fort Scott National Historic Site, at Fort Scott, operated by the National Park Service. The Eisenhower Center contains the Dwight D. Eisenhower Presidential Library, the Eisenhower Museum, the Eisenhower boyhood home, and the Place of Meditation—burial spot for President and Mrs. Eisenhower. The refurbished Fort Scott Historic Site presents that fort as it existed in the 1840's, and the late 1860's is the period represented at the Fort Larned Historic Site.

Nineteen museums and parks in various parts of Kansas are operated by the state through the Kansas State Historical Society.

Seven of these sites are related to Indians and Indian affairs and are located at Highland, Republic, Lyons, Topeka, Shawnee Mission, Council Grove, and Pawnee Rock. Closely identified with the territorial period and early statehood are the eight museums and parks at Muncie, Osawatomie, Manhattan, Fort Riley, Hanover, and Hays, and the two in Linn County. Museums at Iola and Cheney and in Sheridan County concentrate on the late nineteenth and early twentieth centuries, while the new Kansas Museum of History, in Topeka, covers all eras in Kansas history.

There are two museums in Kansas operated by the United States Army—at Fort Leavenworth and at Fort Riley. In addition, there are numerous local and county museums in the state.

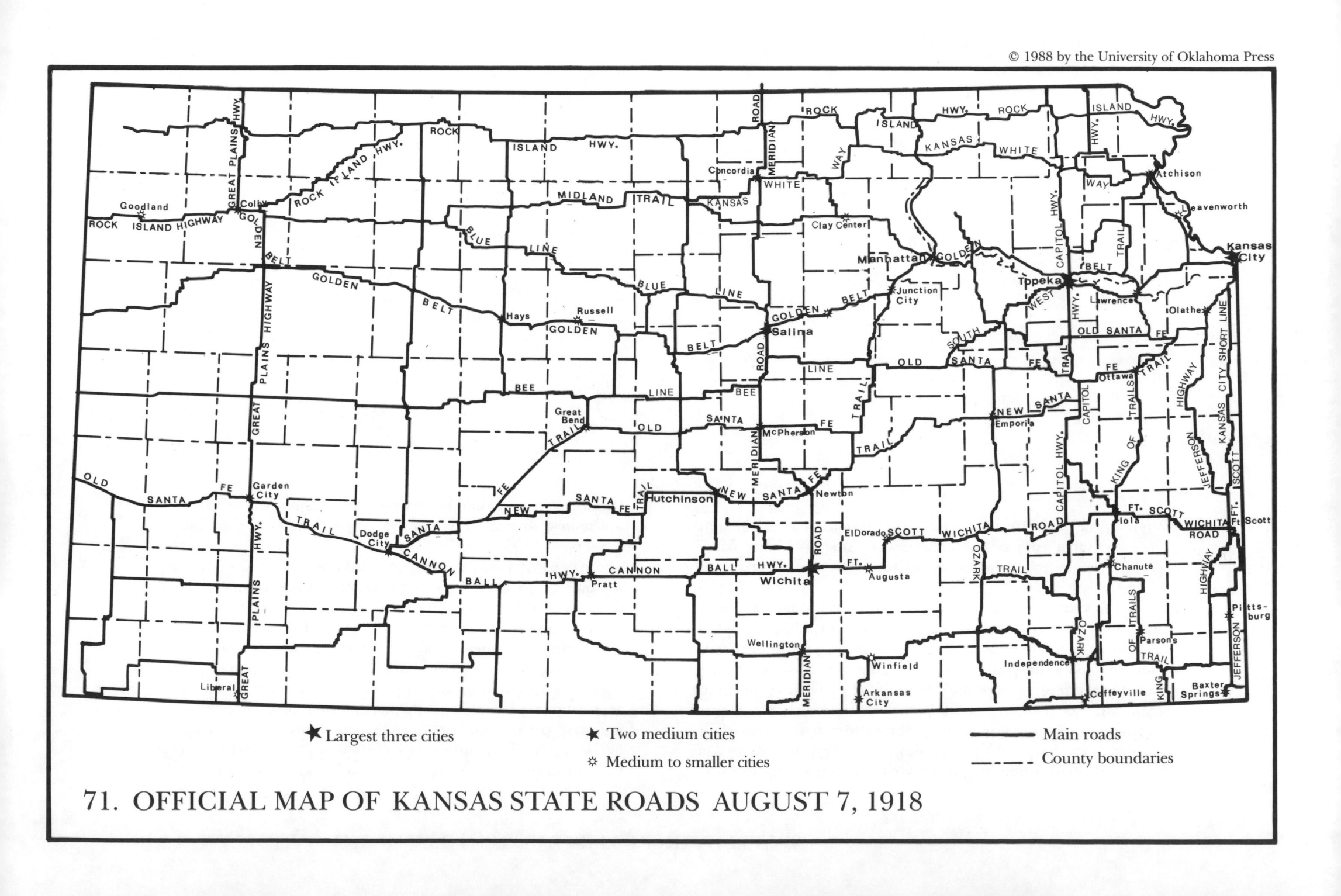

71. OFFICIAL MAP OF KANSAS STATE ROADS AUGUST 7, 1918

★ Largest three cities

★ Two medium cities

✷ Medium to smaller cities

——— Main roads

—·—·— County boundaries

THE KANSAS CONSTITUTION, created at Wyandotte in 1859, prohibited the state from participating in "internal improvements," legally defined as the construction and maintenance of roads and highways, canals and waterways, railroads, and other economic developments. In the previous twenty years several states had been bankrupted by their involvement in internal improvements, so the framers of the Kansas constitution were cautious.

Following the federal highway law of 1916 that provided matching funds for major roadways, the state of Kansas created a State Highway Commission to serve as the state's agency for receiving federal money. The agency had very few employees since the state could not build roads until 1928, when the constitutional restraint was repealed. Almost all of the federal funds it received were passed on to the counties. In the transitional period when the State Highway Commission served only as an advisory agency, the existing roads were drawn into a state system and given names. When improved, many of these early roads were paid for by taxes on adjoining property.

While the State Highway Commission printed the map from which Map 71 was produced, there generally were no official road signs along the margin of the roadway, such as expected in later years. Roads were marked by private citizens for use by the motoring public in a variety of ways. For instance, road markers could be bands of paint in various colors or color combinations on existing fence posts or telephone poles. Corners were not marked, and enterprising Kansans printed booklets with detailed information for each highway. Road users could then get information on how far it was to the next turn and descriptions of what they would see along the way.

Many of the highway names, in use until they were replaced in 1925 by the federal numbering system, drew on historic or regional names, such as the Old Santa Fe Trail, the Golden Belt Route, or the Cannon Ball Highway. These existing roads had been opened for horse-and-wagon traffic, and noticeable on this map are the frequent right-angle corners. Early automobile traffic over these roads was conditioned by the weather. It was foolhardy to travel these roads during rainy weather. Slowly the roads were surfaced and improved for speedier automobile traffic. Citizens of almost every town and city wanted the highway to go down their main street—for many places that was the first all-weather surface for that street.

Communities on these early named highways were in a strategic location and remained on the improved roads of later years. Community leaders throughout Kansas organized highway associations in which they banded together to support their particular road and to enter into decisions involving its location. This map of an elementary state system of 1918, when compared to highway maps of the late twentieth century, shows many changes. The basic highway pattern, however, conditioned by early transportation routes, the lay of the land, and the development of Kansas communities is shown in this historic map.

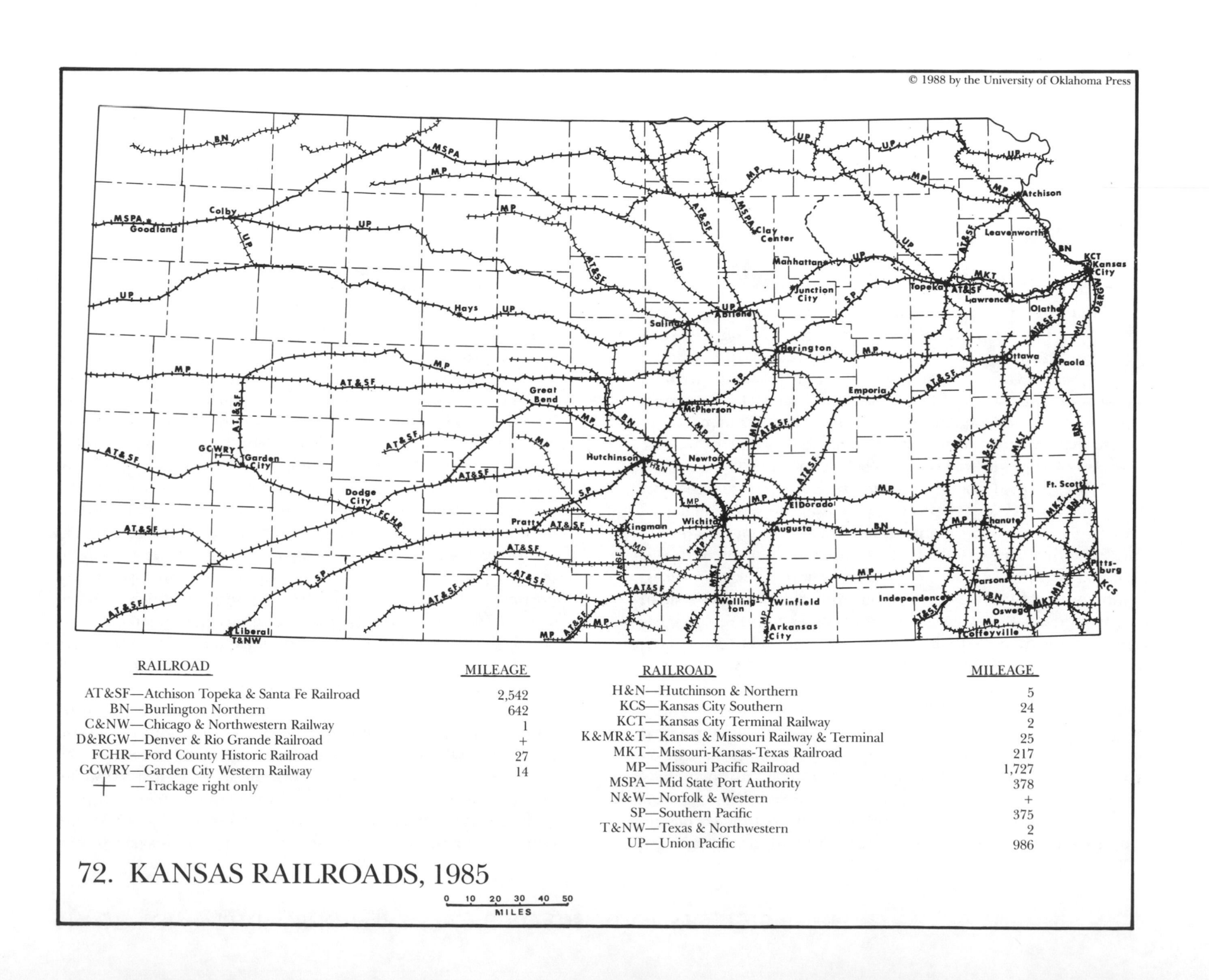

RAILROAD	MILEAGE	RAILROAD	MILEAGE
AT&SF—Atchison Topeka & Santa Fe Railroad	2,542	H&N—Hutchinson & Northern	5
BN—Burlington Northern	642	KCS—Kansas City Southern	24
C&NW—Chicago & Northwestern Railway	1	KCT—Kansas City Terminal Railway	2
D&RGW—Denver & Rio Grande Railroad	+	K&MR&T—Kansas & Missouri Railway & Terminal	25
FCHR—Ford County Historic Railroad	27	MKT—Missouri-Kansas-Texas Railroad	217
GCWRY—Garden City Western Railway	14	MP—Missouri Pacific Railroad	1,727
┼—Trackage right only		MSPA—Mid State Port Authority	378
		N&W—Norfolk & Western	+
		SP—Southern Pacific	375
		T&NW—Texas & Northwestern	2
		UP—Union Pacific	986

72. KANSAS RAILROADS, 1985

0 10 20 30 40 50
MILES

72. KANSAS RAILROADS, 1985

DEREGULATION OF AMERICAN RAILROADS and the bankruptcy of the Chicago, Rock Island and Pacific Railroad had greatly altered the railroad mileage in Kansas by the mid-1980's. In 1985 the Kansas Corporation Commission report showed 3,823 main-line miles and 3,108 branch-line miles of track in the state, with trackage rights to other railroads on 998 miles of that track. The total rail mileage in Kansas in 1985 was 6,831 miles, very close to the track mileage in Kansas a century earlier. Freight tonnage hauled on Kansas railroads in 1985 was far larger than that of 1885, and it moved far more swiftly on much better track and roadbeds.

Mergers of long-time railroad companies have been a recent phenomena. For much of the past century railroad companies have been relatively stable enterprises, with no changes in company names. But the recent merger of the Missouri Pacific and the Union Pacific, shown separately on this map, into the Union Pacific System, created a total mileage within Kansas of 2,713, largest for a single line in Kansas. The attempted merger of the Santa Fe and the Southern Pacific railroads was unsuccessful. Such a merger would have produced the largest single line in Kansas.

The breakup of the Rock Island resulted in some track re-moval and the entrance of new companies into Kansas, or the creation of some new railroad companies, such as the Mid-States Port Authority. This new company, the product of special state legislation, permits continued freight service in twelve counties along or near the Nebraska border. Its trains are operated by the Kyle Railroad Company. Without this adjustment five county seats in that area would be without rail service. A small new enterprise, the Ford County Historic Railroad Preservation Foundation Company, operates 27 miles of track from Dodge City to Bucklin on an infrequent basis for passengers and freight. Nostalgia for the old-time steam engines is shown when one of the few remaining operating steam engines passes through the state on its way to a world fair or a special railroad show. Large numbers of onlookers gather along the right-of-way and for a brief moment relive the old days.

AMTRAK continues to provide the only regularly scheduled passenger trains in Kansas over the Santa Fe track from Kansas City, Newton, Dodge City, and on west. Neither passenger nor freight trains carry United States mail over Kansas rail lines in the 1980's. Instead, diesel-powered engines move massive quantities of freight over Kansas track at speeds incomprehensible to citizens of a hundred years ago.

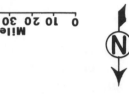

Miles
0 10 20 30 40 50

73. ALL RURAL ROADS IN KANSAS

THE TERRITORIAL KANSAS LEGISLATURE and the earliest state legislatures provided laws for opening roads along each section line. If all section lines had become roads, Kansas would have 130,000 miles of roadway. Actually, about 134,000 miles of public roads, including streets in towns and cities, exist in the state in the late twentieth century, ranking Kansas behind Texas and New York in the mileage of public roads. Ninety-one per cent of these roads are in the rural areas shown on this map, and 75 per cent are all-weather roads.

Most section lines were opened as legal roads, defined as four rods (sixty-six feet) wide from private property line to private property line. Thus, eight acres of land was taken from each side of a section for public use. Roads were generally opened, because of local decisions, soon after settlement. The whiter areas on this map roughly outline the extent of the Flint Hills in east-central Kansas, the area of the Fort Riley military reservation, pasture lands elsewhere, and major rivers. For instance, there are large white areas on the south side of the Arkansas River in southwestern Kansas where roads have not penetrated stretches of sand dunes. In all of these areas, existing roads do not conform to the sectional division of the land.

The vast extent of road mileage in Kansas offers conveniences, but it also becomes a burden. With more than one hundred thousand miles of roadway to maintain, the state, the counties, and local units of government have a responsibility that frequently extends farther than the ability to pay, based on the revenues generally derived from road-user taxes. So priorities have to be established, and some of the less used thoroughfares receive very little maintenance.

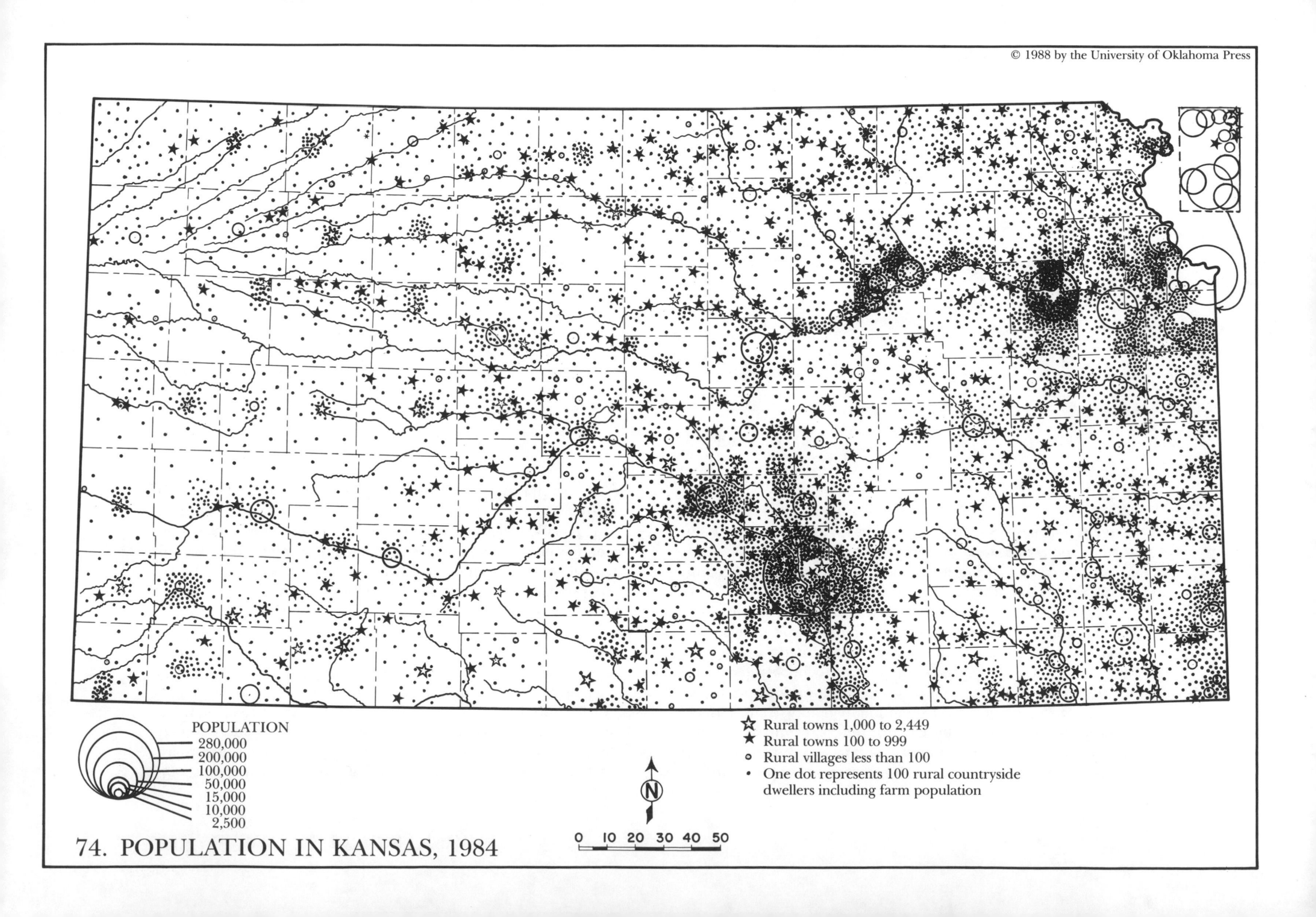

POPULATION
280,000
200,000
100,000
50,000
15,000
10,000
2,500

☆ Rural towns 1,000 to 2,449
★ Rural towns 100 to 999
○ Rural villages less than 100
• One dot represents 100 rural countryside
  dwellers including farm population

N

0 10 20 30 40 50

74. POPULATION IN KANSAS, 1984

CENSUS FIGURES FOR KANSAS POPULATION in 1980 show two major changes from 1970 and earlier. The rate of urban population increase has slowed, growing only slightly from 66.1 per cent of the total in 1970 to 66.7 per cent in 1980. Secondly, a sizable shift was shown in the population recorded as rural farm, which increased from 11.3 per cent in 1970 to 20 per cent in 1980. This latter figure, in reality, reflects the relocation of employees who work in the city even though they have moved to the country or of countryside farmers who have transferred from a primary occupation of farming to industrial jobs in Kansas cities. Living in the country was no longer isolated such as it was prior to 1940. Rural electrification extended to practically all Kansas rural homes, permitting rural Kansans to have most of the amenities found in every home. Hard-surfaced home-to-work or home-to-market roads and improved automobiles allowed rural dwellers easy access to urban jobs and markets. Buses from unified school districts collected schoolchildren for transportation to large, nearby elementary, middle, and high schools.

By 1980, Kansas population was increasing about half as fast as the nation as a whole. Also, there was an average of 28.9 Kansans for each square mile in the state, whereas, nationally, there were 61.1 Americans for each square mile of United States territory. Kansas population was 1.043 per cent of the national total, sufficient to retain five members in the lower house of Congress. There was a great difference, however, in density of population within the state. The ten counties bordering Missouri averaged 208 people a square mile. The seven counties from north to south across central Kansas had 12 people a square mile, while the seven counties bordering Colorado had a population average of 3.7 persons a square mile. The 1980 census also revealed that 56 per cent of all Kansans were born within the state, a figure very close to the national total for persons residing in the state in which they were born.

The map shows the concentration of Kansans in the Wichita, Kansas City, Lawrence, and Topeka Standard Metropolitan Statistical areas. In fact, the ten largest counties contain more than half of the state's population. For the most part these largest counties were in the Kansas or Arkansas river valleys. Rural areas in many of these larger-population counties, because of the large number of population dots, appear almost urbanized. At the other extreme the lighter tones on the map show the least population density within the state.

REFERENCES

References are listed for individual maps. Publication information is given in the first listing of each book and is not repeated in subsequent references.

Map 1. Kansas—Center of the Conterminous United States

American Heritage Pictorial Atlas of United States History (New York, American Heritage Publishing Company, Inc., 1966).

Goebel, Anne M., John B. Heffelfinger, and Delore Gammon, *Kansas—Our State: A Geography of Kansas* (Topeka, State Printer, 1952), 6.

Schoewe, Walter H., "The Geography of Kansas," *Transactions, Kansas Academy of Science*, LI, 253ff.

Schoewe, Walter H., "Kansas and the Geodetic Datum of North America," *Transactions, Kansas Academy of Science*, LI, 117–24.

Self, Huber, *Geography of Kansas* (Norman, Harlow Publishing Corp., 1960), 2.

Map 2. Latitude and Longitude of Kansas

American Heritage Pictorial Atlas, 254–55.

Laws of Kansas, 1967, Chap. 520.

Miller, Nyle H. (ed.), "Surveying the Southern Boundary Line of Kansas: From the Private Journals of Col. Joseph E. Johnston," *Kansas Historical Quarterly* I, 107.

Schoewe, "The Geography of Kansas," 283–84.

Self, *Geography of Kansas*, 3.

Van Zandt, Franklin K., "Boundaries of the United States and the Several States," *Geological Survey Bulletin 1212*, (Washington, Government Printing Office, 1966), 188–91, 223–24.

Map 3. Landforms of Kansas

American Heritage Pictorial Atlas, end cover maps.

Baughman, Robert W., *Kansas in Maps* (Topeka, Kansas State Historical Society, 1961), 8.

Fenneman, Nevin M., *Physiography of Western United States* (New York, McGraw-Hill Book Co., Inc., 1931), 3, 6.

Schoewe, "The Geography of Kansas," 253ff.

Self, *Geography of Kansas*, 13, after Raymond C. Moore.

Self, Huber, *Geography of Kansas Syllabus and Atlas* (Dubuque, Iowa, William C. Brown Book Co., 1967), 19.

Map 4. Distribution of Precipitation in Kansas

Bark, L. Dean, *Rainfall Patterns in Kansas*, Kansas Agricultural Situation Reprint No. 9 (Manhattan, Kansas Agricultural Experiment Station, 1961).

Bark, L. Dean, *Chances For Precipitation in Kansas* Bulletin 461 (Manhattan, Kansas Agricultural Experiment Station, 1963).

Cardwell, A. B., and S. D. Flora, *The Climate of Kansas* Bulletin 302 (Manhattan, Kansas Agricultural Experiment Station, 1942).

Climatography of the United States No. 11–12, Climatic Summary of the United States—Supplement for 1931 through 1952, Kansas (Washington, Government Printing Office, 1956).

Climatography of the United States No. 86–12, Climatic Summary of the United States—Supplement for 1951 through 1960, Kansas (Washington, Government Printing Office, 1964).

Map 5. Native Flora of Kansas

Küchler, A. W., "The Vegetation of Kansas on Maps," *Transactions, Kansas Academy of Science*, LXXII, 141–66.

Self, *Geography of Kansas*, 8.

Self, *Geography of Kansas Syllabus*, 9.

Map 6. Principal Surface Water Resources in Kansas

Kansas State Board of Agriculture, "Municipal, County and Other Dams" ([1985]).

A Kansas Water Atlas (Topeka, Kansas Water Resources Board, 1967).

Murray, Wendy A., ed., *Kansas Statistical Atlas, 1984–85* (Lawrence, Institute for Public Policy and Business Research, The University of Kansas, 1985), 186–87.
Planning for Plenty: The Management of Kansas Water (Topeka, Kansas Water Resources Board, 1966).
Self, Huber, *Environment and Man in Kansas: A Geographical Analysis* (Lawrence, The Regents Press of Kansas, 1978), 128–32.
"State Owned or Administered Areas Under the Jurisdiction of the Kansas Fish & Game Commission," map, 1985.

Map 7. Spanish and French Claims in the United States

American Heritage Pictorial Atlas, 62–63.
Bolton, H. E., and T. M. Marshall, *The Colonization of North America, 1492–1783* (New York, Macmillan, 1922), 32–34, 40–46.
French, Benjamin F. (ed.), *Historical Collections of Louisiana* (New York, Wiley and Putnam, 1846), I, 25ff.
Miller, Theodore R., *Graphic History of The Americas* (New York, John Wiley & Sons, Inc., 1969), 2–3, 6–7.

Map 8. Spanish and French Explorers in Kansas, 16th–18th Centuries

American Heritage Pictorial Atlas, 34–35, 50–51, 52–53.
Bolton, H. E., *Coronado on the Turquoise Trail, Knight of Pueblos and Plains* (Albuquerque, University of New Mexico Press, 1949).
Bolton, H. E. (ed.), *Spanish Explorations in the Southwest, 1542–1706* (New York, Scribners, 1916), 205–12, 250–66.
Hammond, George P., and Agapito Rey, *Narratives of the Coronado Expedition, 1540–1542* (Albuquerque, University of New Mexico Press, 1940).
Jones, Paul A., *Coronado and Quivira* (Lyons, Kansas, Lyons Publishing Co., 1937).
Loomis, Noel M., and Abraham P. Nasitir, *Pedro Vial and the Roads to Santa Fe* (Norman, University of Oklahoma Press, 1967).
Miller, *Graphic History*, 2–3, 7.
Winship, George P. (ed.), "The Coronado Expedition, 1540–1542," *Bureau of American Ethnology Fourteenth Annual Report, 1892–1893*, Part I, 341–593.

Map 9. Spanish and British Claims After 1763

Adams, James Truslow, *Atlas of American History* (New York, Scribners, 1943), 49.
American Heritage Pictorial Atlas, 76–77, 92–93, 114–15.
Miller, *Graphic History*, 14.

Map 10. Louisiana Purchase from France in 1803 and Adams-Onis Treaty in 1819

American Heritage Pictorial Atlas, 118–19, 121, 123, 128–29.
MacDonald, William (ed.), *Select Documents Illustrative of the History of the United States, 1776–1861* (New York, Macmillan, 1901), 160–65.
Miller, *Graphic History*, 17, 20.

Map 11. Early Indian Tribes in Kansas

American Heritage Book of Indians (New York, American Heritage Publishing Co., Inc., 1961), 334.
American Heritage Pictorial Atlas, 23.
Baughman, *Kansas in Maps*, 8.
Hodge, F. W. (ed.), *Handbook of American Indians North of Mexico, Bureau of American Ethnology Bulletin No. 30* (2 vols., Washington, D. C., 1907–10).
Kraenzel, Carl F., *The Great Plains in Transition* (Norman, University of Oklahoma Press, 1955), 74.
Rydjord, John, *Indian Place-Names: Their Origin, Evolution, and Meanings, Collected in Kansas from the Siouan, Algonquian, Shoshonean, Caddoan, Iroquoian, and Other Tongues* (Norman, University of Oklahoma Press, 1968), 5.

Map 12. Homelands of Emigrant Indians of Kansas

American Heritage Book of Indians, 146, 162, 227, 334.
Hodge, *Handbook of American Indians North of Mexico*.
Wright, Muriel H., *A Guide to the Indian Tribes of Oklahoma* (Norman, University of Oklahoma Press, 1951).

Map 13. Indian Reservations in Kansas, 1846

Abel, Annie Heloise, "Indian Reservations in Kansas and the Extinguishment of Their Title," *Transactions of the Kansas State*

Historical Society, 1903–1904, VIII, 72–109.
American Heritage Pictorial Atlas, 148–49.
Baughman, *Kansas in Maps*, 24–25, 26, 27, 31, 40–41.
Zornow, William F., *Kansas, A History of the Jayhawk State* (Norman, University of Oklahoma Press, 1957), 48.

Map 14. *American Explorers, 1804–1854*

American Heritage Pictorial Atlas, 128–29.
American State Papers (38 vols., Washington, D. C., Government Printing Office, 1832–61), *Military Affairs*, V, 373–82.
Barry, Louise, (comp.), "Kansas Before 1854: A Revised Annals," *Kansas Historical Quarterly*, XXIX, 449.
Coues, Elliott (ed.), *The Journal of Jacob Fowler, narrating an Adventure from Arkansas through the Indian Territory, Oklahoma, Kansas, Colorado, and New Mexico, to the sources of Rio Grande del Norte, 1821–22* (2 vols., New York, Francis P. Harper, 1898).
Goetzmann, William H., *Army Exploration in the American West, 1803–1863* (New Haven, Yale University Press, 1959), 28, 35, 71, 114, 215, 276, 348.
Jackson, Donald (ed.), *The Journals of Zebulon Montgomery Pike: With Letters and Related Documents* (Norman, University of Oklahoma Press, 1968), I, 293.
James, Edwin, *The Stephen H. Long Expedition* (vols. XIV–XVII of *Early Western Travels, 1748–1846*, ed. by R. G. Thwaites [32 vols., Cleveland, Arthur H. Clark, 1904–1907]).
McDermott, John Francis (ed.), *The Western Journals of Washington Irving* (Norman, University of Oklahoma Press, 1944, 1966).
Nevins, Allen, *Frémont, Pathmarker of the West* (New York, Unger, 1939, 1961), endpaper maps.
Preuss, Charles, *Exploring with Frémont*, trans. and ed. by Erwin G. and Elisabeth K. Gudde (Norman, University of Oklahoma Press, 1958), 9–10.
Wheat, Carl, *Mapping the Transmississippi West* (San Francisco, Institute of Historical Geography, 1960), IV, 25, 178.

Map 15. *Early Indian Missions and Present Day Indian Reservations in Kansas*

American Heritage Book of Indians, 406–407.
American Heritage Pictorial Atlas, 250–51, 350–51.
Arnold, Anna E., *A History of Kansas* (Topeka, State Printing Plant, 1914), 217.
Connelley, William Elsey, "The Prairie Band of Pottawatomie Indians," *Collections of the Kansas State Historical Society*, XIV, 488–570.
Dickson, E. H., "The 'Boys' Story: Reminiscences of 1855," *Transactions of the Kansas State Historical Society*, V, 76–87.
"Executive Minutes of Governor John W. Geary," *Transactions of the Kansas State Historical Society*, IV, 520–742.
"Explanation of Map," *Collections of the Kansas State Historical Society*, IX, 565–78.
Ferris, Ida M., "The Sauks and Foxes in Franklin and Osage Counties, Kansas," *Collections of the Kansas State Historical Society*, XI, 333–95.
Goodnow, Isaac T., "Personal Reminiscences and Kansas Emigration, 1855," *Transactions of the Kansas State Historical Society*, IV, 244–53.
Gowing, Clara, "Life Among the Delaware Indians," *Collections of the Kansas State Historical Society*, XII, 183–93.
Hobbs, Wilson, "The Friends' Establishment in Kansas Territory," *Collections of the Kansas State Historical Society*, VIII, 250–71.
"Letters Concerning the Presbyterian Mission in the Pawnee Country, near Bellvue, Neb., 1831–1849," *Collections of the Kansas State Historical Society*, XIV, 570–784.
"Letters from the Indian Missions in Kansas," *Collections of the Kansas State Historical Society*, XVI, 227–71.
Lutz, J. J., "The Methodist Missions Among the Indian Tribes in Kansas," *Collections of the Kansas State Historical Society*, IX, 160–235.
McGonigle, James A., "Right Reverend John B. Miege, S. J., First Catholic Bishop of Kansas," *Collections of the Kansas State Historical Society*, IX, 153–59.

Meeker, Jotham, diary of, "High Waters in Kansas," *Collections of the Kansas State Historical Society*, VIII, 472–81.

Merwin, Ray E., "The Wyandot Indians," *Collections of the Kansas State Historical Society*, IX, 73–88.

Morrison, T. F., "Mission Neosho," *Kansas Historical Quarterly*, IV, 227–34.

Plank, Pryor, "The Iowa, Sac and Fox Indian Mission and Its Missionaries, Rev. Samuel M. Irvin and Wife," *Collections of the Kansas State Historical Society*, X, 312–35.

Romig, Joseph, "The Chippewa and Munsee (Or Christian) Indians of Franklin County, Kansas," *Collections of the Kansas State Historical Society*, XI, 314–23.

Ross, Edith Connelley, "The Old Shawnee Mission," *Collections of the Kansas State Historical Society*, XVII, 417–35.

Map 16. Unorganized Territory, 1821–1854

American Heritage Pictorial Atlas, 144–45, 146.

Baughman, *Kansas in Maps*, 54.

Miller, *Graphic History*, 20–24.

Map 17. Trails Through Preterritorial Kansas

American Heritage Pictorial Atlas, 170–71.

Baughman, *Kansas in Maps*, 28–37, 44–45.

Hafen, LeRoy R., *The Overland Mail, 1849–69* (Cleveland, Arthur H. Clark, 1926), 343.

Long, Margaret, *The Oregon Trail* (Denver, W. H. Kistler Stationery Co., 1954), Chapters I and II.

Paden, Irene D., *Wake of the Prairie Schooner* (New York, Macmillan, 1943), 19.

Map 18. Indian Treaties in Kansas

"Indian Treaties and Councils Affecting Kansas," *Collections of the Kansas State Historical Society*, XVI, 746–73.

Kappler, Charles J., *Indian Affairs, Laws and Treaties* (Washington, Government Printing Office, 1902), II.

Map 19. Indian Names in Kansas

Blackmar, F. H., *Kansas: A Cyclopedia of State History* (2 vols., Chicago, Standard Publishing Co., 1912).

Rydjord, *Indian Place Names*.

Map 20. Forts and Military Roads After 1827

Barry, Louise, "Fort Leavenworth—Fort Scott—Fort Gibson Military Road," *Kansas Historical Quarterly*, XI, 115–29.

Frazer, Robert W., *Forts of the West* (Norman, University of Oklahoma Press, 1965).

Jackson, W. Turrentine, "The Army Engineers as Road Surveyors and Builders in Kansas and Nebraska, 1854–1858," *Kansas Historical Quarterly*, XVII, 32–59.

Parkman, Francis, *The Oregon Trail*, ed. by E. N. Feltskog (Madison, University of Wisconsin Press, 1969), 16a.

Strate, David K., *Sentinel to the Cimarron, The Frontier Experience of Fort Dodge, Kansas* (Dodge City, Cultural Heritage and Arts Center, 1970), 14.

Wheat, Carl, *Mapping the Transmississippi West*, V.

Map 21. Kansas and Nebraska Territories, 1854–1861, and Indian Territory

American Heritage Pictorial Atlas, 166–67, 174–75, 196–97, 198–99.

Baughman, *Kansas in Maps*, 6.

Malin, James C., "The Motives of Stephen A. Douglas in the Organization of Nebraska Territory," *Kansas Historical Quarterly*, XIX, 321–53.

Map 22. Locations in Territorial Kansas

Adams, Franklin G., "The Capitals of Kansas," *Collections of the Kansas State Historical Society*, VIII, 331–51.

American Heritage Pictorial Atlas, 196–97, 204–205.

Annals of Kansas, (Topeka, Kansas State Historical Society, 1954), I, 149.

Arnold, *A History of Kansas*, 215.

Adams, *Atlas of American History*, 121.

Baughman, *Kansas in Maps*, 58.

Richmond, Robert W., "First Capitol in Kansas," *Kansas Historical Quarterly*, XXI, 321–25.

Map 23. Territorial Kansas Trails

American Heritage Pictorial Atlas, 122–23.

Connelley, William E., "The Lane Trail," *Collections of the Kansas State Historical Society*, XIII, 268–79.

Connelley, William E., *A Standard History of Kansas and Kansans* (Chicago, Lewis Publishing Co., 1918), I, Chapter VIII.

"Explanation of Map," *Collections of the Kansas State Historical Society*, IX, 565–78.

Root, George A., and Russell K. Hickman, "Pike's Peak Express Companies," *Kansas Historical Quarterly*, XII, 485–526; XIV, 36–92.

"The Pony Express Rides Again," *Kansas Historical Quarterly*, XXV, 269–85.

Richards, O. G., "Kansas Experiences of Oscar G. Richards, of Eudora, in 1856," *Collections of the Kansas State Historical Society*, IX, 545–48.

Map 24. Creation of the State of Kansas

American Heritage Pictorial Atlas, 200–201.

Connelley, William E., "The East Boundary Line of Kansas," *Collections of the Kansas State Historical Society*, XI, 75–80.

Gower, C. W., "Kansas Territory and Its Boundary Question, 'Big Kansas' or 'Little Kansas'," *Kansas Historical Quarterly*, XXXIII, 1–12.

"Kansas Admission to Statehood, 1861," *Kansas Historical Quarterly*, XXVII, 1–21.

Martin, George W., "The Boundary Lines of Kansas," *Collections of the Kansas State Historical Society*, XI, 53–74.

Miller, "Surveying the Southern Boundary Line," 104–39.

Schoewe, "The Geography of Kansas," 283–84.

Map 25. Proposals for Altering the Kansas Boundaries

Kansas Constitutional Convention (Topeka, Kansas State Printing Plant, 1920), 70, 95, 121, 122, 204–19, 229–40, 243–45, 250–64, 384–96, 461–64, 534–37, 546.

Schoewe, Walter H., "Political Geographical Aspect of Territorial Kansas," *Territorial Kansas: Studies Commemorating the Centennial* (Lawrence, University of Kansas Publications, Social Science Studies, 1954), 1–16.

Map 26. Township and Range Lines of Federal Surveys in Kansas

Schoewe, "Geography of Kansas."

Socolofsky, Homer E., "How We Took the Land," in *Kansas: The First Century*, edited by John D. Bright (New York, Lewis Historical Publishing Co., 1956), I, 286–89.

Map 27. Federal Land Offices in Kansas

Greene, Albert R., "United States Land-Offices in Kansas," *Collections of the Kansas State Historical Society*, VIII, 1–13.

Socolofsky, "How We Took the Land," 289–90.

Map 28. The Civil War in Kansas

Bidlack, Russell E., "Erastus D. Ladd's Description of the Lawrence Massacre," *Kansas Historical Quarterly*, XXIX, 113–21.

Castel, Albert E., *A Frontier State at War, Kansas, 1861–1865* (Ithaca, N. Y., Cornell University Press, 1958).

Castel, Albert E., *William Clarke Quantrill, His Life and Times* (New York, F. Fell, 1962).

"A Chronology of Kansas Political and Military Events, 1859–65," *Kansas Historical Quarterly*, XXV, 287–300.

Langsdorf, Edgar, "Price's Raid and the Battle of Mine Creek," *Kansas Historical Quarterly*, XXX, 281–306.

Monaghan, Jay, *Civil War on the Western Border, 1854–1865* (Boston, Little, Brown & Co., 1955).

Prentis, Noble L., *A History of Kansas* (Topeka, Caroline Prentis, 1909), 321–45.

A Survey of Historic Sites and Structures in Kansas (Topeka, Kansas State Historical Society, 1957), 11, 37, 44.

Map 29. Battle Sites in Kansas Other Than Civil War

Baughman, *Kansas in Maps*, 62–63.

Comprehensive Index, 1875–1930 (Topeka, Kansas State Historical Society, 1959), 215. See Indian depredations.

Hafen, LeRoy R. and Ann W., *Relations With the Indians of the Plains, 1857–1861* (Glendale, Arthur C. Clark Co., 1959).

Montgomery, Mrs. F. C., "United States Surveyors Massacred by Indians," *Kansas Historical Quarterly*, I, 266–72.

Oliva, Leo E., *Soldiers on the Santa Fe Trail* (Norman, University of Oklahoma Press, 1967), 52, 164.

Prentis, *A History of Kansas*, 175, 183, 220.

A Survey of Historic Sites and Structures in Kansas, 15, 17, 43.

West, G. Derek, "The Battle of Sappa Creek," *Kansas Historical Quarterly*, XXIV, 150–78.

Map 30. Railroad Development in Kansas, 1878

American Heritage Pictorial Atlas, 202–203.

Baughman, *Kansas in Maps*, 66–79.

Cram's New Sectional Map of Kansas (Chicago, George F. Cram, 1878).

Kansas State Board of Agriculture, *Third Annual Report*, 1874, *Fourth Annual Report*, 1875.

Snell, J. W., and Robert W. Richmond, "Building the Union and Kansas Pacific through Kansas," *Kansas Historical Quarterly*, XXXII, 161–86, 334–52.

Thacher, T. Dwight, "The Railroads of Kansas," *Fourth Annual Report of the Kansas State Board of Agriculture* (Topeka, Geo. W. Martin, Public Printer, 1875), 102–105.

Map 31. Railroad Land Grants in Kansas

American Heritage Pictorial Atlas, 254–55.

Baughman, *Kansas in Maps*, 68–69, 72, 75, 82–85.

Gates, Paul W., *Fifty Million Acres* (Ithaca, Cornell University Press, 1954), 252.

Gates, Paul W., *History of Public Land Law Development* (Washington, Government Printing Office, 1968), 372, 384.

LeDuc, Thomas, "State Administration of the Land Grant to Kansas for Internal Improvements," *Kansas Historical Quarterly*, XX, 545–52.

Map 32. Major Cattle Trails and Cattle Towns

American Heritage Pictorial Atlas, 246–47, 248–49.

Baughman, *Kansas in Maps*, 80–81.

"The Chisholm Trail," *Kansas Historical Quarterly*, XXXIII, 129–37.

Gard, Wayne, *The Chisholm Trail* (Norman, University of Oklahoma Press, 1954), 77, 229.

Long, Richard M., "Wichita Cowtown," *Kansas Historical Quarterly*, XXVI, 92–100.

Prospector, Cowhand, Sodbuster (Washington, National Park Service, 1967), 52–53.

Map 33. Cattle Quarantine Lines in Kansas

State of Kansas, *Session Laws*, 1861, 1867, 1872, 1873, 1876, 1877, 1879, 1883.

Map 34. Major Sheep Trails in Kansas

Prospector, Cowhand, Sodbuster, 63.

Map 35. Buffalo Country

Andrist, Ralph K., *The Long Death, the Last Days of the Plains Indians* (New York, The Macmillan Company, 1964).

Baughman, *Kansas in Maps*, 66–67.

Dodge, Richard Irving, *The Plains of the Great West* (New York, Archer House, 1876, 1959), xiv–xv.

Webb, Walter Prescott, *The Great Plains* (Boston, Ginn, 1931), 50.

Map 36. Kansas Railroads, 1918

Baughman, *Kansas in Maps*, 92–93.

Chandler, Allison, *Trolley Through the Countryside* (Denver, Sage Books, 1963), 25ff.

First Report of the Public Utilities Commission, State of Kansas (Topeka, Kansas State Printing Office, 1913), 174.

Fourth Biennial Report of the Public Utilities Commission, State of Kansas (Topeka, Kansas State Printing Office, 1916).

Interstate Commerce Commission, *Statistics on Railways* (Washington, Government Printing Office, 1888–1967).
Official Highway Map, State of Kansas, 1918.

Map 37. Railroad Development in Kansas, 1970

Kansas Corporation Commission, *Official Kansas State Railroad Map* (n.p., 1968) and supplemental matter.

Maps 38–41. Kansas County Organization

Arnold, *A History of Kansas,* 238–41.
Gill, Helen G., "The Establishment of Counties in Kansas," *Transactions of the Kansas State Historical Society,* VIII, 449–72.
Prentis, *A History of Kansas,* 321–45.
Blackmar, *Kansas, A Cyclopedia of State History.*
Mason, H. F., "County Seat Controversies in Southwestern Kansas," *Kansas Historical Quarterly,* II, 45–65.
Rister, C. C., *No Man's Land* (Norman, University of Oklahoma Press, 1948), 129–38.
Socolofsky, Homer E., "County Seat Wars in Kansas," *The Trail Guide,* IX, No. 4.
Vestal, Stanley, *Short Grass Country* (New York, Duell, Sloan & Pearce, 1941), 238–41.

Map 42. Group Colonization in Kansas

American Heritage Pictorial Atlas, 186, 268–69.
Carman, J. Neale, *Foreign-Language Units of Kansas: I. Historical Atlas and Statistics* (Lawrence, University of Kansas Press, 1962).
Zornow, *Kansas, A History of the Jayhawk State,* 174–89.

Maps 43 and 44. Congressional Districts in Kansas

Brier, Jack H. (comp.), *Kansas Directory, 1984* (n.p., n.d.), 244–49, and related news information.
Cabe, June G., and Charles A. Sullivant, *Kansas Votes, National Elections, 1859–1956* (Lawrence, Governmental Research Center, University of Kansas, 1957).
Guynes, Paul R., *Kansas Voter's Guide, 1970* (Lawrence, Governmental Research Center, University of Kansas, 1970).

Hawley, Lorene A., "Kansas Congressmen and Reapportionment," *Kansas Historical Quarterly,* XXVI, 345–54.
Lujan, Herman D., *Kansas Votes, National and Statewide General Elections, 1958–1964* (Lawrence, Governmental Research Center, University of Kansas, 1965).

Map 45. Kansas Ghost Colleges and Universities

Conard, Erik Paul, *A History of Kansas' Closed Colleges* (unpublished doctoral dissertation, University of Oklahoma, 1970).
Edwards, Ralph W., "A History of the Topeka Dental College," *Kansas Historical Quarterly,* XVI, 381–83.
Official state educational reports.

Map 46. Kansas Colleges, Universities, and Vocational-Technical Schools

Kansas Educational Directory, 1969–70, Bulletin 340 (Topeka, Kansas State Department of Education, [1969]), 244–59.
Kansas Statistical Abstract, 1984–85, 71–85, and official state educational reports.

47. State Institutions Other Than Colleges and Universities

Secretary of State, *Kansas Biennial Report, 1970* (Topeka, State Printer, 1970), and related state publications.

48. Minerals of Kansas

American Heritage Pictorial Atlas, 340–41.
Hardy, Ronald G., "Inventory of Industrial, Metallic, and Solid-Fuel Minerals in Kansas," *State Geological Survey of Kansas, Bulletin 199, Part 5* (December, 1970), 3.
Kansas Mineral Industry, 1967 [Special Distribution Publication 35] (Lawrence, State Geological Survey, 1968).
Schoewe, Walter H., "The Geography of Kansas, Part IV, Economic Geography: Mineral Resources," *Transactions, Kansas Academy of Science,* LXI, 359–468.
Self, *Environment and Man in Kansas,* 131–67.

Self, Huber, "Revisions and Corrections for Environment and Man in Kansas," [1986], 8/9-1 to 8/9-5.

49. Major Highways and Scheduled Commercial Airline Routes in Kansas

Airline maps and correspondence with representatives of operating airlines.
American Heritage Pictorial Atlas, 284–85, 346–47.
Aviation Division, *Kansas Airport Directory* (Topeka, Kansas Department of Transportation, 1984).
Baughman, *Kansas in Maps,* 98–103.
Official Kansas Highway Maps.
Using Your Kansas Turnpike, brochure (n.d., n.p.)

Map 50. Average Annual Value of Farm Crops, Livestock, Livestock Products, and Government Payments to Farmers, 1980–1984

Agricultural Stabilization and Conservation Service Annual Report for Kansas, 1964–69 (Manhattan, Kansas).
American Heritage Pictorial Atlas, 336–37.
Bussing, Charles E., and Huber Self, "Changing Structure of the Beef Industry in Kansas," *Transactions, Kansas Academy of Science,* LXXXIV, 173–86.
Farm Facts (Topeka, State Board of Agriculture, years 1958 through 1981).
Kansas Statistical Abstract, annual volumes 1981–82 through 1984–85.
Self, *Environment and Man in Kansas,* 94–126.
Self, "Revisions and Corrections," 7–1 to 7–13.

Map 51. Irrigation and General Availability of Groundwater in Kansas

Kromm, David E., and Stephen E. White, *Conserving the Ogallala: What Next?* (Manhattan, Kansas State University, 1985).
Pfister, Richard, "Water Resources and Irrigation," *Economic Development in Southwestern Kansas, Part IV* (Lawrence, School of Business, 1955).

Schoewe, Walter H., "The Geography of Kansas, Part III, Hydrogeography," *Transactions, Kansas Academy of Science,* LIV, 263–329; LVI, 131–90.
Self, Huber, "Irrigation Farming in Kansas," *Transactions, Kansas Academy of Science* LXXIV, 310–17.
Self, *Environment and Man in Kansas,* 103–107.

Map 52. Average Annual Growing Season in Kansas in Days

Self, *Geography of Kansas,* 38.

Map 53. Employment in Kansas, 1984

American Heritage Pictorial Atlas, 338–39.
Barton-Dobenin, Joseph, "The Top 175," *Management Horizons* (Manhattan, College of Business Administration, Kansas State University, Winter, 1970), II, No. 2.
Kansas Statistical Abstract, 1984–85.
Self, *Environment and Man in Kansas,* 168–86.
Self, "Revision and Corrections," 10–1 to 10–5.

Map 54. Kansas Community Mental Health Centers

Cape, William H., *A Guidebook for Governing Boards of Community Mental Health Centers* (Topeka, State Department of Social Welfare, 1965).
Cram, Margaret, *Mental Health in Kansas, Hospital Treatment and Community Services* (Lawrence, Governmental Research Center, [1957]).
Kansas Directory of Community Mental Health Centers (Topeka, State Department of Social and Rehabilitation Services, 1984.)
Karson, Marc, "Mental Health in Kansas," in *Kansas, The First Century,* edited by John D. Bright (New York, Lewis Historical Publishing Co., Inc., 1956), II.

Map 55. Judicial and State Board of Education Districts

Brier, *Kansas Directory, 1984,* 250–51, 265–67.

Map 56. State Senatorial and Representative Districts

Brier, *Kansas Directory, 1984,* 253–64.

Maps 57–65. Regions of Kansas

American Heritage Pictorial Atlas, 270–71, 272–73, 332–33.
Brier, *Kansas Directory,* 1984.
Kansas Statistical Abstract 1986–87.
U.S. Census Reports.
Provisional estimates, U.S. Bureau of the Census, *Current Population Reports, 1984.*

Maps 66–67. Standard Metropolitan Statistical Areas in Kansas

U.S. Census Reports.

Maps 68, 69, 70. World War II Installations; Home Counties of Persons Elected to Statewide Offices, 1861–1987; and Historic Sites and Museums

"The Battle of Kansas," *Kansas Historical Quarterly,* XII, 481–84.
Brier, *Kansas Directory,* 1984, 6–17, 75–84, 135–36.
Henderson, Harold J., "Ships in World War II Bearing Kansas Names," *Kansas Historical Quarterly,* XV, 113–26.

"U.S. Army and Air Force Wings over Kansas," *Kansas Historical Quarterly,* XXV, 129–57, 334–60.
Ward, Mrs. Leslie A., *History of the Concordia Prisoner of War Camp, Concordia, Kansas,* 1943–1945 (Concordia, The Kansan Printing House, Inc., 1968).

Maps 71, 72, 73, 74. Kansas State Roads, 1918; Kansas Railroads, 1985; Rural Kansas Roads; Population in Kansas, 1984

Official Map, Kansas State Roads, August 7, 1918, reprinted by the Public Information Department, Kansas Department of Transportation.
Self, *Environment and Man in Kansas,* 82–93, 190–207.
Self, Huber, and Stephen E. White, "One Hundred and Twenty Years of Population Changes in Kansas," *Transactions, Kansas Academy of Sciences,* LXXXIX, 10–22.
Self, "Revisions and Corrections," 6-1 to 6-10, 11-1 to 11-5.

INDEX